DISCARD
BETHANY
W9-AHP-892

What Is Language?

AND OTHER TEACHING UNITS
FOR GRADES SEVEN THROUGH TWELVE

Published for the
Indiana University English Curriculum Study Center
EDWARD B. JENKINSON, Director

PREVIOUSLY PUBLISHED

On Teaching Literature: Essays for Secondary School Teachers
Teaching Literature in Grades Seven Through Nine
On Teaching the Bible as Literature: A Guide to Selected Biblical Narratives for Secondary Schools
Two Approaches to Teaching Syntax

FORTHCOMING VOLUMES

Teaching Literature in Grades Ten Through Twelve
Theme Assignments for Grades Seven Through Twelve
Books for Junior and Senior High School Teachers of English: An Annotated Bibliography

What Is Language?

AND OTHER TEACHING UNITS
FOR GRADES SEVEN THROUGH TWELVE

by

EDWARD B. JENKINSON

Coordinator for School English Language Arts
Director, Indiana University English Curriculum Study Center

BLOOMINGTON *Indiana University Press* LONDON

Library of Congress catalog card number: LC 67-63018

Manufactured in the United States of America

Contents

Introduction by Philip B. Daghlian 3

What Is Language? 6

So What's a Dictionary For? 19

How Words Are Formed 48

How Words Change Meaning in Time and Context 68

An Introduction to Phonetic Alphabets and to Morphemes Through Prefixes and Suffixes 93

American Dialects 153

Why Worry About Meaning? 166

A Suggestion for a Unit on the History of the English Language 168

Lexicography from Cawdrey to *Webster's Third* 170

Nothing Moves Without Translation 192

A Selected Bibliography 214

Appendixes 217

ACKNOWLEDGMENTS

The portion of the project of the Indiana University English Curriculum Study Center reported herein was supported through the Cooperative Research Program of the Office of Education, U.S. Department of Health, Education and Welfare.

The IU Center received additional financial support from the Cummins Engine Foundation, which awarded Indiana University a grant providing funds for meetings and equipment that could not be financed by the grant from the U.S. Office of Education.

The staff of the Indiana University English Curriculum Study Center wishes to thank William E. Wilson, former State Superintendent of Public Instruction, for launching this project in 1962, by appointing teachers to committees to help develop the courses of study, and by appointing Edward B. Jenkinson, Coordinator for School English Language Arts at Indiana University, chairman of the committees. The staff further wishes to thank the Indiana State Department of Public Instruction, under the direction of Richard D. Wells, Superintendent, for distributing this volume to all junior and senior high school teachers of English in Indiana's public schools.

Many teachers played a role in shaping this volume. These members of the state-appointed Committee on Language helped with the initial planning:

Miss Ruth Bertsch, Teacher of English, North Central High School, Indianapolis
Harold Garriott, Associate Professor of English, DePauw University
Miss Frances Graybill, Chairman of the Department of English, Paoli High School, Paoli
Sterling Jackson, Teacher of English, New Trier High School, Winnetka, Illinois
Mrs. Joyce Reed, Chairman of the Department of English, Fremont Consolidated School, Fremont

Webb Salmon, Director of Freshman Composition, Florida State University, Tallahassee
Owen Thomas, Associate Professor of English, Indiana University
Mrs. Margaret Walker, Coordinator, Language Arts and Reading, Hammond Public Schools
Thomas Wetmore, Chairman of the Department of English, Ball State University

The author wishes to thank these teachers who commented on several of the units after testing them in their classrooms:

Mrs. Helen Ashworth, formerly Teacher of English, Mt. Vernon Junior High School, Mt. Vernon
Miss Carolyn Bell, Teacher of English, Franklin Community High School, Franklin
Mrs. Frances Blake, Chairman of the Department of English, Franklin Community High School, Franklin
Mrs. Emma J. Cagle, Chairman of the Department of English, Brazil Senior High School, Brazil
Mrs. Jeanne Campbell, formerly Teacher of English, Noblesville High School, Noblesville
Miss Nondace Campbell, Teacher of English, Huntington County Community High School, Huntington
Jack T. Cole, Teacher of English, River Forest Junior High School, Hobart
Miss Christine Counterman, Teacher of English, Portage High School, Portage
Mrs. Margaret Dillard, Teacher of English, Franklin Community High School, Franklin
Miss Sandra Sue Dragoo, Teacher of English, Lakeside Junior High School, Fort Wayne
Miss Thelma V. Feeler, Teacher of English, Northside Junior High School, Columbus
Mrs. Marjorie Foster, Teacher of English, Northside Junior High School, Columbus
Mrs. Florence Fox, formerly Teacher of English, Franklin Community High School, Franklin
Mrs. Jean M. Hawley, Teacher of English, Mt. Vernon Junior High School, Mt. Vernon
Charles Hayden, Teacher of English, Huntington County Community High School, Huntington
Mrs. Gloria Hjerpe, Teacher of English, William A. Wirt School, Gary
Mrs. Ruth Homco, formerly Teacher of English, River Forest High School, Hobart
Miss Catharine L. Howard, Chairman of the Department of English, Mt. Vernon High School, Mt. Vernon
Mrs. Olive Hughey, Teacher of English, Franklin Community High School, Franklin
Mrs. Ernestine Humphreys, Chairman of the Department of English, Glenn Junior High School, Terre Haute

Miss Catherine Jackson, Chairman of the Department of English, Central High School, Fort Wayne
James Larcomb, Teacher of English, William A. Wirt School, Gary
Mrs. Evelyn Lindsey, formerly Teacher of English, River Forest Junior High School, Hobart
Miss Betty Major, formerly Teacher of English, River Forest High School, Hobart
Miss Lois McClure, Teacher of English, Huntington County Community High School, Huntington
Mrs. Isabelle Morris, Teacher of English, Noblesville Junior High School, Noblesville
Mrs. Daphene Morrison, Teacher of English, Joseph P. Tuttle Junior High School, Crawfordsville
Mrs. Neva Mount, Teacher of English, Tipton Junior High School, Tipton
Mrs. Adrian Neptune, Teacher of English, Northside Junior High School, Columbus
Donald Seybold, Teacher of English, Franklin Community High School, Franklin
Mrs. Betty M. Smith, Teacher of English, Penn High School, Mishawaka
Mrs. Viola Soderstrom, Teacher of English, River Forest High School, Hobart
Miss Marguerite Taylor, Teacher of English, Garfield High School, Terre Haute
Mrs. Annie Wilkerson, Teacher of English, Beckman Junior High School, Gary
Fred E. Wolfe, Teacher of English, Wilson Junior High School, Muncie
Mrs. Juanita Young, Chairman of the Department of English, Huntington County Community High School, Huntington

Special thanks are due these teachers who prepared the first rough drafts of two units: Mrs. Margaret Walker, Coordinator for Language Arts and Reading, Hammond Public Schools, and Mrs. Mary Lou Garriott, Teacher of English, Greencastle High School, who wrote some of the exercises at the end of "So What's a Dictionary For?"; Mrs. Edna Houze, Teacher of English, Columbus High School, and Miss Frances Graybill, who wrote a first draft of the unit on dialects. Some of their ideas and original sentences remain; they are not responsible for the errors in thought and construction, which are the responsibility of the author.

Special thanks also go to Charles Billiard, English Consultant, Fort Wayne Public Schools, for collaborating on the unit, "How Words Change Meaning in Time and Context," and to James R. Jones, Chairman of the Department of English, Würzburg American High School, Würzburg, Germany, for collaborating on the unit on "Lexicography from Cawdry to *Webster's Third*." Ashley Hastings, former instructor in the Intensive Language Program,

Indiana University, deserves thanks for preparing the phonetic transcriptions appended to the unit on prefixes and suffixes.

Grateful acknowledgment is also due Sister Mary Xavier and Brother Thomas Corbett, English Supervisors for the Archdiocese of Cincinnati, and the teachers in the Middletown, Ohio, parochial schools for continuing to test these units after publication so that refinements will be possible.

Grateful acknowledgment is also due Professor Philip B. Daghlian, Department of English, Indiana University, for reading each of these units, for offering helpful suggestions, and for detecting errors. The errors that remain are the responsibility of the author.

These units could not have been tested in public and private schools without the great help of three secretaries—Mrs. Robert D. Spencer, Mrs. James Louden, and Miss Donna Holtel—who patiently retyped several drafts, mimeographed hundreds of copies of each unit, and proofread the final draft.

What Is Language?

AND OTHER TEACHING UNITS
FOR GRADES SEVEN THROUGH TWELVE

Introduction

PHILIP B. DAGHLIAN
PROFESSOR OF ENGLISH
INDIANA UNIVERSITY

For some years now it has been traditional to divide the study of "English" into three component parts, literature, writing, and the language. Language has unfortunately been the most difficult part to communicate, chiefly because its teaching has for so long been complicated by a "totally prescriptive outlook on English usage" and a widespread "subscription to a Latin-oriented grammar."* Too often language study has been merely a series of rigorously applied rules. This practice has had two unfortunate results: the rules seem to have had no effect whatever on the quality of student writing, and many informative and fascinating aspects of the study of language have been ignored in the classroom.

Professor Edward Jenkinson's aim in *What Is Language?* has been to make available to teacher and student alike materials demonstrating some of these interesting aspects of language. At the start he suggests procedures by which students may speculate on the nature of language and formulate their own definitions of it. In connection with a unit on the uses of the dictionary he presents the concepts of denotation and connotation. The next unit proceeds to the formation of words, and the following unit to the process of change of meaning considered both historically and contextually.

**Freedom and Discipline in English:* Report of the Commission on English (CEEB: New York, 1965), p. 18.

The next unit, through a rather extensive examination of prefixes and suffixes, communicates a great deal of information about the meanings of words; it also introduces the students to phonetic alphabets, as used in dictionaries for example, and to the idea of morphemes. Then follows some discussion of American dialects and a treatment of semantics, although the latter is relatively brief because earlier units touch on semantic matters and because teachers are likely to be familiar with the writings on semantics of people like S. I. Hayakawa. A treatment of the history of English lexicography is followed by a brief discussion of the history of the English language.

The final unit, "Nothing Moves Without Translation," is recommended for the beginning of the senior year before students begin reading literary works in translation. The unit presents enough evidence to show the student that reading a translated work presents esthetic and critical problems differing from those evoked by reading a work in the original.

So much for a brief account of what this volume contains. The various units constitute a general, largely non-technical introduction to many aspects of language. But there has been no attempt to be compendious. Many aspects of language are omitted altogether. The very important matter of syntax, for instance, is treated in a separate volume in this series. (See *Two Approaches to Teaching Syntax,* by Marshall Brown, Elmer White, and Edward Jenkinson.) Other aspects are deliberately treated briefly, as is the case with semantics. The often vexing problem of usage has received a great deal of attention over the years. In an appendix Professor Jenkinson makes a few remarks about usage and then reprints an excellent essay by Professor Pooley as representative of enlightened current thinking on the matter. Another appendix contains examples of linguistic change in English relevant to the brief history of the English language in the text. A third contains a brief look at the history of the English language by J. N. Hook and E. G. Mathews. The fourth appendix indicates why roots and combining forms cannot profitably be treated in the same extensive way as were prefixes and suffixes.

It may be appropriate to make a few observations on how all

these materials may be used. Since this series is concerned with the secondary school curriculum, our materials have been prepared for grades seven through twelve. We are quite certain, however, that "What Is Language?" and other units might well be introduced at lower grade levels. We look forward with interest to the trial of some of these materials in the elementary school.

We cannot emphasize too strongly our sense that the materials in this volume should be presented solely in terms of their intrinsic interest. Language is a fascinating phenomenon, with facets that can and do appeal to young and old alike, to the amateur and the professional, to the layman and the scholar. Since we are concerned with this aspect of language, we urge that the teaching of it be done in as relaxed a way as possible. The teacher is guiding his students on a trip through new territory. He will point out matters of interest along the way, but he will not be foolish enough to insist that every student be able to describe in detail every wonder he has observed. If the student's interest in the area is properly engaged, he may well want to make return journeys to the territory of language at later stages in his life. Thus it is most important that a teacher present small amounts of these materials over extended periods of time, rather than try to "cover" everything rapidly. For example, the role of prefixes and suffixes in the meanings of words is fascinating in small doses, but to assign all the lists at one time would be an almost certain way to kill all interest in language.

If the teacher can communicate the sense that permeates this volume, that language is one of the most fascinating of human activities, students will have received a most valuable foundation on which to base all their subsequent thinking about language, in whatever form it may reveal itself.

GRADE 7

What Is Language?

Language plays such a constant, vital role in our daily lives that we rarely—if ever—pause to think about it. Most of us simply take language for granted. Asked to define it, we would probably dismiss the question as being silly. "Of course I know what language is. It's . . . well, it's . . . ."

We teachers of English may not be able to define language to the satisfaction of linguists, but we—and our students—do know a great deal about it. But many of us also entertain a number of misconceptions about the nature of language which we may share with our students, particularly if we are content to teach only those matters of language commonly presented in the traditional "grammar" textbooks. If we do not explore matters of language other than those included in such texts, it is unlikely that our students will ever discuss the nature of language in our classes and correct some of their—and our—misconceptions. A seventh grader, for example, has been learning, playing with, and communicating with language for approximately ten years; he has been studying aspects of language in school for seven years. Yet it is highly unlikely that he has ever been asked, "What is language?"—a question that he would probably consider stupid.

Why trouble seventh graders with a discussion of language? Why lead them to form their own definitions of language?

If language is basic to civilization, we and our students should understand what it is and how it works. If language is man's most important invention, we and our students should know more about it than the fact that we use it every day. If problems in communication arise because people fail to understand the nature of language, then we need to discuss language with students at the earliest age they can contribute to the discussion.*

This unit is designed to lead students to discover for themselves what language is. The teacher serves as guide and referee, keeping the discussion on the right track, giving every student an opportunity to contribute, helping students arrive at intelligent conclusions and thereby enjoy personal discovery. To put it another way, by giving students challenging questions and by setting the proper climate for discussion, the teacher encourages students to find out for themselves how language operates instead of making the discovery for them and passing along information.

To launch the discussion, the teacher might ask questions like these:

1. What kinds of noises can we make with our mouths? Do all of those noises mean something? Are some of the noises more meaningful than others? Do you know exactly what's wrong when a baby cries? Does the cry tell you something? Does it tell you everything you need to know to stop the baby from crying? Or is it just a clue? Are there different kinds of cries? Do they all mean something? If you hear a person whistle, what does that tell you about him? Do some whistles mean something while others do not? Can you tell your neighbor something just by whistling? What noises do you make when you hurt yourself? What noises do you make when someone tells a funny story? Do the noises of pain and happiness mean anything? Can you tell by the noises he makes that a person is in pain or that he is happy?

2. Do you make noises when you talk? Or, to put the question another way, is talking just making noises? If so, what kinds of noise? Must you make certain kinds of noise when you want to talk to someone? What kinds of noise do you make when you talk to someone? What do you call those noises? When did you start

*The project of the Indiana University English Curriculum Study Center is to prepare courses of study for grades seven through twelve; thus this introductory unit is designed for grade seven. However, it could be taught earlier than grade seven, and teachers in some school systems are experimenting with elementary school pupils to determine just how early pupils can discuss intelligently the nature of language.

learning how to make them? How did you learn to make them?

3. Is talking a form of communication? What is communication? How many kinds of communication can you think of? How many different methods can we use to communicate our thoughts and feelings? Must we rely solely on spoken words? Can we communicate our feelings by facial expressions such as a scowl, or an arched eyebrow, or a smile? Can we communicate our feelings by gestures?

4. Do animals communicate? Do they learn how to communicate, or do they do this instinctively? To clarify that question we can ask: Does a puppy learn to growl when a stranger is near or does a puppy just growl instinctively?

5. Does man communicate instinctively or does he learn how to communicate? Or does man communicate both instinctively and non-instinctively? To clarify that question, we can ask students: A small baby cries for food long before he learns how to talk. Does he cry instinctively? Later, he learns to ask for milk, or a sandwich, or a steak. Does he do this instinctively?

Thus far our questions have concentrated primarily on communication in its various forms. We should have led students to see that they communicate with the noises they make with their mouths, but they can also communicate thoughts and feelings in other ways. We have more questions to ask if we want our students to discover for themselves what language is, how it is developed, and how it works. But to ask those questions in a context that will free students' minds to explore language and discover some basic concepts for themselves, we need to set up a situation that can lead to the process of discovery. The thrill of discovery should not be minimized, because students are more likely to remember concepts if they are given the opportunity to explore a subject themselves and arrive at their own conclusions. Therefore, we set up a situation like this for our students, and we ask teachers to guide them on this mental journey by saying something like this:

Let's pretend that this class has been transported back in time more than five thousand years. Each of you lives in the same area. All of you want to get along. You nod at one another. You grunt. But you do not communicate by any means other than grunting, pounding your fists on logs, nodding your heads, grimacing, and, perhaps, hitting one another with clubs if two of you decide that you want the same thing. Now how would you go about developing a system of communication? In other words, how would you develop a language?

If the teacher has succeeded in arousing interest, he may wish to describe the problem further before students attempt to answer this question. The teacher may wish to say something like this:

Let's suppose that you want to tell your neighbor that you are hungry. You could rub your stomach, or you could smack your lips. Or you could do both and also cry. But your neighbor might think you have a pain in your stomach instead of thinking that you are hungry, so you try verbalizing. You say, "Glizzle." Now what does that mean? Does it mean "I'm hungry," or just "hungry," or "Let's go kill a dinosaur"? Or perhaps you say, "Ee glizzle" or "Glizzle ee," either of which could mean "I'm hungry."

Suppose that you and your neighbors agree that when you say "Glizzle," this utterance means "I'm hungry." But when you say "Glizzle?" with a rise in pitch on the last part of the word, it means "Are you hungry?" And if you say in a very high tone "Glizzle!" it means "I'm starved." If you say glizzle in a very low tone with a stress on the first part of the word, it might mean "There's a dinosaur."

All of this may seem like nonsense, but it does focus students' attention on a problem that probably had to be solved by our ancestors. How did they learn to communicate if they had no language and had to form their own? To rephrase an earlier question for our students, If you had no language, what would you and your neighbors need to do to devise a system of communication? What methods of communication are possible? What are the problems that you must solve?

That line of questioning could continue until students realize that, put into the situation described above, they would need to agree on what sounds stand for certain things; on how the sounds are to be put together in a pattern or system; on whether they would rely on word order, inflection, intonation, or all three.

To lead students to an understanding of what word order, inflection, and intonation are, the teacher might, during the discussion, note that students have perhaps agreed that "Eeek glizzle dong" means "I killed a dinosaur." Would it mean the same thing if they said "Dong glizzle eeek"? Or would that mean "The dinosaur killed me"? By developing that kind of questioning students should see the importance of word order in some languages. They might be led to see that English relies heavily on word order by examining several sentences like these: John loves Mary. Mary loves John. The boy hit the ball. The ball hit the boy.

To lead students from word order to inflection, the teacher might note that in some languages the words need not be put into a definite order; instead, the endings on the words are changed like this: "Ee glizzle dongun" means "I killed a dinosaur." "Dongun glizzle ee" means "I killed a dinosaur." And "Glizzle dongun ee" also means "I killed a dinosaur." But "Dong glizzle eeek," "Eeek glizzle dong," and "Glizzle dong eeek" all mean "The dinosaur killed me." (Students should readily see that we do not have endings like those in English. Nor can we change the meaning of a verb like glizzle simply by saying: glizzlo, glizzlas, glizzat, glizzamus, glizzatis, glizzant—which means I kill, you [singular] kill, he kills, we kill, you [plural] kill, and they kill.)

To illustrate the role that intonation plays in language, the teacher might note that when a student gives his mother a present, the mother might respond exclaiming "That's nice," or "It's beautiful," or "That's great." How would a mother say each of those expressions if she were happy? Students might say each aloud, noting what they do with their voices to show they are delighted. Then the student spills coke on the rug and mother says "That's nice," or "That's beautiful, just beautiful," or "That's great." How would a mother say those phrases if she were unhappy? Again, students might say the phrases aloud, noting what they do with their voices to show that they are unhappy.

After students have arrived at an understanding of word order, inflection, and intonation, the teacher might have them review the problem of designing a language to determine just what they need to know, and on what they would need to agree, before they could begin communicating satisfactorily with one another in a new language. The teacher might divide the class into groups of four to six, assigning each group the task of attempting an initial design of a new language. To get started, each group might answer questions like these:

1. How will we express such basic feelings as "I am hungry," "I am thirsty," "I am sleepy," "I am sick," "I am afraid"? (As students begin supplying words for those phrases, they should note the emergence of a thread of a pattern. For each of those statements, for example, students need to agree on one group, or several groups, of sounds to express "I am." They also need to decide on the arrangement of the words. Do *hungry, thirsty, sleepy, sick,* and *afraid* come before or after *I am*?)

2. What sounds will we put together to designate boy, girl, young man, young woman, man, woman, old man, old woman? (Is there any pattern to the sounds they designate for those words? Did one group use the same word for girl, young woman, woman, and old woman, for example, but say it in a different tone to signal the difference in meaning? If a group is so inventive, the teacher might want to spend a minute or two talking about tonal languages.) What sounds will we use to designate various animals? (Again, do the sounds have anything in common? A thread of a pattern may not become apparent until students attempt to distinguish age and sex of the same family of animals, e.g., cow, calf, bull, steer, heifer. Of course, it is readily apparent after saying those English words that a pattern of sounds may not emerge.)

3. What sounds will we use to name the objects immediately around us?

4. After we have named objects around us and have decided on sounds to express basic feelings, what sentences can we make with the new words we have invented? What patterns begin to emerge? (Do students rely on inflection, word order, intonation? Can they find a pattern in their new language?)

The teacher will probably not have students spend more than two class periods designing their new language. After they have attempted to put together sounds for a spoken language, they are ready to work on the problem of recording that new language on paper. What problems must students solve now? What are the differences between written and spoken language? What ways do men use to record their thoughts and feelings on paper? To record their new languages on paper, must each group of students devise an alphabet, or can they record their languages some other way? (The teacher may assign several students the task of preparing oral reports on writing systems before the groups of students meet again to design a means of recording their new languages on paper. The teacher might refer students to chapter two of Margaret Schlauch's *The Gift of Language* [New York: Dover Publications, 1955], or to Gerd Fraenkel's *Writing Systems* [Boston: Ginn and Company, 1965], or to encyclopedias.)

After students have worked on the problems of developing a spoken language and then of attempting to record that language on paper, each student is ready to arrive at his own definition of language. The teacher should give the class one period in which each student attempts to write his own definition of language—a definition that he can remember for years to come. As students attempt to write their definitions, the teacher should wander around the room, talking with students about their definitions, helping them include items that they might have left out, but encouraging them to arrive at comprehensive definitions of their own, written in their own words. If the teacher collects the definitions, he should not grade them; instead he should write useful comments on the papers that would help the students revise their definitions to make them more comprehensive and easier to remember.

The teacher may want to examine with students one or more definitions of language prepared by linguists. But such an examination should come only after students have arrived at their own definitions and may not be necessary if the students' definitions are adequate. If the teacher reads one or more of the following definitions, he might have students discuss the selection, indicating why they agree or disagree with the definition and noting how they might want to add to their own definitions to include some ideas about language that they left out.

In *The Structure of American English,* W. Nelson Francis offers his brief definition: "A language is an arbitrary system of articulated sounds made use of by a group of humans as a means of carrying on the affairs of their society."

Archibald Hill gives this definition in his *Introduction to Linguistic Structures* (published by Harcourt, Brace & World):

> Language is the primary and most highly elaborated form of human symbolic activity. Its symbols are made up of sounds produced by the vocal apparatus, and they are arranged in classes and patterns which make up a complex and symmetrical structure. The entities of language are symbols, that is, they have meaning, but the connection between symbol and thing is arbitrary and socially controlled. The symbols of language are simultaneously substitute stimuli and substitute responses and can call forth further stimuli and responses, so that discourse becomes independent of an immediate physical stimulus. The entities and structure of language are always so elaborated as to give the speaker the possibility of making a linguistic response to any experience. Most of the above can be paraphrased by saying that every language is a model of a culture and its adjustment to the world.

In *The Development of Modern English,* Robertson and Cassidy define language as "the vocal and audible medium of human communication." Then they consider each part of the definition, "clarifying where necessary." Their clarification is extensive, but part of it is reprinted here:

> To say that language is vocal and audible immediately puts aside everything written—and that is as it should be. For writing is a *record* of language, and is therefore on a different plane altogether. People spoke long before any means of record was invented, and the records we make today (in print, or on disks, wires, tapes, photographic film, and so forth) would have no meaning if they could not be translated back into speech. True, they do not always need to be translated so; communication may take place altogether on this second level, as when we correspond with people we have never seen or heard, or when a deaf person learns to read silently the new "visible speech." For to a practiced reader the words on a page need not suggest sounds at all. He has learned to respond directly to what he sees: he has a short cut through the eye that eliminates the ear. This does not change the system, however, which began as a record of speech, and is always potentially retranslatable.

The dots and dashes of the Morse Code are on still a third level, since they are substitutes for the letters with which we spell out our records of speech; and with them are the gestures of the deaf-mute, also substitutes for the letters of a system of writing. In short, our definition recognizes that the basis of language is speech, whatever other structures may be built upon it.

Since gesture has been mentioned, we may ask here whether it is not language. The American Indians had a system of signs once widely used as a kind of diplomatic code by tribes whose dialects were mutually unintelligible. The gestures were conventionalized, and they served for communication, but (unlike deaf-mute gestures) the system bore no relation whatever to vocal sounds. Thus, though it was certainly language in the broader sense, it does not come under our definition. Had vocal communication never been discovered, this kind of sign language might have had to serve for all human communication, though it is hard to imagine how it could have undergone the high degree of elaboration that speech permits of.

Gesture surely preceded speech as a means of human communication and will never be wholly displaced. Some nations and individuals use it more than others, and the gestures themselves differ in meaning from place to place—for example, a nod of the head, which to us means "yes," means "no" in some parts of the East; we clap our hands in applause, but in the Orient this means a summons. However, we all communicate by gesture to some extent. A frown or a shaken fist will everywhere be recognized as threatening. We indicate the sizes of things with our hands ("about *so* long"), and some shapes and movements are far easier to show than to describe (a spiral staircase, or the playing of a concertina). Gesture, then, though it may serve alone up to a point, is usually no more than an aid to speech, which can be far more detailed and precise, and which can proceed with perfect efficiency (as gesture cannot) even when the speakers do not see each other.

Returning to our definition, we find that the use of the word *human* raises a second question: Is it correct to deny the name of language to the sounds made by the "lower animals"? Such sounds are certainly vocal and audible, and many animals appear to be able to communicate a variety of notions to each other by means of sound. Crows and other birds post sentinels to give the cry of alarm when danger threatens, and the barnyard hen makes quite different noises when searching for food for her chicks and when warning them that a hawk is near. But even if there is some likeness in kind, the difference comes in degree, and there it is vast. The language of even the most primitive humans known is enormously more complex than the range of distinctive sounds made by the highest apes. Human speech employs the symbolic process, by which a sound or sound-group is made to "stand for" something with which it may have only a conventional connection—that is, a connection which depends solely upon the tacit agreement, among speakers of the same language, that those particular sounds ("words") will always be interpreted in the same way when used in similar conditions.

Our use of this process is very highly developed; the animals do not appear to use it at all. Their signals seem to refer to broad situations and to concrete things present to their senses; besides, their range of distinctive sounds is too small to permit much elaboration. When (as in the case of bees) they communicate relatively detailed information, this is done by actions, not by speech. Human speech, on the other hand, always has enough distinctive sounds (phonemes) so that their combinations may produce many thousands of "words," which may, in turn, be attached by general agreement to as many things and concepts. It is the possession of this kind of language which separates us widely—one might say essentially—from the rest of the animals.

The third limitation in our definition, that language is a *medium of communication,* will probably raise the largest question, since it is clear that language is not used exclusively for communication. What Madame de Staël has written of the French language surely applies to all others too: "It is not only a means of communicating thoughts, feeling and acts, but an instrument that one loves to play upon, and that stimulates the mental faculties much as music does for some people and strong drink for others." Children discover very early, and adults never forget, that language may give kinesthetic enjoyment through the mere exercise of the vocal organs, and (what is far deeper) esthetic pleasure by expressing whole complexes of inward sensations.

When we talk at length to animals—as Alice in Wonderland does to her cat Dinah, which is not even present—we do not expect to be understood; like a baby babbling, or like Wordsworth's solitary reaper singing to herself, we often make sounds merely for the enjoyment of utterance. In short, language has an important expressive function, as well as the communicative one. Much of what we say in social intercourse, while ostensibly communicative, is no more than vaguely so and is quite as much expressive. The words we use in greeting or in being pleasant to people are not to be taken literally; they, and the tone in which they are said, are mostly a means of establishing a friendly atmosphere.

It is probably safe to conjecture that expressive sounds preceded communicative language, since they require a single speaker only, and the noises made are not necessarily conventionalized. As a speaker repeatedly made sounds, however, he might well find them falling into habitual patterns—like the songs of some birds—and another creature, hearing them in connection with particular situations, might interpret them accordingly. Thus the person expressing himself would quite incidentally be communicating. When, for example, he howled with hunger, smaller creatures would keep out of his way. So expression would pass insensibly into communication as the expression became more willful or as one creature's expression brought a reply from another. Cries evoked by pain, fear, anger, love-longing, and such elemental sensations were surely as much the property of primitive man as of modern man and the lower animals. Out of some such crude beginnings must have come the highly developed structure of language—a primarily social thing as we know it, and primarily communicative rather than expressive.*

In *Language in the Modern World* (published by Penguin Books), Simeon Potter offers this description of language:

Effective language is ever two-way. It is, first of all, an instrument of communication. It consists of an arbitrary system or pattern of speech-sounds by means of which man imparts to others, and shares with others, his thoughts, emotions, and desires. Inasmuch as language is human and non-instinctive, it is raised above the noises made by animals, birds, and insects, such instinctive forms of self-expression as the neighing of a horse, the barking of a dog, the croaking of a frog, the hooting of an owl, or the stridulation of a cricket. Language is a series of sounds or air-vibrations produced by the articulating organs of the speaker and received by the auditory organ or ear of the hearer, and implying a highly complex network of adjustments in the nervous systems and the brains of both speaker and hearer. Such arbitrary series of sounds are theoretically infinite in number. No one will ever know how many languages have been devised by man in the course of his long history. Many have disappeared without a trace. In the modern world their number is between two and three thousand.

In *A Linguistic Introduction to the History of English,* Morton W. Bloomfield and Leonard Newmark describe language as:

. . . a subject of great complexity. It is a connecting medium: it connects men with other men, men with the world, men with themselves, parts of

*From *The Development of Modern English,* 2nd ed., © 1953; reprinted by permission of Prentice-Hall, Inc.

the world with other parts of it, and, in terms of time, the present with the past and the future. It forms a complex series of intricate relationships. We must even use language in our analysis of language. In order for us to see it as a whole satisfactorily, we must regard a language from a variety of perspectives. In both its oral and written forms, it is an aspect of human behavior; a biological and sociological phenomenon with a survival role in evolution; the basis for all education in the broadest sense of the word; a consistent structure with dynamic possibilities; a key to the intellectual structure of various cultures; an esthetic and magical phenomenon. It is a process, a structure, and a preserving medium all at once. It is no wonder that the word "language" is full of ambiguities and that scholars attempt to resolve them by distinguishing terms such as speech, language, tongue, discourse, utterance, and so forth.

Language is not only a creature of society, but like other social institutions, it is also a creator of society: sharing a language is a necessary result and a necessary condition of people living together. But a language is also of the most intimate importance for individuality as such. The acquisition of language in the life of an individual is closely bound up with his mental development and growth. His sense of the world, for example, depends to a great extent on the language he uses. Language enables man both to express himself and to orient himself to the world and society. Because the structure of an individual's personality is so intimately bound up both genetically and systematically with the language he speaks, it is very difficult for people to be objective about their own language. We are so conditioned to these conventionally accepted noises that it is hard for us even to think of them as noises. Thus, to become linguistically aware requires a special concentration on language as an object, which, for humans, who tend to regard the vagaries and accidents of their own language as having an inherent universal and permanent validity, is difficult and perhaps even shocking. We should remind ourselves that linguistics, the objective study of language, can serve not only its own proper function of adding to our general knowledge about language, but can also serve to liberate us from the tyranny, in its subtlest form, of the word. In the course of his life each human being discovers his language, and comes to think of it as a given natural object, rather than as the product of human behavior that it is. One of the reasons we find it difficult to look at our own language objectively arises from the way by which we come to know it. A horse is really a "horse" because our experience tells us it is a "horse."

As Julian Marias writes, "Language is something which each of us encounters; we have not made it ourselves; no one in particular has made it; it is 'there,' with its precise phonetic laws, with a phonetic system, with a vocabulary and a syntax; it is a *social* reality and it serves us precisely for that reason: a language is understood because it is apart from the individuality of each one of its speakers, because it is valid for all, and therefore recourse to it is automatically effective. . . . There is, then, a linguistic ambit which is prior to individuals, in which the latter find themselves immersed, just as they do in the physical world or in the system of beliefs and customs."

GRADE 7

So What's a Dictionary For?

We live in a world of words. With words we imagine, we dream, we think, we believe, we feel, we scream, we sing, and we communicate. The more we control words, the more orderly our own private world becomes, the more we appreciate it, the more we expand it, and the more we contribute to the public world. And the more we know about words, the better we can control them and our worlds—both private and public.

But what is a word? How is it formed? What are its limits? What does a word mean? Or better, how does a word mean?

In his conversation with Alice, Humpty Dumpty declared:

"When *I* use a word . . . it means just what I choose it to mean—neither more nor less."

"The question is," said Alice, "whether you *can* make words mean so many different things."

"The question is," said Humpty Dumpty, "which is to be master—that's all."*

The question really is, Who are to be the masters? Perhaps Humpty Dumpty could make words mean just what he wanted them to—for himself. (In "The Jabberwocky" he adequately dis-

*Lewis Carroll, "Through the Looking-Glass," in *Alice in Wonderland and Other Favorites* (New York: Washington Square Press, 1960), p. 190.

played his ability to coin words.) But he had no control over Alice and her experiences with the same words. So the question of mastery must take into account both the speaker or the writer and his listener or reader.

Had Humpty Dumpty commanded Alice to bring him a table, for instance, he could have meant a piece of furniture, or a systematic list of details about a certain thing, or a thin, flat tablet of metal or stone to write on. Had he meant furniture, he might have intended table to mean a particular kind, such as kitchen, dining room, dressing, coffee, or writing. And he could further have wanted a specific style of one of those tables. But he could not have counted on Alice's bringing him the right table had he not been specific. For to Alice, table could have meant any piece of furniture that had a flat top made of any substance set horizontally on from one to four or more legs.

As children we learned that the word table can refer to several things. We learned the word by imitating the sounds made by our parents and others around us, and we became unconsciously aware of groups of sounds that refer to certain things, or of sounds like *at* and *to* that we constantly use in sentences. As we grew older, we learned that these groups of sounds are called words. And as we continued learning language, we attached certain meanings to these groups of sounds. Some of us grew up thinking that groups of sounds have fixed meanings and that words can be used only in certain ways. Some of us still believe, or we have been taught, that we can always check the "meaning" of a word by referring to a dictionary. We sometimes further believe, or we are told, that if we cannot find in the dictionary the meaning we intended a word to mean we have used the word incorrectly. And therein lies the problem.

No matter how hard we try, we teachers of English can never fix meanings of words so that language study will be easy for students, nor do we want to freeze meanings of words if we prize our living, changing language. We can, however, help students to understand what words are, how they are formed, what and how they mean, and how they work in sentences.

Frequently we hear this question: "What does this word mean?" The question is misleading, for most words do not have a single meaning, but meanings. And that's one of the main points we want to make in this second unit of the language study sequence.

This unit presents several steps in a sequence designed to acquaint students with words, what they are, and how they work. The unit includes basic material that all students—academically talented, average, and slow-learning—need. The teacher can adapt the material to any class. A slow-learning student, for instance, need not learn the terms connotation and denotation, but he can learn those concepts inductively by following the steps presented here.

The first part of this unit deals with denotations and connotations, leading logically to answers to the question, "So what's a dictionary for?" This unit and the preceding one on "What Is Language?" lay the foundation for the units in grades eight through twelve.

This unit is also part of the total junior high school language study sequence that includes units on syntax, usage, and spelling. The unit further provides information on words that students need to write themes and to read with comprehension the literature assigned in the junior high school.

Familiarity with only one dictionary does not give a student an adequate introduction to the study of words. Therefore, this unit considers dictionaries, not a dictionary. In preparing this unit, we have referred to these dictionaries: *The American College Dictionary, Funk & Wagnalls Standard College Dictionary, The Oxford English Dictionary, The Oxford Universal Dictionary on Historical Principles, The Random House Dictionary of the English Language, The Thorndike-Barnhart High School Dictionary, Webster's New World Dictionary of the American Language, Webster's Seventh New Collegiate Dictionary, Webster's Third New International Dictionary*. We recommend that a teacher have a class set of one of those dictionaries and that several copies of each of the other dictionaries be available to the class, excluding *The Oxford English Dictionary,* which, it is hoped, will be available in the library in at least its shorter, two-volume form.

DENOTATIONS

To launch this unit, the teacher may wish to write a list of words like this on the chalkboard:

spring	friend	average	no
astronaut	hate	cat	old
love	insubordinate	enemy	green
fall	contact	television	run
to	strike	jazz	bank

What do we call each of these groups of letters? Students may think such a question ridiculous since it is obvious that the answer is *a word*. But the question and its answer are basic to the understanding of the material that follows. If students agree that every group of letters on the list is a word, how do they know this? What do these letter-groups have in common? What is a word?

Any definition of *word* will be controversial from a linguist's point of view. For years linguists accepted Aristotle's definition that a word is the smallest significant unit of speech. Today, however, linguists have found a significant unit of meaning smaller than a word, the morpheme, which will be explained to students in the unit on phonetic alphabets and morphemes in grade nine. For the time being, however, it would be useful to have students examine the letter-groups on the chalkboard and attempt a definition of *word*. Typical responses might include: "A word is a group of letters that has meaning," or, "A word is a series of sounds that we can produce and that make sense." Such definitions are acceptable at this point, but they will need clarification and expansion later.

Let's leave the list for a moment if students agree that it contains words, and let's ask them if the following is a list of words:

wamtupper	erg	zppg	clarkle
iggle	ogn	img	swicky
slibble	doncuted	skeif	syzygy

Students will probably laugh when they see this list and will probably agree that each of the letter-groups is a nonsense word.

Probably no student will know that *erg, skeif,* and *syzygy* are words. Students need not be troubled with the dictionary definitions of *erg, skeif,* and *syzygy;* they need only realize that real words can be buried in a list of nonsense words.

But why did students reject the second list of letter-groups? Why didn't they think the list contained words? They probably agreed that the groups of letters did not have meanings; consequently, they decided that letter-groups that have no meanings for them are not words. They have chanced upon one important point: a word contains no meaning until a person experiences the word. "Words do not have meanings; people have meanings for words."*

Now let's return to the first list. Do all words on it have meanings? Students will probably answer yes. But what about *to*? Can students define *to* as it stands alone? Or can they only tell what it "means" when they see it in sentences? Even in a sentence, does *to* actually "mean" something, or does it indicate relationships between words, or the position of one thing to another, or the result of an action? Does *to* have "meanings" in these sentences?

1. He wanted to help the woman across the street. (Here, *to* has no meaning *per se;* it is the sign of the infinitive.)
2. Willie Mays ran to first base. (*To* is used as a function word indicating where.)
3. The early Greeks built temples to their gods. (*To* is used as a function word to indicate purpose.)
4. The prisoner was sentenced to death. (*To* is used as a function word to indicate determined end.)
5. She rose to fame rapidly. (*To* is used as a function word to indicate condition.)

We could give many more examples of the multiple functions of *to*, but each example would only show that *to* does not, by itself, denote or connote anything; it serves to indicate some relationship of the word it connects to the rest of the sentence. Students can find denotations of *to* in dictionaries; however, they will note that in al-

*W. Nelson Francis, *The English Language: An Introduction* (New York: W. W. Norton, 1965), p. 121.

most every instance an example of the word as it is used in a phrase is given to indicate its meaning in a particular context. A few other words that do not "mean" by themselves, for the most part, but indicate relationships are *at, from, in, of, on,* and *with.*

"Then, are sounds like *to* and *at* words?" a student might ask. Of course they are, but they do not "mean" in the same way that most other words do. A connecting word "means" in a different way from a word which by itself has a core of meanings. The "meaning" of *to* and *at* derive from their use in sentences, not from a core of definitions that we give those words.

MEANINGS—NOT A MEANING

Now let's look again at that first column of words. If we ask students what *spring* means instead of asking for the meanings of *spring,* at least one student might ask what kind of *spring* we mean. He should be congratulated for seeing that the word *spring* can refer to a number of things; for example, a season of the year, a leap or jump, an elastic or bounding movement, a stream of water flowing from the earth, or a device, usually made of wire or steel coiled spirally, which recovers its shape after being compressed or bent. These, of course, are only a few meanings of *spring. The American College Dictionary* includes fifteen entries for *spring* used as an intransitive verb, ten as a transitive verb, fourteen as a noun, and two as an adjective. Consequently, we can see that *spring* does not have one meaning, but several meanings.

Let's go on with the set of words on page 22 to make students aware of the many meanings words have. For the second word, *astronaut, Webster's Third New International Dictionary* gives two definitions: "1. a traveler in interplanetary space, and 2. a pupil, devotee, or advocate of astronautics." Although we do not plan to go into connotations at this point, the teacher may wish to ask students what they think of when they hear the word *astronaut.* Students will probably respond with words like hero, brave, courageous, superman, and so on. Some of the boys may become quite excited and want to talk about the latest exploits of the astronauts. The teacher may simply note at this stage that the mere mention of *astronaut* excites some students. Why? When students hear the word, do they think only of its dictionary meaning? Or do other thoughts enter their minds?

It would be useful at this stage to have students go through the list of words in the first two columns and give as many meanings as they can for each word, and then have them check dictionaries for the body of meanings that the dictionaries include. Class time can be well spent if the teacher has students examine all the words on the list and try to give meanings for these words. Students should conclude that most of the words on the list have more than one meaning. Therefore the question, "What does a word mean?" should seem inadequate to them. They should learn that a more appropriate question might be, "What are the dictionary meanings of a given word?" For example, students will find more than fifty meanings of *run* in some dictionaries. *The American College Dictionary* lists 104, *Webster's New World Dictionary of the American Language* lists 87, and *The Thorndike-Barnhart High School Dictionary* lists 37.

How do some words have so many meanings? How do the makers of dictionaries decide what these words mean? How can we be certain that we are using a word correctly if it means so many different things? These are some of the questions that should occur to students as they become aware of the many dictionary definitions of a word. We will not attempt to answer these questions fully at this point; however, we will try to give students enough information to stimulate their interest and to make them curious about words. The answers to the three questions we have raised in this paragraph, as well as answers to additional questions, will grow clearer as students work through the language sequence.

Let's take those first three questions one at a time and give students some information.

How do some words have so many meanings? Language is a miracle—a miracle of man. As early man examined his environment, he learned that he must give names to the objects around him in order to communicate with his fellow man. For years linguists have advanced theories about man's method of attempting to affix a series of sounds to an object as an oral symbol for that object.

Many of those theories have been discredited. However, it is safe to theorize that as man gave names to objects his fellow man accepted the series of sounds that were put together to make the name and that they agreed that these sounds referred to a specific object. As man developed a more complex society, he discovered that he needed many more words, or series of sounds, to name the objects around him. He formed new words, borrowed words from other languages, and extended the meanings of existing words in his vocabulary to refer to different objects. Thus, in many instances, a single word could be made to refer to a number of different objects. Therefore, a speaker using a word that could refer to a number of different objects found it necessary to make it clear by the rest of the words in his sentence which object he was referring to.

Uses of Run

Let's take *run* as an example of a word that has come to refer to a number of different things. The teacher will want to mimeograph either these sentences or sentences like them and give them to students, or he may prefer to read the sentences and ask students what the word *run* refers to in each of the sentences:

1. Willie Mays hit his five hundredth home run on September 12, 1965.
2. "That was a good run," the track coach said.
3. He told his wife that she should not run up big bills.
4. That man never stops; he is always on the run.
5. That ill-mannered child has the complete run of the house.
6. The run on the banks in 1929 caused serious trouble for the United States.
7. In the long run you are better off if you do not buy too many things that you cannot pay cash for.
8. That musical composition is difficult because of its intricate run.
9. The mine had a huge run of silver.
10. The candidate announced that he will run for office.
11. When the smelt run, the fishermen in northern Michigan get excited.

12. The rapid reader is one who has learned to run his eyes down a page quickly.
13. He wants to run up to Chicago for the weekend.
14. The trainer said that he will not run the horse in the next race.
15. She had a run in her stocking.

Students will have little difficulty making additional sentences in which the word *run* stands for a different action or thing. By examining such sentences, they should see that man has extended the meaning of *run* to refer to a great number of objects or actions.

When students hear or read the word *run* in a sentence, how can they tell which *run* is meant by the speaker or writer? By reexamining the sentences above, they should conclude that they can learn the meaning only from the entire sentence. Thus they have concluded that words sometimes can be dealt with only in context. In other words, the listener or reader can only infer what is meant after he has examined all the words surrounding the word in question.

A unit for grade eight deals with how words change meaning in time and context, so we will not go into contextual meanings of words in great detail now. However, we feel that it is necessary for students at this stage to recognize that the "meaning" of a word can frequently be determined only after a careful examination of its use in a sentence. Other clues to meaning must also be considered. For example, words change meaning in time and they also change meaning by intonation. Students will become well aware of these changes after they have studied the unit in grade eight. For the time being, it is necessary only for them to be aware of other clues to meaning besides context.

Let's take the word *nice* as an example of a word to which men have given a number of different meanings in its four hundred year history in the English language.

In 1513, for example, a writer might have used the word *nice* to mean that a piece of work to which he was referring required or involved great precision, accuracy, or minuteness. Therefore, if a writer wrote that something was "a *nice* piece of work," he meant that it required great skill to make. The word *nice* still retains this meaning in some contexts today. Only thirty-eight years later, a writer may have used *nice,* in referring to a person, to mean that the person was extremely careful and precise or that he was punctilious or difficult to please or satisfy. Nine years later, in 1560, men also used the word *nice* to mean that a person was foolish or stupid. By 1604 the word had acquired the additional meanings of unimportant and trivial. Not until 1830 did people use the word *nice* in the way that we most frequently use it today, that is, to mean kind, considerate, or pleasant.

Since words change meaning in time, it is necessary for the sensitive reader of literature to be aware of these changes so that he can understand what the writer means by a certain word. These changes of meaning in time are frequently radical changes as will be discussed in the unit, "How Words Change Meaning in Time and Context."

Another important clue to meaning comes in oral discourse. We can frequently tell what a person means by the ways he says a word. Again, let's take the word *nice* as an example. If a student gives his mother a present for her birthday, she may exclaim, "That's nice." In such a context, the student's mother is probably very pleased with the present and she means that not only the giving of the present was a pleasant surprise but that the present itself was appreciated. On the other hand, if a student comes home from school late and gives a lame excuse for his tardiness, his mother may exclaim, "That's nice." By the way that she says the word and by the expression on her face, the student can immediately infer that his mother does not accept his action as being something pleasant but that she is using the word *nice* sarcastically.

Words, then, take on different meanings in context, in time, and through intonation patterns.

But we still have not answered this question, "How do dictionary makers decide the meanings of words?" The dictionary maker, or lexicographer, collects many examples of different uses of a word by well-known writers and speakers, and he studies these uses very carefully in context. After studying numerous uses of a word, he arrives at definitions of the word which he records in the dictionary. (To compile a dictionary like *Webster's Third, Webster's New*

World Dictionary, or *The Random House Dictionary*, large staffs of specialists spend years examining many uses of words in context before they arrive at a definition.) These definitions can be called dictionary, or lexical, definitions. They can also be called the word's denotations. (It is not our purpose here to give students a number of terms that they must memorize or that they must define in examinations. However, it is important for students to learn the word denotation.) A word's denotation is the dictionary entries for that word, or to put it another way, it is the core of meanings that a word has. For example, the word *sleep* has a definite denotation; it means the act of bodily rest that we perform in the evening in a reclining position. If we check the entry for the word *asleep* in *The American College Dictionary*, we find these definitions: "1. in or into a state of sleep.—adj. 2. sleeping. 3. dormant; inactive. 4. (of the foot, hand, leg, etc.) numb. 5. dead."

These entries give us the common core of meanings assigned to the word *asleep*. From this common core of meanings, we can infer what a writer or speaker means when he declares: "Harry was asleep at the switch and did not do what we wanted him to." Or, "His mind was asleep during the test."

Let's look at a very common word that has a definite core of meanings, or denotations. *The Thorndike-Barnhart High School Dictionary* lists these denotations for *cat*: "1. a small, four-footed, flesh-eating mammal often kept as a pet or for catching mice. 2. any animal of the group including cats, lions, tigers, leopards, etc. 3. animal something like a cat. 4. a mean, spiteful woman. 5. catfish. 6. cat-o'-nine-tails. 7. tackle for hoisting an anchor. 8. *let the cat out of the bag*, tell a secret. —v. hoist (an anchor) and fasten it to a beam on the ship's side."

According to *The Thorndike-Barnhart High School Dictionary*, cat has the above core of meanings, or denotations. The dictionary also defined the word cat as it is used in the idiomatic expression, "let the cat out of the bag." But are these the only meanings of cat? What associations do we make when we hear the word cat? If students understand that the dictionary definitions give us the common core of meanings the word has and that this core is called the word's denotations, then they are ready to move on to another group of meanings that are equally important.

CONNOTATIONS

As an introduction to connotative meanings of words, the teacher may wish to read this verse by John E. Donovan, printed in *The Saturday Evening Post* on July 13, 1946.

Semantics

Call a woman a kitten, but never a cat;
You can call her a mouse, cannot call her a rat;
Call a woman a chicken, but never a hen;
Or you surely will not be her caller again.

You can call her a duck, cannot call her a goose;
You can call her a deer, but never a moose;
You can call her a lamb, but never a sheep;
Economic she lives, but you can't call her cheap.

You can say she's a vision, can't say she's a sight;
And no woman is skinny, she's slender and slight;
If she should burn you up, say she sets you afire,
And you'll always be welcome, you tricky old liar.*

As the teacher read "Semantics," students probably laughed because they grasped the connotative meanings of the words. They knew, for example, that words like cat, kitten, mouse, and rat when applied to a person mean totally different things from what they mean when applied to the animals that bear those names. They associate certain meanings with such words. To illustrate these associations, the teacher may want to take several of the words from the verse and put them on the board like this:

cat

sample responses: a four-legged animal, a fur-bearing animal with a long tail, a pet, an animal that purrs, a feline, an animal with claws

also: a player or devotee of jazz, a hep cat, a person who swings

possibly: the nickname for Caterpillar tractor

The teacher asks what the word implies in the poem. Students will see that none of the definitions they have given works. Next the teacher will write these words from "Semantics" on the board and ask students to define them:

kitten	goose	cheap	hen
duck	economic	slight	lamb
sheep	slender	chicken	sight
skinny	rat	moose	set you afire
mouse	deer	vision	burn you up

For each of the words or phrases, the students will probably give responses like those given for *cat*. Then the teacher will ask if the students would have laughed as he read the poem if they thought of only these meanings of the words. Students will probably admit that these denotative meanings never occurred to them as the teacher read the poem. Then what did they associate with the words? Why? Are these associations always found in the dictionary?

At this point the teacher may read the poem again, pointing out that students were amused by the associated, not the lexical, meanings of the words. When students were asked to respond to the word *cat*, in isolation, they gave the denotative meanings of the word, i.e., they listed the set of characteristics that the word *cat* signifies. They reacted to the word by giving its conventional definitions. But as they listened to the poem, they recognized the context that the word was used in, and they associated an altogether different kind of meaning with the word.

In *Thinking Straight*, Monroe Beardsley prefers to speak of a word's *designation* instead of its denotation. The change in term is not important for our purposes; however, Beardsley's definition of *designation* is most useful.

> When a term acquires a fairly fixed conventional meaning, it applies to a distinct set of things, and these things are its *comprehension*. They are grouped together in a class. But on what grounds? Well, ordinarily such a group is like a club or organization of some sort—there are rules of membership, or qualifications that each thing has to possess in order to be admitted. The class of *cots*, for example, includes all light-weight

beds; in other words, to be included in this class, an object must be (1) a bed, or something you can sleep on, and (2) light in weight. This pair of characteristics marks off the class of cots from all other classes in the world, and we shall say that the term "cot" *designates* these two characteristics. The designation is part of its signification.

Of course, individual cots have a lot of other characteristics besides being light in weight and being a bed: some are wooden, some metal; some are stretched with canvas, some with wire mesh; some fold up, some don't; some are comfortable, some are not. But being light in weight and being a bed are the indispensable characteristics of cots, and only these two characteristics are involved in the standard, or customary, meaning of the term "cot."*

From Cots to Cats

To go then from cots to cats, we can easily determine the characteristics of the term *cat.* To be a member of the class of cats, a thing must be (1) a four-legged carnivorous animal with (2) retractile claws. A cat can be any color, or almost any size, but it must have four legs and retractile claws. It may have a tail, or it may not. But it does fit into the class because of its two distinguishing characteristics.

People commonly associate another meaning with the word *cat.* In a given context, *cat* can refer to a woman who is guilty of backbiting, who verbally claws her neighbor. These associative meanings of the word *cat* are its connotations. These associative meanings are so common that they have become a part of *cat's* common core of meanings, or denotations.

Instead of telling students that they responded to the poem because of the connotative meanings of the words, perhaps we can get them to arrive at the meaning of connotation by another step. The teacher writes these words on the chalkboard and asks students to write what comes to their minds when they see them:

carnival nurse airplane dog lake

Several students may be reminded of the fun they had at a carnival and associate the word with pleasant memories. They may write

*Monroe C. Beardsley, *Thinking Straight,* 2nd ed., © 1956, p. 230; reprinted by permission of Prentice-Hall, Inc.

such responses as ferris wheel, merry-go-round, cotton candy, taffy apples, fun house, or just fun. But one student may recall that she got cotton candy all over her good dress and that her mother was cross with her when she got home. Another student may recall that he overate; therefore, a carnival is associated with a stomach ache.

Without identifying the students, the teacher may read several of the responses that will help students to see that some words, even in isolation, call to mind a variety of experiences and feelings. But if they are asked to define the words written on the board, all students may arrive at the same general definitions. In other words, carnival designates the same *thing* to all students, but not all students feel the same way about carnivals because they have had different experiences at them.

As the teacher reads the responses to the words, he may point out the two kinds of associated meaning: the public and the private. For example, most students associate fun with a carnival; this is a public meaning, i.e., a meaning generally associated with the word by most people. On the other hand, the girl who associates carnival with cotton candy and a ruined dress has a private meaning, i.e., an association that rarely comes to the mind of more than one person since it arose from an individual experience.

To show students how the process of association works, the teacher may wish to read Lewis Carroll's delightful poem, "Jabberwocky."* A skillful reading of this poem will introduce students to words that they have not heard before, and which they cannot find in the dictionary. (It should be pointed out to students that these words do not have denotative meanings.) However, several questions will lead students to see that they almost automatically associate meanings with Carroll's coined words as a result of their sounds and as a result of how they are used in context.

Jabberwocky

'Twas brillig, and the slithy toves
Did gyre and gimble in the wabe:
All mimsy were the borogoves,
And the mome raths outgrabe.

*The poem is included in a Caedmon recording, "Nonsense Verse of Carroll and Lear," TC 1078.

"Beware the Jabberwock, my son!
The jaws that bite, the claws that catch!
Beware the Jubjub bird, and shun
The frumious Bandersnatch!"

He took his vorpal sword in hand:
Long time the manxome foe he sought—
So rested he by the Tumtum tree,
And stood awhile in thought.

And, as in uffish thought he stood,
The Jabberwock, with eyes of flame,
Came whiffling through the tulgey wood,
And burbled as it came!

One, two! One, two! And through and through
The vorpal blade went snicker-snack!
He left it dead, and with its head
He went galumphing back.

"And hast thou slain the Jabberwock?
Come to my arms, my beamish boy!
O frabjous day! Callooh! Callay!"
He chortled in his joy.

'Twas brillig, and the slithy toves
Did gyre and gimble in the wabe:
All mimsy were the borogoves,
And the mome raths outgrabe.*

As students analyze this poem, the teacher will ask them what these words mean:

brillig	mome
slithy	raths
toves	outgrabe
gyre	Jabberwock
gimble	Jubjub
wabe	frumious
mimsy	borogoves

*Carroll, p. 133.

The teacher may ask these questions:

1. Do these words have denotative meanings?
2. What words are pleasing to you? Why?
3. Do you like or dislike slithy? Why?
4. What is a Jabberwock? Should you be cautious around a Jabberwock? Why?
5. What is frumious?

This line of questioning can continue as long as the students are interested in the words. If students ask, "But what do the words actually mean?" the teacher may go to Lewis Carroll to prove that they are just wonderful nonsense. This passage from *Through the Looking-Glass* may help:

"That's enough to begin with," Humpty Dumpty interrupted: "there are plenty of hard words there. '*Brillig*' means four o'clock in the afternoon—the time when you begin *broiling* things for dinner."

"That'll do very well," said Alice: "and '*slithy*'?"

"Well, '*slithy*' means 'lithe and slimy.' 'Lithe' is the same as 'active.' You see it's like a portmanteau—there are two meanings packed up into one word."

"I see it now," Alice remarked thoughtfully: "and what are '*toves*'?"

"Well, '*toves*' are something like badgers—they're something like lizards—and they're something like corkscrews."

"They must be very curious-looking creatures."

"They are that," said Humpty Dumpty; "also they make their nests under sun-dials—also they live on cheese."

"And what's to '*gyre*' and to '*gimble*'?"

"To '*gyre*' is to go round and round like a gyroscope. To '*gimble*' is to make holes like a gimlet."

"And '*the wabe*' is the grass-plot round a sun-dial, I suppose?" said Alice, surprised at her own ingenuity.

"Of course it is. It's called '*wabe*' you know, because it goes a long way before it, and a long way behind it—"

"And a long way beyond it on each side," Alice added.

"Exactly so. Well then, '*mimsy*' is 'flimsy and miserable' (there's another portmanteau for you). And a '*borogove*' is a thin shabby-looking bird with its feathers sticking out all round—something like a live mop."

"And then '*mome raths*'?" said Alice. "I'm afraid I'm giving you a great deal of trouble."

"Well, a *'rath'* is a sort of green pig: but *'mome'* I'm not certain about. I think it's short for 'from home'—meaning that they'd lost their way, you know."*

Students will realize immediately that Humpty Dumpty knows little more about the words than they do; however, this lack of knowledge does not prevent students from associating certain meanings with the words just as Humpty Dumpty did. Why do they associate certain meanings with words? Perhaps students will realize that they do so because of the sounds of the words and because of the ways that they are used in the poem.

Many persons learn to associate definite meanings with words because of the way the words sound when they are spoken. For example, the words sneak and snake. Both begin with *sn,* and both are frequently hissed when they are spoken. As a person grows up, he becomes aware of the feeling of a speaker toward a certain word by the tone the speaker employs as he pronounces the word. Have students think of words that have unpleasant connotations because of the way they are used in sentences and because of the ways they are pronounced. For example, in the sentence, "He's a weasel," the very tone employed by the speaker may give the listener an unpleasant connotation. Have students make up sentences in which, by their tone, they give an unpleasant connotation to a word that may normally carry a pleasant connotation. For example, the word *carnival* in the following sentence can carry either a pleasant or unpleasant connotation depending on the tone the speaker employs and depending on how he emphasizes the word. "The dance had a *carnival* atmosphere." If the speaker hits the word lightly, he conveys that a carnival atmosphere is desirable since it is pleasant, gay, full of fun. If he hits the word hard and spits it out, he may convey that such an atmosphere is sinful or otherwise unpleasant.

Two Kinds of Meaning

At this point students should understand that many words have two kinds of meaning. The first kind of meaning is that which is designated, i.e., the characteristics of the object named by the

*Carroll, pp. 191-93.

word. This kind of meaning can be found in the dictionary. The second kind of meaning is the associated meaning, i.e., the thoughts that run through a person's mind when he hears a certain word because of his experiences with it, or because of the way it is pronounced, or because of the way it is used, or because of the various meanings attached to the word by society.

Students should be asked to determine how words take on particular associations that they may not be able to find in the dictionary. Some of the reasons have been listed above, and there are others.

Some words take on an aura of respectability because they are normally associated with religion, with the happy home, with formal education, or with undisputed greatness. Others words take on the aura of respectability because they are associated with a branch of knowledge that many persons are not familiar with. For example, in advertising products, advertisers will frequently say that a certain product contains *hexasodium* or some such compounded scientific term. What do students think when they hear the word *hexasodium*? Does the mere fact that *hexasodium* is an ingredient mean that the product is good? Why is the product good? What do students associate with *hexasodium*? Have students listen to commercials for words that have this scientific respectability. Ask them if they would use the products only because they contain "hexa-X". Do they know what "hexa-X" is? If they do not know what it is, and if they have answered that they would use the product because it contains "hexa-X," then why would they use this product? Are they unconsciously aware of the scientific respectability that comes with certain words? Are they afraid to challenge certain words because they do not know what they mean? Or do they think that because a product is advertised that it must be good regardless of what it contains? What makes them associate goodness with a certain product? Is it the words used? Is it the context in which the product is presented? Is it the tone of voice that the announcer uses in pronouncing certain words?

The power of words, then, lies not only in their designated meanings but also in their associated meanings. The emotions that they evoke, the images that they create in the mind, and the sensory reactions that they create all add to the power of words through their associated meanings.

The teacher will probably call students' attention to connotative meanings of words in poems that appear in the seventh grade program. He will also want to call attention to the connotative meanings of words as students read both fiction and non-fiction. From this unit on, the teacher can always call attention to the various meanings and shades of meanings of words. Students should learn that if they begin responding to language by thinking of the various meanings associated with words that they will begin enjoying literature more and they will become much more aware of what people might actually mean when they talk.

SO WHAT'S A DICTIONARY FOR?

After seventh grade students have become acquainted with connotative meanings of words, they may wonder just how valuable their dictionary is. In other words, they may ask: "So what's a dictionary for?"

Seventh grade students have long been using dictionaries of one kind or another. And, perhaps, some have even acquired skill in using a good standard dictionary to check such items as spelling, definitions, synonyms, antonyms, syllabication, pronunciation, and capitalization. Therefore, some students may wonder why they should examine the dictionary again. If a teacher asks questions like these, students may become aware of their need to explore the dictionary once more:

1. If you look up a word in a dictionary and you find that it has two possible spellings, how do you know which spelling is preferred?
2. If a dictionary entry gives more than one definition of a word, how can you tell which is the most common meaning?
3. How do you pronounce *presentation*? Is there a preferred pronunciation? How do you know which pronunciation of a word is considered standard?
4. How can you tell if a word is usually used only in slang expressions? How can you tell if a word is used primarily

in everyday speech but not in writing, or if it is used primarily by uneducated persons?

5. If you are writing a composition and you need to divide a word at the end of a line, how can your dictionary help you? What marks are used to show syllabication?
6. What are synonyms? antonyms? homonyms? homographs? Does your dictionary contain examples of each?
7. Does your dictionary tell you the origin of a word? If so, where is this information given in the entry?
8. Does your dictionary ever help you to see what a word refers to? In other words, are there maps, pictures, or diagrams?
9. Does your dictionary tell you how a word is used in a sentence? Does it tell you whether a word can function as a noun, a verb, an adjective, or an adverb?
10. Does your dictionary show you how to form the past tense of a verb? the plural of a noun? the comparative degree of an adjective?
11. Does your dictionary identify prominent persons? literary characters? Biblical characters? prominent places?

If students can answer those questions without difficulty and if they can show the teacher that they know how to find various kinds of information about words, then they may not need this section of this unit. If, however, they are not certain just what information they can find in a dictionary, they may need to cover all or part of the exercises in this section.

The questions included here should be adapted to fit the classroom situation. These items are covered:

1. arrangement of entries
2. pronunciation
3. spelling
4. syllabication
5. pictures, diagrams, maps
6. inflected forms (plurals and principal parts of verbs)
7. parts of speech
8. levels of usage

9. synonyms, antonyms, homonyms, homographs, and idiomatic phrases
10. etymology and derivatives
11. literary allusions

To acquaint students with dictionaries, not just *a* dictionary, the teacher should have, in addition to the class set, single copies of four of five other dictionaries. The activities in this unit are based on these dictionaries: *The American College Dictionary, Funk & Wagnall's Standard College Dictionary, The Random House Dictionary of the English Language, The Thorndike-Barnhart High School Dictionary, Webster's New World Dictionary of the American Language, Webster's Third New International Dictionary,* and *Webster's Seventh New Collegiate Dictionary.*

Arrangement of Entries

Students frequently refer to a dictionary without knowing anything about its system of entries. These questions may prove useful:

1. How are words arranged in the dictionary you are using? in another dictionary?
2. Which is the most common definition in the dictionary you are using? in another dictionary?
3. Where can you find information about the listing of definitions?
4. What information is given with each entry in the dictionary you are using? in another dictionary?

Pronunciation

How do you know how to pronounce the words in the dictionary you are using? in another dictionary? Is the same pronunciation key used in all dictionaries? What do you need to read before you try to pronounce the first word you look up in a dictionary other than the one you are using? (The teacher may decide that it is necessary to review the pronunciation keys.)

Spelling

Some words can be spelled in more than one way. The question is, which is correct or more acceptable? To become familiar with how dictionaries treat variant spellings, students may be asked these questions:

1. How can you tell which spelling is preferred if more than one spelling is listed in the dictionary? Where do you find the answer to that question in your dictionary? in another dictionary?
2. Look up the word *enclose* under both *i* and *e*. Which is the preferred spelling? How do you know?
3. Look up the word *color* in your dictionary. What does "also esp. Brit." mean? Where does it appear in the dictionary you are using? in another dictionary?
4. Look up the word *adviser*. Are two spellings of the word given in your dictionary? If so, is there any explanation of the two spellings?
5. How do you know when a word can be abbreviated? Look up the abbreviation *mag.* in *The Thorndike-Barnhart High School Dictionary*. Compare the entry with entries in other dictionaries.

Syllabication

These questions may help students understand how words are syllabicated:

1. Look up the word *machinery*. How is the word divided into syllables? What mark is used in your dictionary to show syllables? in another dictionary?
2. Look up *made-up*. How is it divided? What mark is used in the entry? Is the entry *make up* also hyphenated? How do you know that it is two words? Is *make up* listed as two words in all dictionaries, or is it hyphenated in some? In which dictionaries is it hyphenated?
3. Look up the word *making* in several dictionaries. Which dictionaries give you compound words that are formed with making? Which of the compounds are two words? Which are one word?

Pictures, Diagrams, and Maps

Pictures, diagrams, and maps are valuable additions to any dictionary. Although students may be aware of their inclusion in the dictionary they are using, they seldom realize the importance of these items. These activities may make students more aware of the usefulness of pictures, diagrams, and maps:

1. Draw an *English horn.*
2. What is unusual about *Pegasus*?
3. Describe a *flamingo.*
4. What bodies of water border *India*?
5. Draw a diagram showing the *apogee* of the orbit of the moon around the earth.
6. Thumb through the pages of your dictionary noting the maps, diagrams, and drawings. What generalization can you make about their inclusion in dictionaries? Or, to put it another way, why do you think editors decide to include visual aids with certain words? What kinds of words do they select?

Inflected Forms of Nouns and Verbs

The dictionary gives inflected forms of nouns and verbs. These questions may make students more aware of these aids:

1. Are the plural forms of all nouns given in your dictionary? in another dictionary? What system did the editors of the dictionary you are using follow for giving inflected forms? Where do you find an explanation of their system? Are the systems the same for all dictionaries? If not, how do they differ?
2. What is the plural form of *brother-in-law*? of *index*?
3. What is the past tense of *ricochet*? If more than one form is given, which is preferred? How do you know?
4. What are the principal parts of the verb *climb*? Are all given in your dictionary? in another dictionary? What are the principal parts of the verb *open*? Are all given in your dictionary? in another dictionary? Why, or why not?

5. Is there a principal part of the verb *picnic* that is spelled *picnicking*?
6. What is the singular form of *data*? Is *alumnus* the singular or plural form? Does *alumnus* refer to a man or a woman?

Parts of Speech

These questions may be of value:

1. Does your dictionary list the parts of speech of a word? Can one word, according to the dictionary you are using, be used as more than one part of speech?
2. Look up the word *accord*. As what part(s) of speech can it be used?
3. Does the dictionary you are using indicate that a verb may be of a particular kind? What distinction among verbs does your dictionary make? Can some verbs be used in more than one way (i.e., transitive or intransitive)?
4. Look up the word *contact* in your dictionary. What is the complete entry? Now look up *contact* in *Webster's Third New International Dictionary*. Does the entry in the *Third* differ from the one in your dictionary? How? Why do you think the entry differs from those in other dictionaries? (The teacher may wish to comment on the work of a lexicographer at this point. Since the furor about *Webster's Third* has been raised, many articles have been printed in both professional journals and popular magazines. Several of these articles are included in Jack C. Gray's *Words, Words, and Words about Dictionaries* [San Francisco: Chandler Publishing Company, 1963]. The teacher may wish to read several articles about the role of the lexicographer before discussing it in class.)

Levels of Usage

Lexicographers record language as it is used; most do not prescribe how words must be used or which words should not be used in formal conversation or writing. Lexicographers know that time, place, and occasion govern a person's choice of words. To indicate how words are used, some lexicographers label words as slang, informal, standard, colloquial, obsolete, archaic, poetic, and British. Levels of usage should be explained fully to seventh graders, and these activities may help:

1. What is a colloquialism? Look up the word in more than one dictionary.
2. What is slang? Are slang words included in the dictionary? If so, why?
3. What is a dialect? Can you find words in your dictionary that are labeled *dial.*?
4. What labels indicating levels of usage do the editors of your dictionary use? How do they define the various levels? Do their labels differ from those used by editors of other dictionaries? If so, how? (The teacher may wish to introduce the concept of usage levels employed by the editors of *Webster's Third.* He will want to read the introductory material carefully before discussing *Webster's Third* with the class.)
5. Look up the words *ain't, corn, drop, adorable, make-up* in your dictionary. What usage labels are given for each word? Compare the entries of these words in your dictionary with those of several other dictionaries.
6. When can you use *dove* as the past tense of dive?
7. What is the level of usage given in the entry for *ball up*? What usage label do you find behind the word *belike*?
8. In which part of the country is the word *arroyo* used?
9. Check several dictionaries for the entry of *poke*, meaning a bag or sack. What label(s) are given?
10. Entries for some words are labeled *Naut., Bot., Biol.,* and so forth. Are these usage levels? If not, what are they?

Synonyms, Antonyms, Homonyms, Homographs, and Idiomatic Phrases

Students sometimes use a dictionary to find a synonym for a word that they have used twice or overused in a composition. Occasionally, they do not discriminate in their choice of synonyms, but merely take the first one they find. These activities may help them make proper use of the dictionary as a writing tool:

1. Look up the words *imagination* and *make up* and check the entries after the abbreviation *syn.* What information are you given? Write sentences in which you use the synonyms for *make up* and *imagination.*
2. What is a synonym? How did the editors of the dictionary you are using select words for which they recorded synonyms? What do the editors say about their presentation of synonyms?
3. Look up the word *absolve.* What appears in the entry after *ant.*? What is an antonym? Does your dictionary give antonyms? If so, for which words? What do the editors say about the inclusion of antonyms?
4. What are homonyms and homographs? Give examples of each. In the dictionary you are using, have the editors explained homonyms or homographs? If so, what do they say?
5. Look up the words *account* and *advantage* in *Webster's New World Dictionary of the American Language.* What are the final entries under these words? What are these phrases called? What do the editors say about idiomatic phrases? Are idiomatic phrases included in other dictionaries? How are they entered? How does the listing of idiomatic phrases help you?

Etymology and Derivatives

As students become increasingly familiar with the wealth of material contained in dictionaries, they will begin to realize that many words, or their ancestors, have been with us for centuries. They will also realize that English has borrowed thousands of words from other languages. To get students interested in word origins, these exercises may help:

1. Look up these words in the dictionary: alumnus, induce, portico, beau, drive-in, bambino.
   Are they English words? If not, from what languages do

they come? Can you tell how long they have been a part of the English language?

2. Have you noticed the abbreviations OE or ME in the dictionary entries? What do these abbreviations mean? In which section of the dictionary would you look if you did not know the meanings of these abbreviations? What does the symbol < mean? What do these abbreviations stand for?

   AF, Am.E., Am.Ind., Am.Sp., E, F, G, Gk., Gmc., HG, Hindu., Ital., L, LG, LGk., LL, M, ME, Med., Med.Gk., Med.L, MF, MHG, MLG, NL, O, OE, OF, OHG, Pg., Scand., Skt., Sp., VL

   Can you find additional abbreviations in the language keys in other dictionaries?
3. What is a derivative? What are prefixes? What are suffixes? How does a knowledge of them help you increase your vocabulary?
4. Look up the prefix *mal-* in the *Funk & Wagnalls Standard College Dictionary*. Why are 33 words listed in this entry?
5. What does the suffix *-able* mean? What are the variant forms of this suffix?

Literary Allusions

As seventh graders read the literature suggested for their grade level, they will encounter Biblical, mythical, and literary allusions. The students may know some of the persons mentioned in the stories, but they may be stumped by others. A few minutes with the dictionary will give them some help, and questions like these may pave the way:

1. Who are the following? Mercury, Atlas, Pegasus, Narcissus, Nathan, Esther, Mars, Haran al-Rashid, Helenus, Scrooge
2. Can you find the following in your dictionary? Hudson Bay, Helena, Heliopolis, Cornhusker State, Hoosier State

3. Who were the following persons? Is your dictionary of help in identifying them? John Drew, Anthony Drexel, Alfred Dreyfus, Hans Driesch
4. Do you find proper names in *Webster's Third*? If not, why?

Review

Students may now be asked the same questions that were given them before they started these exercises. They should be able to answer them readily and clearly. They should also be able to generalize about dictionaries and what they are for. The teacher may decide to conclude this unit by assigning a theme topic like one of these:

1. In a letter to a friend who doesn't like to look up words, persuade him that a dictionary is a warehouse of information that can be useful.
2. In a short theme, explain why usage labels appear in most dictionaries and tell why they can be useful.
3. In a short theme, indicate why a knowledge of word origins is or is not valuable.

GRADE 8

How Words Are Formed

Language is man's most important invention. Without it, he would have been unable to build bridges and empires, to harness the elements of nature for his own use, or to acquire knowledge of the world around him and to impart that knowledge to others. Without language, man would have lived as the other animals live.

With language, man examined the world around him and communicated his knowledge to his fellow man. As his awareness of his world increased, man found that he needed to add words to describe his surroundings, to name his neighbors, to express his thoughts, to convey his attitudes, and to explain his inventions. Taking advantage of his own language, he formed new words by combining two words or by adding prefixes and suffixes to existing words; taking advantage of other languages, he borrowed words, combined two borrowed words, or added prefixes and suffixes to borrowed words. As he borrowed words, man changed them slightly in spelling or pronunciation—if at all. If he could not get the word he needed by borrowing, by adding a prefix or suffix to an existing word, or by combining two words, man coined new words.

This unit is concerned with the addition of words to the English language through affixation, compounding, coinage, and borrowing. Prefixes and suffixes are also treated in units for grade nine. Therefore, this unit will not emphasize those methods of language development.

WHAT'S IN A NAME?

Every student takes pride in his own name. Taking his surname for granted, he rarely, if ever, pauses to consider how it was formed.

He knows that he has a given name and a surname and that the two are useful for identification. He probably has never considered the confusion that would arise if he and his classmates had only given names.

In a class that has several students named Bill, Bob, Jane, or Mary, the teacher may be able to illustrate the value of surnames and launch this unit by making a statement like "Language is man's most important invention" and asking "Do you agree with that statement, Bill?" Without an indication of which Bill, the Bills will probably wonder which should answer. Giving little time for response, the teacher asks the same question of the Janes, Marys, or Bobs without indicating which Jane, Mary, or Bob he means. After the students ask which is being called on, the teacher can have them consider the confusion that would arise if students had only given names. Through discussion, students should conclude that it would be necessary to devise some system of distinguishing the Janes, Marys, Bobs, and Bills. Students may even suggest that they be called Jane One, Jane Two, Jane Three, and so forth. But the questions that should arise are "Who will be Jane One? Who will make this decision?"

Centuries ago English-speaking man had to solve the problem of confusion with names. Most men had only given names. In small towns where only one William lived, there was no problem. But if a second William moved to the town, problems of identification arose. Therefore, man began devising methods of distinguishing himself and his sons from others who had similar given names. And man let his imagination and inventiveness have free rein.

Have students consider the ways that early man could distinguish between the two Williams living in the same town. If one came from Westchester, he might be called William of Westchester, which of course man would shorten, because he has a tendency to shorten things, to William Westchester. But only one of the two Williams has been taken care of. What do we do with the other? Is he bold? If so, why not call him William Bold or William Hardy? Or is he strong? If so, why not call him William Strong or William Stout? If he's dark in coloring, he could be called William Black, or Brown, or Dunn, or Schwartz if he's from Germany. If he's red-haired or red-faced, he could be called William Reed, or William Reid, or William Roth, or William Russell.

Other means of identification occurred to man in the early period of English history. If one William was a tailor and the other a miller, they may have been known as William Taylor and William Miller. If one was the son of Thomas and the other the son of John, they could have been called William Thompson and William Johnson. Or, if one lived on or near a hill, he may have been known as William Hill, and the other, who lived near a well, may have been known as William Wells. If one William came from Scotland and the other from Ireland, they may have called themselves William Scott and William Irish. Or possibly, as was the case with the Jews living in Central Europe who were not permitted to have family names, the two Williams may have named themselves after objects they admired: thus William Jewel, or Gold, or Rose, or Prince, or Stein (stone, usually meaning a gem).

Thus in early England man found that he could distinguish himself from others by adding a name to his given name, and he passed this family name, or surname, on to his sons and daughters. One of the foremost ways of identification was to name a child after his father. This was done by adding a prefix or suffix to a father's name or nickname. The most common prefixes that mean *son of* are O-, Mac-, Mc-, Fitz-, and B-. Thus today we have the surnames O'Brien, MacDonald, McCain, Fitzpatrick, and Bowen. Some of the suffixes meaning *son of* are -son, -sen, and -s. Thus we have Johnson, Petersen, Davis (son of David), and Jones (son of John).

Speakers of other languages have also named themselves after their parents. In German, for example, the suffix -sohn appears in such names as Mendelssohn and Heinsohn. In Spanish, a native may carry both his mother's and father's last names in his own; consequently, we read such names as Pedro Gonzalez y Sanchez. Russian has a number of suffixes indicating *son of* or *daughter of*. These include -ov and -ova, -ev and -eva, -in and -ina, -oy and -oya, -ovich and -ovna, and -evich and -evna.

The Ukranian suffix -enko gives us an excellent opportunity to show students how many different objects persons name themselves after and how their children retain these family names by adding

-enko to them. This suffix literally means *son of,* and it has been attached to many different names, as the list below indicates:

Ivanenko—son of Ivan (John)
Andrijenko—son of Andrig (Andrew)
Babenko—son of Baba (grandmother)
Bratunenko—son of Bratun (brother)
Bondarenko—son of Bondar (hooper)
Teslenko—son of Teslja (carpenter)
Usenko—son of a man with a long mustache
Turcenko—son of a Turk
Dniprenko—son of Dnipro (Dniper River)
Bobrenko—son of the bibr (beaver)
Losenko—son of the *los* (elk)
Caplenko—son of a heron
Koropenko—son of a carp
Komarenko—son of a gnat
Dubenko—son of an oak
Bilenko—son of white
Cornenko—son of black
Bidenko—son of misfortune

As was already pointed out, and was so graphically illustrated with the suffix -enko, a person's surname could be arrived at in a number of ways: from his occupation, from personal characteristics, from his nationality, or from the place where he lived. Thus we have the names Smith, Bailey (bailiff), Cantor (singer), Turner (woodworker), and Zimmerman (carpenter); Armstrong (strong arms), Cruikshank (crooked leg), Fairfax (fair-haired), and Weiss (fair in coloring); Dane, English, Hollander, and Welsh; and Bach (brook), Baum (tree), Field, Hurst (wood), and Steinway (stone road).

Students may be interested in learning the ten most common surnames in the United States. As the teacher writes these names on the board, the students should have little difficulty figuring out how they came into the language: Smith, Johnson, Brown, Miller, Jones, Williams, Davis, Anderson, Wilson, and Taylor.

Suggested Activities

1. The teacher may wish to write the names of all students in the class on the chalkboard and have students try to decide what these surnames mean. Each student should attempt to tell what his name means and what its origin is.

2. Students should look in novels for names that the novelists chose purposely to describe the traits of their characters. Dickens provides a goldmine of descriptive names. Students may also want to discuss the names of television characters. Are the names of certain characters significant? If so, what do the names reveal about the characters? Do they appeal to you, or are they so obvious that they insult your intelligence?

This assignment might extend to the assumed names of Hollywood or television personalities who have, for some reason or other, changed their names. Students may be led into a discussion of the public's acceptance of Hollywood or television stars on the basis of their names. They should also realize, through class discussion, that exotic names catch a fickle public's fancy.

3. In addition to the methods of selecting names that are referred to in this unit, what other ways do students discover as they examine surnames?

COMPOUNDS

One of the oldest and most frequent ways of forming new words is by taking two separate words and joining them together to describe something new. This process has been going on from Old English, which gave us seacliff, to present-day American English, which gave us babysitter. The process of compounding does not confine itself to only two words. Consequently, we have the expressions fare-thee-well, off-the-cuff, and nonetheless.

By combining noun with noun, we get such words as airplane, apron-string, arrowhead, bearskin, bedclothes, bedside, bedtime, birthday, bondman, boyfriend, clothesbasket, congressman, countryman, deliveryman, disc jockey, footman, frogman, girlfriend, handbook, hangman, headache, heartache, highwayman, horseman, lipstick, necklace, policeman, postman, railroad, rainbow, rifleman, roller-coaster, schoolmaster, showman, signalman, slave girl, swordfish, thumbnail, timecard, trainmaster, wagonload, waistcoat, waistline, wallboard, wallflower, watchman, warehouse, warhead, wastebasket, waterpipe, woodman, vest-pocket, and vestryman.

Combining a possessive or genitive noun with a noun, we get such compounds as bridesmaid, draftsman, herdsman, plainsman, marksman, salesclerk, salesgirl, saleslady, salesroom, sheepshead, spokesman, sportsman, tradesman, tribesman, woodsman, and yachtsman.

By combining adjective with noun, we have such compounds as blackbird, briefcase, greenhouse, halfway, heavyweight, highway, hotshot, lightweight, livestock, madcap, madman, middleweight, nobleman, shortcake, shorthand, smallpox, strongbox, sweetheart, sweet potato, tenderfoot, third-rate, threefold, vainglory, and woodenhead. There are also many words that are formed with the adjective new and a place name, such as New Hampshire, New York, or New England.

By combining noun with adjective, we get such words as airtight, jet-black, threadbare, and timeworn.

Placing an adverb before a noun, we get afterthought, alongside, downtown, offbeat, off-Broadway, off-color, offspring, outlaw, underarm, underdog, underfoot, undergraduate, underhand, and underwater.

By putting a verb with an adverb, we have such compounds as dugout, holdup, kickoff, markup, takeoff, throwaway, throwback, tie-up, tip-off, toss-up, write-up, and workout.

Putting noun with verb, we have babysit, handpicked, manhunt, nosebleed, sideswipe, tape-record, toothache, and viewpoint.

By putting verb with noun, we get such words as crybaby, paydirt, playmate, tugboat, turntable, snapdragon, vouchsafe, wanderlust, workhouse, workingman, and workwoman.

The combination of adjective and verb gives us such words as highflown, highjack, rapid-fire, short-circuit, shortcut, and whitewash.

The combination of adverb with verb gives us such words as bypass, downcast, onrush, outfit, output, outreach, overprice, overthrow, undercharge, underdevelop, underplay, understaff, and underwrite.

By putting a noun with an adverb, we get such expressions as feet first, hands-down, and head-on.

The combination of adverb with adjective gives us such words as evergreen, overripe, past due, and wellworn.

The combination of pronoun with noun gives us he-man, she-devil, she-lion, she-oak, she-pine, and she-witch.

Suggested Activities

1. Students should list as many words as they can that have been formed by compounding two words, noun with noun, noun with verb, verb with noun, and so forth.

2. Students should list as many words as they can that have been formed by compounding more than two words.

3. After students have examined a number of these compound words, can they arrive at some general rule for spelling compounds, i.e., certain types of compounds are hyphenated while others are spelled as one word? Can students also see that hyphenation or single-word spelling sometimes depends on whether the compound is used as an adjective or as a noun?

PREFIXES AND SUFFIXES

With the help of prefixes and suffixes, both native and borrowed, speakers of English have formed new words. This method of word-making is one of the most common. Since a later unit will treat base prefixes and suffixes, this unit will not go into Latin and Greek prefixes and suffixes in great detail; however, it may be useful to point out to students that they may be able to infer meanings of certain words if they understand the meanings of prefixes and suffixes like *in-*, *ir-*, *im-*, *un-*, *-ly*, *-ful*, and *-ize*. It may be useful to introduce students to a portion of the unit on prefixes and suffixes to acquaint them with the meanings of these bound morphemes.* It may also

*See the discussion of bound morphemes on page 94.

be useful to point out to them that a morpheme is the smallest meaningful unit of language. A free morpheme is a word like *boy, girl, cat,* and *dog.* A bound morpheme is a unit like *-ly, -ful,* and *in-,* which cannot stand alone but which changes the meaning of the word to which it is added.

Students may already know that certain prefixes and suffixes have been borrowed from other languages. For example, *ir-, im-, in-,* and *il-,* meaning not, come from Latin. Since these are Latin prefixes that are normally used with Latin roots, English has developed the prefix *un-,* meaning not, which is normally used with English free morphemes.

But we do not always use foreign prefixes only with foreign roots. For instance, we use the proper prefixes before the words inglorious, impossible, impatient, infer, and inexperienced. On the other hand, we have the native prefix *un-* in front of borrowed words in the words unpleasant, undesirable, and unprogressive. Occasionally, we have a regional preference. For example, the British say insanitary and the Americans say unsanitary.

Some persons dislike the indiscriminate use of prefixes and suffixes to form new words. In a few instances, these persons are probably justified in criticizing the extensive use of these bound morphemes.

The suffix *-ize,* for example, has been most useful in our language in such words as antagonize, disorganize, and baptize. Today, it seems to be one of the favorite suffixes employed by advertising copywriters. We find the suffix appearing frequently in such new words as tenderize, customize, winterize, and motorize. We also see the words finalize, regularize, and actualize in some of our commercial publications.

Another favorite suffix is *-ee.* The use of it has given rise to such words as draftee, trainee, employee, addressee, and selectee.

Other widely used suffixes are *-ette, -eer, -orium, -ster, -ery, -burger,* and *-cade.* We find these suffixes in words like kitchenette, dinette, bathinette, farmerette, usherette, bachelorette, tusslerette (lady wrestler), majorette, fashioneer, vacationeer, budgeteer, upperbracketeer, lubritorium, shavatorium, corsetorium, spaghettorium, gangster, mobster, pollster, hashery, beanery, cheeseburger, steakburger, pizzaburger, cavalcade, motorcade, aquacade, and musicade.

Another frequently used, or overused, suffix is *-wise.* This bound morpheme can obviously be applied to almost any word in the language. Consequently, we hear speakers saying, "Economywise, this is unsound." "Religiouswise, he should not do this." "Schoolwise, this is a good idea." "Stock-marketwise, he should not invest now."

In the same category as *-wise,* we have the many combinations with *-crazy, -happy, -conscious, -struck, -minded.* Using these suffixes, native speakers form such words as girl-crazy, slap-happy, trigger-happy, class-conscious, race-conscious, stagestruck, thunderstruck, social-minded, and security-minded.

With prefixes, we have the typically American usage of *para-* in such words as paratroops, paratrooper, and parachute. And, of course, the use of *super-* in such words as supercolossal, superhighway, and supermarket.

In *Words & Ways of American English* (New York: Random House, 1952), Professor Thomas Pyles points out that most of the ways of forming new words are not exclusively American. "But the freedom with which they are employed and the attitude towards life they sometimes mirror may certainly be regarded as characteristic of the America of our times."

Suggested Activities

1. Students should list as many American English words as they can that have been formed by adding these suffixes: *-ize, -ette, -ee, -buster, -eer, -ine, -orium, -ery, -cade, -mobile,* and *-wise.*

2. Students should list as many words as they can that are typically American formations made by the addition of these prefixes: *de-, super-, semi-,* and *near-.*

3. Students should examine advertisements to see what new words they can find that have been coined by the addition of prefixes or suffixes to existing words. Can students think of prefixes or suffixes that have not been treated in this unit?

4. Students should be reminded that we frequently judge a person by his use of language. Then they should react to these sen-

tences by writing a paragraph in which they comment on the person who may have uttered them. "Saleswise, we must finalize our arguments before we prepare our supercolossal advertising campaign." "Emergencywise, you will be better off in the long run if you customize your car and have it winterized by our service station now." "Stagewise, we must finalize our plans so that we can wow the yokels."

BLENDS, MANUFACTURED WORDS, AND ACRONYMS

Blending is taking parts of two words and putting them together to form a new word. This process seems to be very popular today, especially in the business world. As a result of this blending, or forming a portmanteau word, we have *motel,* which is a combination of motor and hotel. And the blight of the West Coast, the combination of smoke and fog, gave us *smog.* When a minister was forced to use a public auditorium for his services, he called it an *evangelorium.*

Other popular blends include *brunch* (breakfast and lunch), *flush* (flash and blush), *squash* (squeeze and crush), and *splatter* (splash and spatter). Lewis Carroll gave us *chortle* by combining chuckle with snort.

One of the most interesting blends is gerrymander, which is a combination of Gerry and salamander. This word combines the last name of a former Governor of Massachusetts and Vice-president of the United States, Elbridge Gerry, and salamander. While Gerry was Governor of Massachusetts, his party attempted to stay in power by dividing the state into electoral districts with more regard for politics than for geography. One district somewhat resembled a salamander. When artist Gilbert Stuart added head, wings, and claws to a map of the district, the result was called a gerrymander. This word caught on immediately and has become a derisive term in politics.

Businesses have manufactured words by taking several letters from each of the words in their titles. Thus, we have Socony (Standard Oil Company of New York), Nabisco (National Biscuit Company), Alcoa (Aluminum Company of America), and Sunoco (Sun Oil Company). Students should have little difficulty in supplying other manufactured words that have been made by blending either the names of the manufacturers or the products they produce. They may also suggest some of the blends that have been formed from cafeteria and another word. Today we have gaseteria, lubriteria (also lubritorium), auditeria (a schoolroom that is used as a cafeteria and auditorium), buffeteria, and so forth.

In the United States the acronym, or tip name, has become very popular. Acronyms are words made from the initial letters of other words. Some of the most common are CARE, which stands for Committee for American Relief in Europe, SHAPE (Supreme Headquarters of the Allied Powers in Europe), UNESCO (United Nations Educational, Scientific, and Cultural Organization), UNICEF (United National Children's Fund—note the insertion of the I and E so that it can be pronounced), WAC (Women's Army Corps), WREN (Women's Royal Naval Service—note the insertion of the E so that it can be pronounced), and AWOL (absent without leave). Since many of these acronyms arose during World War II, the GI, with his droll sense of humor, coined the acronym to end all acronyms—SNAFU (situation normal, all fouled up).

Probably the most widely used of all acronyms is O.K. Of the many stories that have been written about the origin of O.K., the most colorful is the one that attributes the coining of the acronym to a sign painter who could not spell. For a Whig demonstration on September 15, 1840, in Urbana, Ohio, a sign painter allegedly wrote in large letters, "The people is oll korrect." This sign was in support of the candidacy of General William Henry Harrison for President. According to this story, the persons who saw the sign were so attracted by the misspelling and by the politician identified with it, that they began saying, "Everything is oll korrect," or simply "O.K."

The origin of O.K. that seems to be most accurate also dates to the same Presidential campaign, but it is attributed to Martin Van Buren, the opponent of General William Henry Harrison. President Van Buren was born in the little town of Old Kinderhook, and his birthplace became a sort of rallying cry for the Democrats in the days of Van Buren's power. He became known as Old Kinderhook, which was shortened to O.K. Regardless of its origin, the acronym O.K. is used around the world. It also illustrates how a word can be used in many different ways through the process known as functional shift, which will be described later. Although O.K. originally came into the language as an adjective, it can be used as a noun (We need your O.K. on the paper) or as a verb (Will you O.K. this?).

Suggested Activities

1. Students should list as many blends as they can. They should analyze the blends to see what words are used to form them. Is the blend a more descriptive term than the two words that would originally have been used to describe the same object?

2. Students should list a number of acronyms. They should analyze the acronyms very carefully to attempt to determine which came first, the acronym or the name of the organization. In some cases, linguists think that the organization decided its name after it had chosen an acronym.

3. During the administration of Franklin Delano Roosevelt, acronyms became extremely popular in this country. Students might check with their parents to learn what organizations their parents remember by their initials but cannot remember what the initials stood for.

ONOMATOPOETIC OR ECHOIC WORDS

Some early students of language thought that man learned how to speak by imitating sounds that he heard. This theory, which has been derisively labeled as the "bow-wow theory," has long been discredited. Obviously, these early linguists based their theory on the number of words that attempt to recreate the sounds described. Any student would not be hard-pressed to think of a number of onomatopoetic or echoic words such as meow, bow-wow, clink, clank, or clunk. A reading of Edgar Allen Poe's *tour de force* in onomatopoeia, "The Bells," will graphically illustrate how poets have made full use of onomatopoetic words.

Instead of spending much time on this method of word formation, the teacher may simply want students to list all the words they can that imitate sounds.

Closely related to the echoic or onomatopoetic words are the iterative or reduplicative compounds. In one type of these compounds, the base is exactly duplicated in the second form. Thus we have such words as tweet-tweet, cuckoo, mama, click-click, clop-clop, clump-clump, and thump-thump. In nursery rhymes we also have quack-quack and choo-choo.

In a second type of iterative words, the second element is changed slightly. Thus we have bow-wow, tick-tock, zigzag, chit-chat, click-clack, clitter-clatter, and fiddle-faddle.

A third type of iterative form rhymes the second element with the first. Thus we have walkie-talkie, peepie-creepie (a portable television camera), hotsy-totsy, hoity-toity, okey-dokey, heebie-jeebies, palsey-walsey, killer-diller, and jeepers-creepers.

New iterative forms are frequently found in slang expressions. Students should have no difficulty adding many words to the examples given.

Suggested Activity

Students should suggest onomatopoetic or echoic words that are relatively new to the language. How many of these are slang expressions? What do they mean? If they are slang expressions, students might discuss the possibility of these words staying in the language.

FUNCTIONAL SHIFTS

Many words that first came into the language as nouns now also function as verbs. For example, to contact, to date, to elbow, to package, to park, to program, and to vacation. New verbs are also made by shortening nouns. For example, to emote, to perk, to phone, and to typewrite.

Frequently the stress we place on a syllable shifts to another syllable when we change the function of a word from noun to verb. Linguists call this shift a superfix, a term which may intrigue some students. They may arrive at an understanding of this change in stress if they are asked to use the following in sentences first as nouns and then as verbs:

combat	permit
content	predicate
contract	subject
object	suspect

Is there a noticeable change in stress in each of the above words when it is used first as a noun and then as verb? Can students add other words that function as both nouns and verbs? Are these words pronounced differently as they change function?

The shift from noun to verb is not the only kind of functional change that occurs in American English. There are occasional verb to noun shifts, e.g., dump and scoop (getting a news story first) and adjective to noun, e.g., personal (item in a newspaper column) and basic (a fundamental point or issue). Some words can be used to serve more than two functions, e.g., down, run, and bank.

Suggested Activity

Students should write as many sentences as they can in which they change the functions of the words *down, run,* and *bank.* What other words can they think of that can serve more than two functions in sentences?

OTHER METHODS OF FORMING WORDS

Clipping is the process of shortening a word to give us an abbreviated version that is used more commonly in speech. As a result of the clipping or shortening process, we have hypo for hypodermic, photo for photograph, gas for gasoline, and prof for professor. Other examples of clipping are plane for airplane, lab for laboratory, gym for gymnasium, math for mathematics, mike for microphone, memo for memorandum, and grad for graduate.

In spoken language, first names are frequently clipped. Examples are Al for Albert, Fred for Frederick, Sue for Susan, Sam for Samuel, Pat for Patricia, and so forth.

Some men find themselves immortalized in words that bear their names. For example, watt, ohm, gerrymander, Edisonphone, and bowie knife. Other words can be traced back to characters in mythology, e.g., mercury. Still others are formed to describe something that is new, e.g., Sputnik, jeep, and Telstar.

Some persons have made serious attempts at coining new words. A few of these survive in the language. Hollywood has given us the Oscar and television has given us the Emmy. *Time* magazine has coined such words as cinemactress, steelionaire, millionheiress, and socialite. Included among the words that have been coined by individuals are bromide, blurb, yes man, infanticipate, high brow, and momism.

This unit does not treat every method of word formation, nor does it cover in depth those methods listed. The teacher may wish to have students do research on word formation and also have them listen carefully to language for other processes of word formation that have not been covered here.

Suggested Activities

1. Each student should write a paragraph in which he traces the history of a word that has been formed by blending, compounding, affixing, or coining. If students do not have access to *The Oxford English Dictionary,* they may find help in one of the books listed in the bibliography. Some words that have interesting histories include:

bluff	cybernetics	mockingbird
carpetbagger	G-man	mugwump
caucus	gouging	O.K.
charley horse	lightning rod	popcorn
chortle	linotype	razorback
copperhead	lynch	smog

2. To describe the landscape, colonists used such words as barrens, bluff, bottom land, bottoms, branch, clearing, cliff, creek, divide, foothill, hollow, neck, pond, rapids, run, swamp, underbrush, watergap, and watershed. Students might talk to "oldtimers" in the area to learn colorful names for features of the American

landscape. Are these words commonly used today? If not, can students decide why they are not?

3. After students study this unit, they should realize that American English is not a static language. It changes daily. The teacher may have students write a theme in which they discuss why a living language changes.

BORROWED WORDS

Our language is richer because our ancestors have borrowed words from other languages to name items for which there was no word in English. To show students how freely English has borrowed words from other languages, the teacher might ask them to open their dictionaries to any page and count the total number of entries. Then they should count the words that have been borrowed from another language and subtract that number from the total number of entries to determine how many native words are recorded on that page of the dictionary. (On page 589 of the *Thorndike-Barnhart High School Dictionary*, of 53 entries, 36 are borrowed words or forms of borrowed words.)

In a *History of Foreign Words in English* (New York: E. P. Dutton & Company, 1936), Mary S. Serjeantson lists thousands of words that have been borrowed from other languages and cites their first recorded use in English. A few examples from different languages may prove interesting to students. (Note: Only a very small portion of the listing is given for each language.)

Latin

cadaver (1500); integer (1509); genius (1513); pollen (1523); junior (1526); alias (1535); circus (1546); medium (1551); omen (1582); militia (1590); radius (1597); virus (1599); premium (1601); census (1613); focus (1644); album (1651); lens (1693); antenna (1698); alibi (1727); bonus (1773); duplex (1817); and bacillus (1883)

Greek

irony (through the Latin in 1502); alphabet (through Latin in 1513); trophy (through French in 1513); drama (through Latin in 1515); phrase (1530); cube (through French in 1551); topic (1568); epic (through Latin in 1589); orchestra (through Latin in 1606); hyphen (through Latin in 1620); tonic (1649); camera (through Latin in 1708); phase (1812); acrobat (through French in 1825); and agnostic (1870)

Scandinavian (Since Middle English)
link, silt, smelt, rug, kink, skit, snag, scuffle, snug, scrub, simper, oaf, squall, keg, gauntlet, smut, cozy, muggy, tungsten, trap, nag

French (Since Middle English)
pioneer (1523); colonel (1548); machine (1549); gauze (1561); grotesque (1561); vase (1563); cartridge (1579); unique (1602); fanfare (1605); crayon (1644); detour (1738); glacier (1744); rouge (1753); restaurant (1827); coupon (1864); and garage (1902) [Note: Like the borrowings from Latin and Greek, the borrowings from French could fill many pages.]

Low German
[Under the term Low German, Miss Serjeantson includes the dialects of Dutch, Flemish, and continental Saxon. Only a small part of the list is included here.]
spool (1440); rack (1440); sled (1440); buoy (1466); deck (1466); snap (1495); hose (1495); uproar (1526); reef (1584); wiseacre (1595); drill (1611); brandy (1622); furlough (1625); tattoo (1644); easel (1654); slim (1657); hustle (1684); smuggle (1687); spook (1801); waffle (1808); boss (1822); and dope (1880)

High German
sauerkraut (1617); zigzag (1712); cobalt (1728); poodle (1825); yodel (1830); kindergarten (1852); and seminar (1889)

Italian (since 1600)
attack (1600); gazette (1605); umbrella (1609); intrigue (1612); parasol (1616); balcony (1618); ditto (1625); balloon (1634); monsignor (1635); opera (1644); serenade (1649); cartoon (1671); piano (1683); sonata (1694); solo (1695); portfolio (1722); trombone (1724); soprano (1730); studio (1819); figurine (1854); and vendetta (1855)

Spanish (since 1550)
Negro (1555); cask (1557); alligator (1568); renegade (1583); comrade (1591); spade (on cards—1598); booby (1599); bravado (1599); desperado (1610); cockroach (1624); guitar (1629); parade (1656); cargo (1657); turtle (1657); vanilla (1662); plaza (1683); mustang

(1808); picaresque (1810); rodeo (1834); cigarette (1842); bonanza (1878); bronco (1883); and cafeteria

Celtic
inch (1425); gull (1430); bog (1505); slogan (1513); galore (1675); and banshee (1771)

Portuguese
caste (1613); tank (1616); pagoda (1634); and veranda (1711)

Slavonic
mammoth (1706); vodka (1802); polka (1844); pogrom (1905); soviet (1917); and robot (1923)

Arabic
mattress (1290); camphor (1313); cotton (1381); zenith (1387); almanac (1391); ream (1392); syrup (1398); artichoke (1531); assassin (1531); algebra (1541); alcohol (1543); magazine (1583); giraffe (1594); zero (1604); sofa (1625); ghoul (1786); alfalfa (1845); and safari (1892)

Indian Dialects
pundit (from Hindu, 1672); bungalow (from Hindu, 1676); bandana (1752); cheetah (1781); shampoo (1762); sari (1785); bangle (1787); thug (1810); beri-beri (1879); and pyjamas [Brit. sp. (1886)]

Persian
scarlet (1250); azure (1325); salamander (1340); taffeta (1373); tiger, check, checkmate, and chess (14th century); arsenic (14th century); mummy (1400); spinach (1530); jasmine (1548); naphtha (1572); divan (1586); caravan (1599); julep (1624); jackal (1603); lilac (1625); shawl (1662); seersucker (1757); and khaki (1848)

Turkish Dialects
tulip (1554); horde (1555); turban (1561); coffee (1598); fez (1802); and bosh (1834)

Dravidian (non-Indo-European dialects of Southern India)
calico (1540); coolie (1598); curry (1598); atoll (1625); and teak (1698)

Semitic Dialects (excluding Arabic, Phoenician, Hebrew, and Aramaic)
amen, hemp, rabbi, Sabbath, Satan, tunic, seraphim, cherubim, endive, emerald, coral, cinnamon, sapphire, lotus, torah, hallelujah, and kosher

Tibeto-Chinese
silk, tea, pongee, ketchup, and pekoe

Japanese
kimono (1637); soy (1696); hara-kiri (1856); jinricksha (1874); and jujitsu (1904)

Malay-Polynesian
bamboo (1598); gong (1600); junk (meaning a ship, 1613); gingham (1615); launch (1697); orangutan (1699); bantam (1749); kapok (1750); aye-aye (1781); caddy (1792); sarong (1834); poi (1840); and ukulele (1920)

African Languages
ebony, banana, drill (a kind of baboon), okra, chimpanzee, cola, voodoo, zebra, and gnu

South American Languages
canoe, hurricane, iguana, savannah, potato, maize, petunia, llama, cocaine, cashew, tapioca, jerk (verb), and cougar

American Indian
hominy, hooch, pemmican, pone, succotash, supawn, cayuse, chipmunk, moose, muskrat, possum, raccoon, skunk, terrapin, woodchuck, menhaden, musellunge, porgy, quahog, catalpa, catawaba, hickory, pecan, persimmon, poke, scuppernong, sequoia, squash, tamarack, pow wow, totem, papoose, squaw, machinaw, moccasin, tomahawk, wampum, hogan, igloo, kayak, teepee, wigwam, mugwump, Tammany, chautauqua, and podunk

Suggested Activities

1. The teacher might ask students to examine a list of borrowed words, attempting to determine why our ancestors borrowed the words from other languages. Can some of the words be classified into groups, for example, articles of clothing, or kinds of food, or different animals?

2. To illustrate how heavily English has borrowed from other languages, a teacher might have students write a paragraph in which they use only English words. Can students describe any of their activities or any item in their environment by using English words only?

Bibliography

Baugh, Albert C. *A History of the English Language*. 2nd ed. New York: Appleton-Century-Crofts, 1957.

Greenough, James Bradstreet, and George Lyman Kittredge. *Words and Their Ways in English Speech*. Boston: Beacon Press, 1962. (This book was first published by Macmillan in 1900.)

Groom, Bernard. *A Short History of English Words*. New York: St. Martin's Press, 1965.

Laird, Helene and Charlton. *The Tree of Language*. Cleveland: The World Publishing Co., 1957.

Marckwardt, Albert H. *American English*. New York: Oxford University Press, 1958.

Pyles, Thomas. *Words & Ways of American English*. New York: Random House, 1952.

Robertson, Stuart, and Frederic G. Cassidy. *The Development of Modern English*, 2nd ed. Englewood Cliffs, N. J.: Prentice-Hall, 1953.

GRADE 8

How Words Change Meaning in Time and Context*

Students are sometimes surprised to learn that a word to which they give special meaning in teen-age conversations means little or nothing when used in the same manner before adults. To teen-agers, the words *tough, cool,* and *neat* have additional meanings that are not always included in the entries in standard dictionaries, even as slang, because the meanings are too ephemeral to record. Like adults, teen-agers sometimes invent words when they think they are needed; also, like adults, they frequently give well-established words new meanings to convey their thoughts and feelings to their friends.

English is a living language, and because it is, some of its words are given additional meanings or the meanings of the words are changed slightly from generation to generation because people change with time and progress. Some words retain essentially the same meanings for centuries; others undergo quite radical changes in meaning. For example, the word *nice* has undergone an elevation in meaning from foolish and stupid, first recorded in 1560, to these present-day meanings recorded in *The Random House Dictionary of the English Language* in 1967:

> 1. pleasing, agreeable: delightful: *a nice visit.* 2. amiably pleasant: kind: *They are always nice to strangers.* 3. characterized by or requiring great accuracy, precision, skill, or delicacy: *nice workmanship: a nice shot.* 4. requiring or showing tact or care: delicate: *a nice handling of the situation.*

*This chapter was written by Charles Billiard, Consultant for English, Fort Wayne Public Schools, and Edward B. Jenkinson.

5. showing minute differences: minutely accurate, as instruments: *a job that requires nice measurements.* 6. minute, fine, or subtle: *a nice distinction.* 7. having or showing delicate, accurate perception: *a nice sense of color.* 8. refined as to manners, language, etc.: *Nice people wouldn't do such things.* 9. virtuous: chaste: respectable: decorous: *a nice girl.* 10. suitable or proper: *That was not a nice remark.* 11. carefully neat as to dress, habits, etc. 12. (esp. of food) dainty or delicious: *That was a nice dinner.* 13. having dainty or fussy tastes: *They're much too nice in their dining habits to enjoy an outdoor barbecue.*

As *nice* illustrates, in time people can give a single word a number of different meanings. People retain some meanings for words for generations; they discard other meanings, thus the entry *Obs.* in many dictionaries; and they add some meanings. To illustrate how people can give one word a number of meanings, even to the extent that they have it refer to a number of different things, we give these meanings of *gig*—some of which we still recognize today and others of which are obsolete:

Middle English—something that whirls
1651—to throw out (a smaller gig), which apparently referred to the whipping-top of a particular construction that does this
1693—to move to and fro
1722—a kind of fish-spear
1777—an oddity; in dialect, a fool
1777—fun, glee
1780—a flighty, giddy girl
1789—to raise the nap of cloth with a gig
1790—a light, narrow, clinker-built ship's boat
1791—a light two-wheeled, one-horse carriage
1807—to travel in a gig
1816—to fish, also to spear fish with a gig
1821—a joke
1865—a form of a ship's boat used for racing purposes
1875—to move backward and forward

1881—a wooden box, with two compartments, one above the other, used by miners in ascending and descending a pit-shaft

Present—an official report of a minor infraction of regulations, as in school or the army; a demerit; also a punishment for a minor infraction of rules

We can see from the various meanings that people have given to the word *gig* and from the various objects to which people have had the word refer that, to understand *gig* as it is used by writers during the last four centuries, we must find a source that lists the word's various meanings. The most complete record is given in *The Oxford English Dictionary; The Shorter Oxford English Dictionary* is also helpful. Other sources indicate the ranges of a word's meanings but do not, of course, record the dates when a word was first found in print because that is not their purpose. Such sources include: *The American College Dictionary, The Random House Dictionary of the English Language, The Standard College Dictionary, Webster's New World Dictionary of the American Language, Webster's Seventh New Collegiate Dictionary,* and *Webster's Third New International Dictionary.*

Students should report on the various meanings from the earliest recorded use to the most recent for the following words:

propaganda, virtue, chisel, bolster, derby, Scotch, take, fine, mystery, spleen, picture, lewd, marshal, minister

As students note the changes in meanings of those words, they may realize that some words that once stood for a special thing now have a more general meaning, e.g., *picture;* other words that once had a general meaning now have a specialized meaning, e.g., *virtue.* Students may also notice that a word that once referred to something bad or neutral has come to refer to something good, e.g., *marshal* and *minister;* whereas, other words that may have referred to something neutral or good have come to refer to something bad, e.g., *lewd.* If students do note these changes, they are recognizing the processes of generalization, specialization, elevation, and degradation without using the terms.

As students note that words seldom remain static, with no change in meaning, the teacher should stress that words usually do one of four things: they become (1) more specialized or (2) more generalized in application; or the meaning becomes (3) more elevated or (4) degraded. Occasionally a word will move from a specialized meaning to a general meaning and back to a specialized denotation.

Those four processes have contributed greatly to changes in meanings of words from one generation or one century to another. As an example of specialization, people once used the word *girl* to refer to a young person of either sex; now, of course, English-speaking people use it only to refer to a young female. Another example: an *undertaker* was once used to refer to a person who could undertake to do anything, but today one would hardly refer to a mayor who has undertaken to improve city planning as an undertaker.

Another word that has become specialized in meaning is *meat*. Of course students normally think of *meat* as edible food from an animal. Actually, the word *meat* was originally used to refer to any kind of food for humans or animals. Not until the nineteenth century did people use it to refer specifically to the flesh of animal's prepared for human consumption. Therefore, the word *meat* moved from a general category of words referring to any kind of food to a specialized category referring to only one type of food.

As some words have taken on specialized or narrower meanings, other words have taken on more general meanings. The word *butcher* has changed meaning toward a broader, more general connotation. In its earliest use, the *butcher* was one who killed goats. The word was used in this narrow meaning as early as 1100 in Anglo-French dialects. By 1440, a *butcher* had become any slayer of animals who provided food for human use. In the sixteenth century we find the word applied to any men of cruel and inhuman behavior who wantonly slew humans in war or peace. In 1529, Rastell in the *Pastyme History of Britain* wrote about the infamous lord, "Erle of Worcester whiche for his crueltye was called bocher of Englande." The word *butcher* today retains two general meanings of a killer of animals for meat and of an inhuman slayer of people. Therefore, in time people have broadened or generalized the meaning of the word *butcher*.

We have given some words that we use daily so many meanings that they can be used to refer to any of a number of objects. In *The Development of Modern English* (2nd ed., Englewood Cliffs, N.J.: Prentice-Hall, 1953), Robertson and Cassidy list such words as *thing, business, concern, condition, matter, article,* and *circumstance* as examples of words that have taken on general meanings to the extent that readers or listeners cannot always determine the referent.

Words that were once used to refer to something good or neutral now are used to refer to something bad. Such words have undergone the process of degradation. Robertson and Cassidy note:

> Many terms that are now descriptive of moral depravity were once quite without this suggestion. *Lust,* for example, meant simply "pleasure," as in German; *wanton* was "untaught"; *lewd* was merely "ignorant," "lerned and lewed" being a phrase commonly standing for "clergy and laity"; *immoral* was "not customary"; *vice,* "flaw"; *hussy,* "housewife"; *wench,* "young girl"; and *harlot,* "fellow" (of either sex).

The word *knave* developed in just such a downward direction. In Old English, a knave referred to a youth. It later applied to a male servant who was young in years. By 1400 it came to mean a rascal or prankish one. This was a natural development, for boys tend to be playful and tricky. Therefore, all boys tending to be incorrigible became knaves. Finally, the knave dropped to its lowest pitch and became one involved in petty crimes.

On the other hand, words that people once used to refer to something bad or neutral "have traveled the opposite path, from the humble to the exalted, or from the base to the refined." Robertson and Cassidy list, among others, these words that are examples of elevation of meaning: knight, bard, enthusiasm, marshal, chamberlain, minister, constable, governor, steward, angel, martyr, paradise, pretty, nice.

We can illustrate this elevation process with the word *knight.* As early as 893, this word meant just a boy, a youth, as did the word *knave* in its earliest meaning. By 1000 it had come to mean a servant, but still a young boy servant. Five hundred years later, the word added the meaning of military servant to the king. Interestingly enough, while the king was away at war, his lady needed a protector at home. The word *knight* by 1500 took on the special meaning of a young man devoted to the service of a lady. Since these two duties were special privileges bestowed upon worthy young men, trusty and brave, between the years of 1400 and 1800 the word *knight* denoted an order or rank of respect and attainment. *Knight* thus moved from the Old English meaning of any lad or youth, an ordinary category, to the area of a privileged rank in medieval history. This word is an example of elevation in meaning.

Certainly it is true that people do not move words so simply in a single direction. People move some words in two directions at once and still retain perfectly clear meaning in each category. The word *go* provides an interesting example.

Go as a verb has from the earliest time meant movement, especially to talk. In 1605 Shakespeare used this connotation in *Lear,* I, iv, 134, "Ride more than thou goest. . . ." In 1684, Bunyan's *Pilgrim's Progress,* II, has this statement: "I have resolved to run when I can, to go when I cannot run, and to creep when I cannot go." By the eighteenth century the meaning of *go* had broadened to include movement of any kind, as "Let's go." With this development of meaning, the word shaded into meaning a journey or even distance to travel. In 1847, Marryat in *Children of the Forest* uses the word as we would today: "We shan't have far to go. . . , the horse is done for."

However, at the time of Marryat and before, the word *go* used as a substantive had other meanings. It seemed to encompass the idea of the action of going, the manner of going, the gait, dash, or vigor. For example, Boyer in a *French Dictionary* in 1727 described a horse as having "a good go with him." He meant the horse paced well. In 1825 Westmacott expressed the same idea in *English Spy,* I, 178: "She's only fit to carry a dean or bishop. There's no go in her."

But the expression was not confined to horses. In 1882, *The Daily Mirror* of October 27 reported "Mr. Grossmith's music is . . . full of humour and go." *The Congregationalist,* February, 1885, reported "Numbers of people who like the 'swing and go' of these popular ballads. . . ."

People gave *go* colloquial and slang meanings between 1700 and 1800. Using *go* to mean an unexpected turn of affairs, Robinson, 1796, in *Angelina,* II, 168, records this conversation: " 'You may take off the four horses; the gentlewoman rides in the stage.' 'That's a good go enough!' cried one of the postboys." Likewise, Bennet, in *Beggar Girl,* III, uses *go* as slang: " 'There's a go now,' cried Miss with a hoyden laugh." Kenny does this also in 1803 in *Rising Wind:* "Ha! Ha! Ha! Capital go! Isn't it?" And finally, George Eliot uses it in this connotation in *Daniel Deronda,* I, vii: "I see a man with his eye pushed out once—that was as rum a go as I ever see!"

Still another meaning for *go,* added in the 1800's, is a turn at doing something, especially an attempt to make a success of it. Froude uses *go* in this sense in 1835 in *Reminiscence,* I: "And now I will have another go at you about your rules of faith." Mrs. Carlyle uses *go* as we often do today. She says in 1848 in *Letters,* II: "Amusement after a certain age is no go . . . , merely distraction." In *Vanity Fair,* Thackeray has a character remark in Chapter 34: "You want to trot me out, but it's no go."

During that same era people also gave *go* the meaning of "the style," "height of fashion," "the rage." Coleridge used it in this connotation in 1793 in his *Letters,* 50: "Have you read Mr. Fox's letter to the Westminster electors? It's quite the political go at Cambridge." In *Babylon,* Sims states, "All day long there's a crowd stops to look at this lady who's all the go."

Thus we have a word to which people have given a number of meanings; the context determines the sense for the reader. The word *go* has undergone the processes of elevation, degradation, generalization, and specialization. Its meanings vary and wander. We find these same meanings often being used for *go* in our conversations.

To enable students to experience the elevation or degradation, generalization or specialization of words, we suggest the following exercise. Each section of this exercise consists of a word with its several meanings as it moved through eras of language use. These definitions are from *The Oxford English Dictionary*. The teacher should have the student study each word with its definitions and then conclude that the word has been degraded, elevated, specialized, or generalized in meaning.

1. Bonfire (spelled bonefire until 1760). Samuel Johnson decided to use bon + fire to mean a "good fire."
   a. A fire of bones burnt in the open air (14th c. to 15th c.)
   b. A fire to consume corpses (16th c. to 17th c.)
   c. A fire for destruction, as of heretics, proscribed books, trash (16th c. to 18th c.)
   d. A large fire for any celebration, e.g., Halloween, fall festivals, homecomings, Christmas (19th c. to 20th c.)
   This word has been ________ (generalized) in meaning.
2. Villain
   a. A low born, base-minded rustic, country fellow, villager (1303 A.D.)
   b. A person of troublesome character, ignoble ideas (15th c. to 16th c.)
   c. An unprincipled, depraved scroundrel (17th c. to 18th c.)
   d. A man naturally disposed to base or criminal actions (18th c. to 20th c.)
   This word has been ________ (degraded).
3. Boor (from the Dutch *boer*). Means farmer.
   a. A Dutch lowland farmer
   b. A German peasant or countryman called a Bauer
   c. A Dutch colonist in South Africa
   d. Any foreign peasant
   e. An ill-mannered fellow, tiresome, annoying
   This word has been ________ (degraded and generalized).
4. Chest
   a. A coffin
   b. A box for the safe-keeping of articles of value, e.g., a treasure chest or jewel box
   c. A container for various commodities or money, e.g., safe-deposit box, shipping crate
   This word has been ________ (generalized).

To illustrate graphically that despite all the thousands of words we have in our English language we still need to use one word in many ways, the teacher might have each student write on a sheet of paper as many meanings as he can think of for the word *pad*. At the end of a specified time, the teacher might ask who has the largest number of definitions. The teacher should then write the word *pad* on the chalkboard and under it list the definitions as the students contribute them. After students have given all the denotations and connotations of *pad* they know, the teacher should ask them which definition they think is the most recent and which is the earliest or most archaic meaning for the word. Have people changed its meaning throughout the years, or do they use it to refer to the same things today as they did centuries ago?

It is possible that even the best students will not have recalled all of the meanings people have attached to *pad*. To give students many definitions and also give them an exercise in inferring the meaning of a word from context, the teacher might use the following definitions. The student has to use all the clues at his disposal to determine the meaning of *pad* as it appears in that particular context. This exercise might reveal new meanings for *pad*, illustrate how words change meaning in time and context, and stimulate students to discover contextual help for word meaning. It might also be interesting to students if attention is called to the dates when the word was used in a particular sense. These meanings and examples were taken from *The Oxford English Dictionary*.

	AUTHOR AND TITLE OF BOOK	DATE	WORD IN CONTEXT	DEFINITION
1.	Topsell, *Serpents*	1608	"There are three kinds of frog: the first is the little green frog; the second is this *pad* having a crook back; and the third is the toad."	________
2.	More, *Song of a Soul*	1647	"The equall *pad* of justice now alas! is seldom trad."	________

3. Farquarr, *Beaux-Strategem*	1706	"Do we know of any other gentlemen of the *pad* on this road?"	________
4 Farquarr, *Beaux-Strategem*	1706	"Her husband was on the *pad* in the country as London was too hot for him."	________
5. DeFoe, *Robinson Crusoe*	1719	"They lay upon goatskins laid over *pads* as they made for themselves."	________
6. Wolcott, *Letters*	1792	" 'Tis better riding upon a *pad* than upon a horse's bare back."	________
7. Lytton, *Pelham*	1827	"But, sir, we must be *padded;* we are all too thin to look well."	________
8. Macauley, *Essays*	1831	"His (Johnson's) constant practice of *padding* out a sentence with useless epithets . . ."	________
9. South, *Household Surgery*	1850	"Surgeons have a brass tourniquet with a handage and a *pad;* the action of the *pad* is to press specially upon the artery."	________
10. Dickens, *Our Mutual Friend*	1865	"A pen, a box of wafers, and a writing *pad*."	________
11. Manson, *Tropical Diseases*	1878	"Prick the congested finger *pad* with a	________

	Source	Date	Quotation	
			clean needle. Then gently squeeze the finger *pad*."	
12.	Todd, *Anatomy II*	1889	"Of special interest is the elastic-like *pad* beneath the foot of the dromedary."	________
13.	Kipling, *Plain Tales*	1890	"There came the soft '*pad-pad*' of camels."	________
14.	*Glasgow News*	1882	"Many an honest man is forced to *pad* the road in search of work."	________
15.	Smith, *North Country Folk*	1883	"We *padded* bare-foot to school."	________
16.	*Life*	May 28, 1965	"The Titan II rises straight from its launching *pad* with a pillar of white vapor."	________
17.	*Movie Mirror*	April, 1965	John Chaplin: "This is my *pad*. What's so queer about it? I like it."	________
18.	Overheard between two traveling salesmen:		"Sure, I *pad* my expense account. Don't tell me the boss doesn't expect it!"	________

For the teacher's convenience, here are suggested definitions for *pad* as it is used in the above exercise:

1. a kind of humped-back frog or toad
2. a path, road, track
3. same
4. same
5. a cushion, especially one made of straw

6. something soft to protect from jarring, friction; a guard or protection for sports
7. to stuff or fill out
8. to fill out or expand, especially with worthless words
9. something soft to protect from jarring, friction; a guard or protection for sports
10. a number of sheets of writing paper fastened together at an edge with glue to form a block-like shape
11. cushion-like part of animal or human anatomy
12. same
13. soft sound made by walking (especially barefoot)
14. to walk on foot
15. same
16. a platform to form a working base, especially for missiles
17. an abode, apartment (slang)
18. to add false figures to data for reimbursement in cash on a business account, tax form, and so forth

As students discover the many meanings people have given an ordinary word like *pad,* they should become aware of the importance of experience in understanding the meaning of words. It should be clearer to them that communication demands care and accuracy. Selecting the right word in conversation and writing helps avoid misunderstanding. Still, what one person understands a word to mean and what this word means to another because of his age or experience can cause problems in communication.

Many words have come into our language as "genteel" substitutes for commonly used words. In an attempt to avoid bluntness or vulgarity, English-speaking people have coined many euphemisms. Some examples of these are *pass away* and *breathe one's last* for die; *custodian* or *sanitary engineer* for janitor; *realtor* for real estate agent; and *junior executive* for clerk. In "Euphemisms," a chapter in his classic book, *The American Language,* H. L. Mencken notes that an engineer is no longer an engineer, but that many groups have succeeded in disguising what they do by referring to themselves as "— engineers," e.g., appearance engineer, clothing engineer, feed-plant engineer, floor-covering engineer, baking engineer, or tonsorial engineer.

Suggested Activities

1. The teacher should have students list euphemisms that they hear daily, and then have them write a theme in which they explain why euphemisms come into our language and how they reflect a particular attitude of people. (Students should note why these euphemisms apparently entered the language and why certain kinds of people use them.)

2. Students should identify the euphemism in each of the following pairs of words and explain why the euphemism was coined.

bricklayer—mason
housewife—homemaker
interior decorator—house painter
cabinet maker—carpenter
patron—customer
cheap—economical
teacher—educator
waitress—hostess
domestic help—servant

In the course of time society often reverses itself. We see this happen in styles, moral patterns, attitudes, and in the history of the rise and fall of great nations. Society does strange things to its language also, as the coinage of euphemisms illustrates. The meanings society chooses to give to a word change as society changes. Slang is an illustration of this trend. A social group may change the meaning of a word several times in slang expressions, but the word remains the same in its basic definition. To understand how a word is used, the listener or reader must be aware of changes brought about both by time and context.

The teacher may want students to comment on the following sentences in terms of how the meaning of the underlined word changes in each sentence and whether persons of the twenty-first century would understand some of the sentences if they could not find the twentieth century meanings in a work like *The Oxford English Dictionary*. Students should also be asked which words have transitory meanings, i.e., which words may be used to mean one thing today but will probably take on totally different meanings tomorrow.

1. The party was a *blast*.
2. He was deafened by the *blast*.
3. He was hurt in the *blast* when the cats rioted.
4. He's a *blast*.
5. That's a fresh *egg*.
6. He's a good *egg*.
7. He's an *egghead*.
8. That is a cool *breeze*.
9. This class is a *breeze*.
10. That car drives as smooth as a *breeze*.
11. Let's shoot the *breeze*.
12. As a child I never owned a *cat*.
13. That *cat* is keeping cool.
14. There goes a cool *cat*.
15. I don't know many *hepcats*.
16. This algebra problem is a *snap*.
17. Don't *snap* your fingers.
18. She fastened her skirt with a *snap*.
19. He likes to eat *gingersnaps*.
20. Don't *snap* at me when you're angry.

Slang words and expressions have become a part of our spoken language. Although their meanings may change rapidly and radically, they are a part of our study of words. Students should understand, however, that slang expressions or words are not always reliable tools for effective communication, since the meanings of the words or expressions may change drastically from one small group to another within the same city. The teacher may be able to prove how slang words or expressions may be misunderstood by different groups in the same city, or even in the same school, by having students define the following words and then by having their parents define the same words. If possible students should also ask their grandparents or other older persons to define the same words. After students have collected various definitions of these words, they should discuss the problems of communication that arise when these, and like words, are used in conversation.

> savvy, trigger-man, hokum, cook, square, cube, fink, jive, skiddoo, pad, glide, whoopee, chick, tomato, go-getter, gas, blast, breeze, snap, egghead, pig

Students should realize, through class discussion, that the meanings of those words change not only in time but the meanings also depend on the context in which they are used.

HOW WORDS CHANGE MEANING IN CONTEXT

To show students how words change meaning in context, a teacher may ask students to arrange the sentences below into groups illustrating the different meanings of *flight.*

1. Under the cover of darkness, the refugees began their *flight* for freedom.
2. Into the marsh, a well-protected nesting place for wild geese and ducks, the *flight* settled gently.
3. Imagining we might encounter the Hunchback, we climbed the spiraling *flight* of stairs to the cathedral bell tower.
4. To stop the *flight* of skilled workmen to West Berlin, the East German government erected a wall of concrete and barbed wire.
5. Each spring, the villagers eagerly watch the sky for the *flight* of swallows.
6. Step by step, we climbed the *flight* to the ghost-infested attic.

After students have grouped the sentences according to the several illustrated meanings of the word *flight,* the teacher should ask them to write a definition for the word as used in each group of sentences.

1 and 4 ________ (act of fleeing or escaping)
2 and 5 ________ (a flock of birds)
3 and 6 ________ (a set of stairs)

Thus students should discover that the word *flight* has at least three meanings and that each meaning is determined by the use of the word in its sentence, i.e., its verbal setting or context. Which of the above three definitions is the "correct" definition? Is there a "correct" definition? How many more meanings of the word *flight* can students think of and illustrate?

To illustrate further how different the meanings of a word actually are in various contexts, students should use a different word for *turn* in each of the following sentences.

1. In the fall in Indiana, the leaves *turn* many colors.
2. If snow *turns* to freezing rain, the pilot knows he must increase his altitude to avoid dangerous icing.
3. The *turn* of events caused the sophomore class to cancel the picnic.
4. *Turn* the key quietly, or you will awaken father.
5. Adlai Stevenson could *turn* a fine phrase.
6. She *turned* him against his family.
7. At the *turn* of the century this country will be colonizing distant planets.
8. My *turn* to stand guard came at the blackest hour of the night.

As a short research project for able students, the teacher might ask them to select one of the following words, or any others the teacher may want to suggest, and to find in newspapers, magazines, and books ten or twelve sentences in which the word is used. Using the system of dictionary editors, students should record the sentences, as well as author and source, on separate cards; then they should separate the cards into groups according to different meanings and write definitions for the words as illustrated in the sentence context.

air bat frame mean paint pair record swing

Students should decide whether the meaning of the word *green* changes in the following sentences:

1. Mary is wearing a *green* bathing suit.
2. The fruit is still *green.*
3. The second team is pretty *green.*

What new meaning does *green* take on in sentence 2? in sentence 3? How is each of these new meanings suggested by other words in the sentences?

Students should consider how the meaning of *run* changes in the following sentences:

1. John can *run* a fast half mile.
2. Bill *runs* an illegal business.
3. He plans to *run* for office.
4. Tom batted in the winning *run.*
5. Mary has a *run* in her stocking.
6. The scandalous Florida land deals of the late twenties started a *run* on the stock market.

Students should be able to explain how the meaning of *run* is controlled by other words in the foregoing sentences.

Suggested Activities

1. Students should write three sentences in which they use each of the following words in different ways:

foot point wing pipe cat rat

2. Students should write as many sentences as they can in which they use the word *bank* in a different way in each sentence. Each student should read his sentences to the class and ask his classmates if they can infer the meaning of the word from its context, i.e., immediate verbal setting.

By this time students should begin realizing that a word can take on any of a number of meanings, depending on its verbal setting, or context. To illustrate how important context is, the teacher may put the word *slide* on the chalkboard and ask students what the word means.

The word *slide,* like the word *run,* should elicit a number of different responses. A particularly bright student may indicate that the word, out of context, can mean any of a number of things; but if he were to see it in a sentence, he could come closer to giving a precise definition of it.

The teacher may then put sentences like these on the chalkboard and ask students how the meaning of *slide* changes.

1. The little boy went down the *slide.*
2. Maury Wills made a great *slide* into second base.
3. He was never able to *slide* on ice without falling.
4. He let the matter *slide* by without doing anything about it.
5. The trombonist *slides* from note to note without difficulty.
6. He will never back*slide* as long as he listens to the Reverend Goodman.
7. That giant *slide* started an avalanche.
8. What I need is a *slide* rule.
9. He had trouble putting the *slide* into the projector.
10. He polished the *slide* on his trombone.

In the preceding exercises, the student, if he has been following instructions faithfully, has tried to determine word meanings without recourse to the dictionary. Knowing how to use surrounding words to unlock the meaning of a familiar or unfamiliar word is a highly useful and practical skill. Since words do change meaning in context, as demonstrated above, the student will increase his ability to read intelligently and sensitively by consciously developing his skill in using context clues.

The following exercise is suggested as one approach for illustrating some of the most useful context clues for tracking down word meanings. First, the teacher might write sentence A of a group on the chalkboard and ask the class to discuss the meaning of the underlined word; then he could present sentence B to demonstrate how the context clue helps to establish and define more exactly the meaning of the word. After each word has been defined by the use of context, the teacher may wish to have students check the dictionary for denotative meanings:

1A. Carefully propelling himself in space with his gun, Astronaut White photographed the Earth 120 miles below. (The sentence as it stands obviously contains a specialized meaning of the word *gun*. As sophisticated about space as they are, some students may even be able to describe in detail the construction and operation of the jet-propulsion gun. Nevertheless, many students will probably have only a vague, generalized notion about the *gun*.)

1B. Carefully propelling himself in space with his *gun*, a jet-nozzled device that spurts compressed oxygen enabling him to move in any direction, Astronaut White photographed the Earth 120 miles below. (What additional information is now supplied about the *gun*? In the original sentence, the reader did not know that the gun was equipped with a jet nozzle, that it used compressed oxygen, nor that it could give motion in all directions. The use of a synonym, in this instance in the form of an appositive phrase, may provide the meaning of an unfamiliar word or a more specific meaning for a familiar word.)

2A. He suffers from *claustrophobia*. (The sentence as it is written gives little help in determining the meaning of the word.)

2B. When a person dreads being in a closed room or narrow space, we say that he suffers from *claustrophobia*. (In this instance, the context clue is an actual definition included in the sentence.)

3A. His analysis of the problem was *superficial*. (In this instance, unless the students are actually familiar with the word or its Latin origin, they will be unable to make an intelligent guess at its meaning.)

3B. His analysis of the problem, far from being careful and thoroughgoing, was *superficial*. (Students who can now supply a satisfactory meaning for the word should be asked to explain specifically how they solved the riddle. The words *far from* introduce an idea of contrast. Whatever *superficial* means, it is, according to the sentence, far from or opposite to the meanings of *careful* and *thoroughgoing,* e.g., careless and hasty. Thus in this instance the context clue tells the reader the meaning of a word by telling what it is not like.

4A. I soon learned that John was an exceedingly *obdurate* person. (Again, unless the students are familiar with the word or its Latin origin, they will find little help within the context of the sentence.)

4B. I soon learned that John was an exceedingly *obdurate* person, as stubborn and unyielding as a mule. (The teacher should ask students who can now supply a satisfactory meaning for the word, how the context clue in this sentence differs from the clue in sentence 3B. The word *as* introduces an idea of likeness or similarity. According to the sentence, being obdurate is like being as "stubborn and unyielding as a mule." Thus *obdurate* must mean *stubborn* or *unyielding* in this sentence. The context clue in this example tells the reader the meaning of the word by telling what it is like.)

5A. The President made plans to counteract the *escalation* of the war. (The teacher should ask students to substitute "tried desperately to prevent" for the words "made plans to counteract" in the foregoing sentence. How do the words "tried desperately to prevent" change the tone of the sentence? Do they provide a stronger clue to the meaning of *escalation* than the original words?)

5B. The President made plans to counteract the *escalation* of the war, the expansion of military power. But the efforts resulted in an increased commitment of men and materiel by the enemy. Thus the conflict enlarged and spread as each side tried to win freedom and justice. (A larger context provided by several sentences often gives the circumstances or situations which make the meaning of an unfamiliar word clearer. The additional sentences suggest that *escalation* has to do with "expansion of military power," "increased commitment of men," and the enlarging and spreading of the conflict.)

To summarize, some of the most useful ways to unlock word meanings in context without immediate recourse to the dictionary are through the use of synonyms, comparisons, contrasts, definitions, explanations, and the larger context of several sentences which explain the general situation or circumstance in which the word is used. While the foregoing exercise is intended to show how useful context clues can be in determining word meanings, it also shows sentences in which virtually no significant clues are available, although the larger context of many sentences may sometimes provide a clue to meaning not given in the immediate sentence environment. A knowledge of Latin and Greek roots may help a person infer meanings of words, and the dictionary remains an invaluable tool in supplying many generally accepted meanings as a check against contextually derived meanings and in providing meanings when context clues are unavailable.

Thus far in this unit, the emphasis has been on the strong influence that word setting or verbal context has on the meaning of a word. But there are other variable factors of prime importance which comprise the total context determining word meanings. Among the many elements affecting word meaning, some significant ones are the background or experience of the individual, the purpose of the speaker or writer, and the nature of his audience. The background and experiences of a person color his use of and reaction to many words. When George Lincoln Rockwell of the American Nazi Party spoke of "America for Christians," he undoubtedly had a different meaning in mind for the word *Christians* than has Martin Luther King, Jr., when he uses the term. When Rockwell used the word *Christians,* he probably was thinking of members of his organization. There are certainly no Negroes in his "congregation." On the other hand, King is probably not thinking of an all-Negro "congregation." King's *Christian* is not equal to

Rockwell's *Christian.* That the thoughts and feelings a word evokes for one may be strikingly different from the associations the word may suggest for another person is a fundamental idea students need to understand.

To illustrate to the class that words do suggest different ideas and emotions to each person, the teacher might try this game of association. He reads or writes on the chalkboard words relating to controversial ideas or persons, such as the following:

Ku Klux Klan	a current TV show that appeals to teen-agers
beatnik	Viet Cong
drag racing	hippies
liberal	Pentagon
love-ins	dropout
school	surfing
parents	Governor Wallace
egghead	de Gaulle
a current, controversial musical group	communist

After each word is read or written on the board, he gives students a brief time, perhaps 20 to 30 seconds, to make a spontaneous written reaction to each term in the form of a word or phrase. He collects the responses and reads and discusses them with the class. Why are there so many different responses to a given word? Are there tendencies toward a common agreement for a given word? For the word *school,* for example, some typical responses might be "building," "prison," "education," "brick and mortar," "friends," "a drag," "misery every hour," "pep sessions," and "homework."

This activity and similar ones should help students realize that the meaning of a word can be colored by highly personal experiences which evoke an emotional response to the idea or object to which the word refers. Thus the potential dropout who is having difficulty reading may find attending school a desperately discouraging experience and may respond to the term *school* with the word *prison.* On the other hand, the potentially brilliant student who is not being challenged by the school's curriculum may describe school as a *drag.*

If the responses given for the words listed on the chalkboard were sufficiently different, students may begin wondering just how they manage to communicate with their classmates, teachers, and parents. Communication, though imperfect, is possible because people have reached general agreement on what many words mean. This general agreement stems from the fact that many words relate to things or situations in the physical world, things which people have observed or have experienced through one or more of the senses. For example, the word *tree* by common agreement among English-speaking people describes an object having particular physical characteristics. It is important for students to see that the word *tree* is a symbol created by the mind to stand for an object in the physical world and that the word is not the same thing as that object. Confusion between the symbol (the word) and the referent (the object) often causes a breakdown in communication. As semanticists frequently say, "The word is not the thing."

The purpose of the writer or speaker is another significant factor contributing to the total context of word meaning. Skillful writers or speakers may deliberately use words which carry emotional connotations favorable to their purposes. Also, writers and speakers sometimes extract words from their context and quote them to serve their own purposes. The result is that the reader or listener receives a distorted message which is often diametrically opposed to the meaning intended in the original quotation.

To illustrate the effect upon meaning when quotations are lifted from context, the teacher may use the following sentence pairs. First, he presents the "lifted" quotation to get the students' impression of the musical or book being described; then he gives them the original quotation. He should discuss the differences in meanings and the apparent purpose of the writer who extracted the phrase from the original description.

1A. "A brilliant work."
1B. "It falls far short of being a brilliant work."

2A. "*Bye Bye Birdie* has emotional delicacy."
2B. "*Bye Bye Birdie* has the emotional delicacy of a teen-age rumble."

It may be useful for students to look at bits of reviews as they appear on covers of paperback books. How appealing is the book when the student sees the word *sensational* on the cover as part of a comment about it by a prominent critic? What does he find when he looks up the original criticism? Students may be asked to read current reviews in popular magazines to lift out of context particular words of praise or condemnation and to read them to their classmates. Then students should read the entire sentence or paragraph from which the complimentary or uncomplimentary words were taken.

KINDS OF CONTEXT

Thus far we have been primarily concerned with written verbal contexts, i.e., with a word's immediate verbal setting. As we already pointed out, the reader must take into consideration the word's immediate verbal environment to understand what the writer means. But equally important, the reader must also consider the writer, his background, and his intentions. As we noted before, George Lincoln Rockwell and Martin Luther King, Jr., do not mean the same thing when they use the word *Christian* or when they refer to their *congregation.* Consequently, the intelligent reader must consider as he reads (1) the word's immediate written setting; (2) the kind of book, magazine, or article in which the word appears; (3) the time at which the book, magazine, or article was written; (4) some basic information about the author; and (5) the author's intentions (if these can be determined by what and how he writes). Perfect communication is impossible since no two people have exactly the same set of experiences with the same words. Therefore, the reader must attempt to take into consideration what experiences might affect the writer's use of particular words, especially motive words.

In conversation, if a listener intends to infer correctly what the speaker is saying, he must consider (1) the word's immediate setting; (2) the situation; (3) the mood of the speaker; (4) his experiential background; (5) his tone as he uses certain words; and (6) his facial expressions and his gestures.

Basically, there are three kinds of contexts: verbal, physical, and psychological. The verbal context is, of course, the immediate oral or written setting in which a word is used. The physical context includes the time, the place, and the activities going on when the word is spoken or written. The psychological context includes the mood of the speaker or writer at the time he uses a particular word and his experiences with it.

To illustrate the three kinds of context, a teacher might give students a nonsense word like *triz*. First, each student is to write a paragraph in which he uses *triz* in such a way that his readers will know exactly what *triz* designates. (This paragraph will illustrate verbal context.)

Second, each student should describe a situation in which a speaker or writer uses *triz* in such a way that it conveys a meaning different from the one in the first paragraph. The meaning of *triz* must be made clear from the way it is used and from the description of the setting. The teacher might encourage students to describe a situation several hundred years ago to show that *triz* has changed meaning in time. (This is an example of physical context.)

Third, each student is to write a paragraph in which he describes how a speaker or writer uses *triz* to convey a meaning slightly different from that conveyed in either of the first two paragraphs. The student is to explain how the writer's experiences with *triz* or his mood change the meaning. (This is an example of psychological context.)

GRADE 9

An Introduction to Phonetic Alphabets and to Morphemes Through Prefixes and Suffixes

Words and dictionaries are a student's most useful tools. If he is to succeed in life, he must know how to use and pronounce thousands of words correctly. He can, and should, rely heavily on his dictionary for the lexical definitions and the key to the pronunciation of many words. But he won't always have his dictionary handy when he reads or hears a new word; he will have to infer the word's meaning from context or from his knowledge of other words.

This unit gives a student clues to the meanings of thousands of words by introducing him to the most productive prefixes and suffixes in the language. Knowing the meanings of these bound morphemes, a student can frequently infer the meaning of a word that is new to him. But he will probably only be confused if he is asked to memorize the meanings of many prefixes and suffixes in a short time. Likewise, he will probably only be confused if he is asked to memorize the phonetic symbols that give him the key to the pronunciation of words new to him. *Therefore, this unit is not designed to be taught in three or four weeks. Instead, it can be divided into small segments that can be presented each week during the year.*

A student is more likely to remember the meanings of a prefix or a suffix if he can examine a number of words containing the same prefix and a number containing the same suffix, and if he can arrive, inductively, at the meanings of the prefix and of the suffix. Therefore, it is recommended that each week a teacher write on the board two lists of words, the first containing the same prefix, and the second containing the same suffix. Then the teacher asks students to infer the meanings of the prefix or suffix and, in the case of the latter, its grammatical functions, by using the words in sentences. In twenty to thirty minutes each week, the teacher should be able to acquaint students with the most productive bound morphemes in the language.*

A morpheme is the smallest meaningful unit of sound. The word *untie* contains two morphemes: *un* and *tie*. *Tie* can stand alone, and is called a free morpheme. *Un* must be combined with another morpheme, and is therefore called a bound morpheme. All prefixes and suffixes are bound morphemes.†

Occasionally the pronunciation of these bound morphemes changes because of the immediate phonetic environment. To acquaint a student with the phonetic alphabets used by major dictionaries, this unit has appended to it the phonetic transcriptions of three dictionaries and the International Phonetic Alphabet transcription of all the prefixes and suffixes that appear in this unit. It is recommended that teachers not have a student memorize these phonetic alphabets. Instead, the teacher can help a student use them properly by introducing him to a few symbols at a time. This can be done by writing the phonetic transcriptions of the new prefixes and suffixes on the board. (These transcriptions appear on pages 147-152.)

Although the present treatment has been to introduce prefixes (pp. 99-119) and suffixes (pp. 119-146) alphabetically within each section, this does not mean that this is an inviolable order. The teacher may wish to combine those prefixes that have nearly the same meanings, or he may wish to introduce a student only to the prefixes and suffixes that are the most productive in the language.

*Some of the words included in these lists will not be readily found in one or more of the dictionaries that students are using. This merely underscores the fact that no single dictionary can include all the words in our lexicon.

†The free morphemes *extra, fore,* and *super* might be confused with the bound morphemes *extra-*, *fore-*, and *super-* which function as prefixes. *Auto-* and *hypo-* are bound morphemes, but we also have the free morphemes, auto (automobile) and hypo (hypodermic). Likewise, the suffixes *-able, -ful, -like, -wise,* and *-worthy* might be considered bound variants of morphemes that also have free variants.

PREFIXES

To introduce students to prefixes, the teacher may wish to write these words on the chalkboard:

unarm	undo	unreel
unbend	unfold	unroll
uncap	unhand	unscrew
unchain	unhitch	unsnap
uncoil	unlatch	untie
uncork	unloose	unwind

These eighteen words have three things in common: all contain the prefix *un-;* all are verbs; all have only two syllables. Students should have little difficulty detecting these points of commonality. They should also see that in each case the prefix *un-* reverses the action of the verb, which is the second syllable in each of the words.

There is nothing wrong with saying that each of the *un-* words contains two syllables, but the term syllable does not adequately cover both parts of these *un-* words. Nor would there be anything wrong with saying that each of these words contains a prefix and a verb. Either method of describing the words is correct. But there is a third, and perhaps more comprehensive description: each of the *un-* words contains a bound and a free morpheme.

As a baby learns to talk, he indiscriminately combines any number of sounds that he can produce or that please him. The result may be an endless stream of gibberish interrupted occasionally by combinations of sounds that we have given meanings. When a baby produces the smallest unit of sounds that we have given meanings, he utters a morpheme.

Let's suppose that the baby is fascinated by the sounds *tie* and *un.* As he says them to himself, only one—tie—contains meaning for us. But if he combines the two in proper order, he utters the word *untie,* which, of course, means something to us. Now as the baby babbles "un, un, un, tie, tie, tie" he is uttering two morphemes, for both are minimal units of sound that contain meaning. *Un-* means not. Or, if it precedes a verb, it means that the action of the verb is reversed. We know *un-* as a prefix that can precede many words. Linguists call this unit of sound a bound morpheme since it cannot stand alone. The second combination of sounds—tie—can stand alone and is called a free morpheme.

All prefixes are bound morphemes,* i.e., they are minimal meaningful units of sound that must be combined with other minimal meaningful units of sound. In the past we would have called sounds like *un-* prefixes and let it go at that. In an age of linguistic science in which our students will be introduced to more and more linguistic terms, it will be helpful to them if they become acquainted with both terms, prefix and bound morpheme. Thus they will have taken a step toward understanding the language of tomorrow's textbooks.

Students should immediately see that the list of words above does not contain all the verbs that can have their meaning reversed by being preceded with the prefix *un-*. They should have little difficulty in adding a great number of verbs to this list. And as they add verbs, they should also see that many probably contain more than one syllable. Some of these verbs will undoubtedly contain more than one morpheme, but an analysis of the morphemes involved will come later. At this point, it is important for the students to see only that by placing the bound morpheme or prefix *un-* in front of a verb, they reverse the action of the verb. They should also see that the word that follows the bound morpheme is an actual word, or as the linguists would call it, a free morpheme.

The prefix *un-* can precede more than just verbs. It can be used with adjectives and adverbs, and occasionally with nouns. As a prefix in front of adjectives, adverbs, and nouns, it means not, or opposed to. The teacher may wish to have students examine this list of *un-* words:

unable	unaware	uncompromising
unaccomplished	unbearable	unconcern
unaccountable	unbelievable	unconformity
unaccustomed	unbiased	unconscious
unaffected	unborn	uncourtly
unapproachable	uncertainty	undaunted
unassisted	unchristian	undeniable
unattached	uncleanly	uneducated

*Please refer to the note on bound morphemes, p. 94.

unemployed	unimproved	unqualified
unexpected	unintelligent	unquestionably
unfeelingly	unjust	unreasonably
ungainly	unprepared	unscrupulous
ungracious	unprofitable	untenable

If students were to use each of the above words in sentences, they would see that some function as nouns, some as adjectives, and some as adverbs. If they are familiar with participles, they will probably recognize that some are past participles of the verbs and that they function as adjectives. Students should also see that the prefix *un-* in each of the aforementioned words means not.

Students should be able to add many nouns, adjectives, and adverbs to this list of words that can be preceded by the prefix *un-*. They should also be led to see that *un-* is not always a prefix. A student may suggest that one of these words be added to the list of *un-* words:

unanimous	unicycle	unite
undulate	unified	universe
unicorn	union	

In the words in the above list, the first syllable is stressed in all but *unanimous* and *unite*. In all but *undulate*, the vowel is different from the *ŭ* in the prefix *un-*; the words *unicorn, unicycle, unified, union,* and *universe* contain *yü,* part of the prefix *uni-*, which means one. When *un-* appears as a prefix, it is a stressed syllable (or stressed morpheme). In the words above, the *un-* is not a bound morpheme that means not or that reverses the action of the verb; the *un-* is simply a part of a combination of sounds that make up different morphemes.

The prefix *un-*, meaning not, comes to us from Old English. In most of the words in the above lists, the prefix precedes a free morpheme that also comes to us from English. Therefore, the free morpheme is a native, not a borrowed word. Some grammarians object to the use of an English prefix with a word that comes from Latin, Greek, French, German, or any other language. Since *un-* is an English prefix, those grammarians would have it precede only English words, although this is not always the case. For example, the word appropriate comes from Latin. Therefore, unappropriate is a combination of an English prefix with a Latin word. At least one student in the class should recall that unappropriate is not the only way of saying that something is not appropriate; another word for the same meaning is inappropriate. In the word inappropriate, we have combined a Latin prefix with a Latin word. Can students find other words in the lists that can have either the prefix *un-* or the prefix *in-*? If they can, the teacher might have them look up the origin of those words to see if they have been borrowed from another language.

Un- is not the only prefix that means not. Students should examine these words:

immodest	immoral	impossible
immoderate	imperfect	implausible

Students should see immediately that all those words begin with the prefix *im-*, which means not. They should have little difficulty giving the definitions of those words. Can they substitute the prefix *un-* for the prefix *im-* in the words in the above list? If so, for which words? If not, why not?

What is the meaning of the prefix *ir-* in the following words:

irrational	irrelevance	irresponsible
irreconcilable	irreparable	irretraceable
irredeemable	irresistible	irreverence
irregular	irresolute	irrevocable

Can students infer the meanings of those words without looking them up in a dictionary? Can they replace the prefix *ir-* with either the prefix *un-* or the prefix *im-*? If not, why not?

Can they infer the meaning of the prefix *in-* in these words:

inacceptable	incohesive	inexcitable
inassignable	inconcealable	inobtrusive
inauthentic	inconsecutive	intranquility
incertain	indeficiency	invital

Can students replace the prefix *in-* with the prefix *un-* in some of the words in the above lists? If so, which words? Why can they use *un-* with some of these words?

What is the meaning of *il-* in the following words:

illegible	illogical
illiberal	illegal
illiterate	

Can students replace the prefix *il-* with *im-*, *un-*, *in-*, or *ir-*? If not, why not?

Students should recognize that the prefixes *un-*, *im-*, *ir-*, *in-*, and *il-* all mean *not* in the words in the above lists. The most common of these prefixes are *in-* and *un-;* however, *in-* cannot precede all words. Therefore, we find the prefix *il-*, meaning not, in front of words that begin with *l*. We have *ir-*, meaning not, in front of words that begin with *r*, and *im-*, meaning not, in front of words that begin with *b*, *p*, or *m*. But the prefixes *im-*, *in-*, *ir-*, and *il-* do not always mean not. *In-*, for example, can mean in or into. What words that begin with the prefix *in-*, meaning in or into, do students know?

Alert students should recognize that a knowledge of prefixes will help them determine the meanings of many words. As they study prefixes, they should also see that although a certain prefix from Old English, for example, meant *on* at the time that it was introduced into the language, it may no longer bear exactly that same meaning today.*

a-

Thus far, we have considered only a few prefixes that mean not. A Greek prefix, *a-*, meaning not, has only limited use. It appears in such words as achromatic, acritical, amoral, aseptic, atonal, asymmetric, and atypical.

The prefix *a-* from Middle English means "being in a state or position of" in such words as these:

aflicker	aflutter	aglimmer
aflower	agleam	aglitter

*Students must realize that many prefixes have more than one meaning. Knowledge of a single meaning only will frequently lead a student astray if he attempts to infer the meaning of a new word by drawing solely upon that knowledge. To appreciate the problems that arise from an overreliance on prefixes, suffixes, and roots, see Appendix D.

aglow	astride	atingle
astir	athrob	awash
astraddle	atilt	awhirl

ab-

From this list of words students might try to determine the meaning of the prefix *ab-*.

abdicate	abnormal
abduct	abscess
abhor	absent
abject	absolve
abjure	absorb
ablaut	abstract

After compiling some possible meanings they should look up the words in a good dictionary to check their derivation.

ad-

The prefix *ad-*, meaning to, toward, or near, appears in the words addict, address, adduct, adhere, adhibit, adjacent, adjective, adjourn, adjudge, adjust, administer, admire, and adsorb.

If the free morpheme begins with the letters *sc* or *sp,* the *ad-* prefix becomes simply *a-*, as in ascend, ascribe, aspect, asperse, and aspire. It becomes *ac-* if the free morpheme begins with *c* or *q* as in acquire; *af-* if the free morpheme begins with *f* as in affect, affirm, and affix; *ag-* if the free morpheme begins with *g* as in aggravate, aggregate, and aggressive; *al-* if the free morpheme begins with *l* as in allay, alleviate, alliterate, allow, allure, allude, and ally; *an-* if the free morpheme begins with *n* as in annex, annotate, announce, and annul; *ap-* if the free morpheme begins with *p* as in appall, apparatus, apparel, appear, append, and appetite; *ar-* if the free morpheme begins with *r* as in arrange, array, arrest, and arrive; *as-* if the free morpheme begins with *s* as in assail, assault, assent, assess, assert, and associate; and *at-* if the free morpheme begins with *t* as in attach, attack, attain, attend, and attract.

As students study prefixes and their meanings, the teacher may wish to assign each student to one word that he writes on the board and have a student look up the word for its meanings, its derivation, and the meanings of the original prefix and free morpheme. Students should find this information fascinating. For example, abduct comes from the Latin *ab-*, meaning away, and *ducere*, meaning to lead. Therefore, to abduct someone is to lead him away. Students may note that the common connotation is a little stronger than simply to lead away.

ante-

As was already pointed out, a teacher will not want to teach this unit at one time; instead, he will probably give students one new prefix and one new suffix each week by putting lists of words containing the prefix and suffix on the chalkboard and by having students first arrive at their meanings before the teacher gives them the meanings or has them look up definitions in a dictionary. Thus the teacher may wish to put these words that contain the prefix *ante-* on the chalkboard and have students first decide the meaning of the prefix, then, only if necessary, look up the bound morpheme in the dictionary. If students can see that *ante-* means "before" in time or order or "in front of," they can probably infer the meanings of these words:

antebellum	antechamber	antemortem
antecede	antedate	anterior
antecedent	antemeridian	anteroom

anti-

The Greek prefix *anti-* means against or opposed to in these words:

antiaggression	antidote	antimilitarist
antiaircraft	anti-Fascist	antimoral
anti-American	antihuman	anti-Platonic
anticlimax	anti-imperialist	antiscientific
anticommercial	antilabor	antiwar

Students should see why hyphens are necessary in such words as anti-American and anti-Fascist. They should also have no difficulty seeing why a hyphen is necessary in anti-imperialist. The prefix *anti-* means the opposite to, or the reverse of, in words like antiseptic, antisocial, antitrust.

In medical terms, the prefix *anti-* means counteracting, curative, or neutralizing. Students may be familiar with these medical terms:

antianemic	antimalarial
antiasthmatic	antirheumatic
antibiotic	antitoxin
anticonvulsive	antityphoid

arch-

The prefix *arch-* comes from the Latin *arch-* through the Greek *archos,* meaning ruler. It means chief or principal in these words: archangel, archbishop, archdeacon, archdiocese, archducal, and archduke. It means very great, or extreme in words like archenemy and archrival.

auto-

The Greek prefix *auto-* means self. It appears in such words as autobiography, autohypnosis, autotherapy, autostability, autosuggestion, autoinfectant, and automotive.

Auto- means self-propelled in such words as autobus and autogiro.

be-

The Old English prefix *be-* means around, all over, or throughout in these words containing verbs:

beclasp	beshadow
beclothe	beshroud
becloud	besmear
bedabble	besmudge
bedrape	betatter

The prefix *be-* means completely or thoroughly in these words:

becrowd	befluster	beshame
becurse	bemadden	bethump
bedamn	bemuddle	bewitch
bedrabble	bescourge	beworry

The prefix *be-* means off in the word behead.

When combined with intransitive verbs, the prefix *be-* means at, on, over, against, or for in words like:

bechatter	begroan
bedrizzle	beshout
befret	beswarm

When the prefix *be-* appears with adjectives and nouns, it can mean to make or to cause to be as in:

beclown	bedwarf
becripple	beknight

In the following words, the prefix *be-* means to provide with or to affect by, or to cover with:

becarpet	beflower	besmoke
becharm	begloom	bethorn
bedrape	bejewel	bewhisker

When the prefix *be-* appears with a participle, it means furnished with excessively or conspicuously as in:

becapped	bejeweled	beruffled
becarpeted	belaced	bestrapped
bechained	beribboned	betinseled
beflowered	berobed	beturbaned
befrilled	beroughed	bewreathed

co- and *com-*

The Latin prefix *co-* or *com-* means with, together, joint, or jointly. It is frequently combined with verbs, nouns, adjectives, and adverbs. Students should have little difficulty inferring the meanings of these words:

coadminister	codebtor	coexist	cooperate
coagent	codefendent	combat	co-owner
coauthor	coenact	combine	copromote
cocaptain	coestablish	command	coproprietor
coconspirator	coexecutor	comply	coreign

The prefix *com-* is changed to *co-* when it precedes words beginning with *gn* or *h* as in cognate, cognomen, cohabit, cohere, and cohesive. It becomes *col-* if the free morpheme begins with *l* as in collide, collect, colloquy, and collusion. It becomes *con-* in words in which the free morpheme begins with *c, d, f, g, j, n, q, s, t,* and *v*. Have students give examples of the prefix *con-*, meaning with or together.

The prefix *com-* becomes *cor-* if the free morpheme begins with an *r*. Examples: correct, correspond, corroborate, corrode (in this case, the prefix means thoroughly).

counter-

The prefix *counter-* comes from Middle English from the French. In the following words it means opposing, contrary, or acting in opposition or response to the action of the free morpheme:

counteract	counterpropaganda
counterargument	counterreform
counterdeclaration	counterreligion
countereffort	counterstatement
counterintelligence	countertheory
countermand	counterthreat

Counter- means corresponding or denoting the duplicate or parallel in these words: countercopy, counterseal, and countersecurity.

In the following words the prefix *counter-* means opposite in direction or position: counterarch, counterclockwise, countercurrent, counterflight, countermigration, counterpressure, counterstep, and counterturn.

de-

The prefix *de-* comes from the Latin *de* meaning from, away, or down.

In the words deflect and decapitate, the prefix carries the meaning away or off. In decline and descend, it means down. In denude it means completely and utterly. It conveys the meaning of reversing the free morpheme or ridding of the element contained in the free morpheme in the words decode, decentralize, and decarbonization.

Students should be asked to infer the meaning of the prefix *de-* in these words:

deacidify	deflea	derestrict
deaerate	defluoridate	desand
debug	deforest	desaturate
declassify	degerm	desex
decolor	deglaze	despecialize
decondition	deglorify	desugar
decongest	demast	detribalize
decrown	denasalize	dewax

dis-

The Latin prefix *dis-* means away from, apart, reversing the action of the free morpheme in the word, the deprivation of some quality of power, not, completely, or thoroughly. Students should be asked to infer the meaning of the prefix in these words:

disable	discard	disinherit
disabuse	discern	disjoin
disaccord	discharge	dislodge
disadvantage	disclaim	dismember
disaffect	disclose	disparage
disaffirm	discontented	dispense
disagree	discontinue	disperse
disallow	discord	displace
disappoint	discriminate	dispose
disapprove	disembody	disquiet
disarm	disgust	disseminate
disassociate	disgrace	dissociate
disaster	dishearten	dissolve
disavow	dishonest	distribute
disbelieve	dishonorable	disturb

Note that *dis-* frequently appears in the language as a variant of the Old French prefix, *des-*.

en-

The prefix *en-* is used to make verbs from nouns and adjectives. It means to cover or surround with or to place into or upon. It appears in such words as encircle, enable, enfeeble, enact, encompass, encourage.

A variant of the prefix *en-* is *em-;* it replaces *en-* in words in which the free morpheme begins with *b* or *p*. Examples include the words embalm, embankment, embark, embellish, embrace, employ, and empower.

ex-

The Latin prefix *ex-* means out in words like exit, exhale, and exonerate. It means thoroughly in words such as exasperate and excruciate. And when it is attached to a free morpheme with a hyphen, it means formerly or sometime as in ex-president, ex-mayor, and ex-wife. Half of the students in the class should list as many words as they can in which the prefix *ex-* appears. The other students should attempt to infer the meaning of the words from their knowledge of the meaning of the prefix.

extra-

The prefix *extra-* means beyond or outside the scope of a certain thing, or beyond the limits of a certain boundary. Students should infer the meanings of these words:

extracelluar	extralegal
extraconscious	extranuclear
extracultural	extraofficial
extracurricular	extraparental
extraformal	extrapopular
extrahuman	extrascholastic
extraintellectual	extrasocial

fore-

The Old English prefix *fore-* means prior in time, place, or rank, and also situated at or near the front. Students should infer the meaning of the prefix after they examine this list of words:

forearm	forebode	foreclose	forefather
forebear	forecast	foredeck	forefinger

forefront	foremast	foresight
foreground	foreordain	forestall
forehand	forerank	foretell
forehead	forerunner	forethought
foreknowledge	foresee	foretop
foreleg	foreshadow	foreword
foreman	foreshorten	

hyper-

The Greek prefix *hyper-* means over, above, or excessive in the following words:

hyperacidity	hypercritical	hyperpersonal
hyperactive	hyperidealistic	hyptertension
hypercivilized	hyperintellectual	hypersensitive
hyperconfident	hyperpatriotic	hypervigilant

hypo-

The Greek prefix *hypo-*, the opposite of the Greek prefix *hyper-*, means under or beneath in words like hypodermic, hypocaust, and hypothesis. The prefix means less than in words like hypoactive, hypodynamic, and hypomania. When used in its medical sense, the prefix *hypo-* denotes a lack of or a deficiency in the free morpheme that follows the prefix. Examples: hypoalkaline, hypocatharsis, and hypothyroid.

inter-

The Latin prefix *inter-* means with each other, together, mutual, mutually, between, or occurring or situated between. Students should be able to figure out the meaning of the prefix *inter-* in the following words:

intercede	intercom	intercurrent
intercellular	intercommunity	interdenominational
intercept	intercontinental	interdependent
intercession	intercostal	interdict
interchange	intercourse	interest
intercollegiate	intercross	interfere

interfold	interlunar	interrelated
intergrade	intermarriage	interrupt
intergrowth	intermediary	intersect
interject	intermediate	interspace
interlace	intermingle	intersperse
interlay	intermittent	interstellar
interleaf	intermixture	intertribal
interlinear	interpenetrate	interurban
interlock	interphone	interval
interlocution	interplanetary	intervene
interlope	interpose	interview
interlude	interracial	interweave

intra-

The Latin prefix *intra-* means situated or occurring within in the following words: intra-abdominal, intra-arterial, intra-aural, intracephalic, intracollegiate, intracontinental, intradermal, intraglandular, intramarginal, intramundane, intranational, and intraurban.

The prefix *intra-* means within or inside of in the following words: intracellular, intracoastal, intramural, intramuscular, intrastate, intravenous.

macro- and *micro-*

The Greek prefix *macro-* means long or enlarged. It appears in such words as macroclimate, macrocosm, and macroeconomics. The Greek-derived *micro-* means small or minute. It has come to mean enlarging or magnifying in size or volume. The prefix *micro-* appears in such words as microbotany, microhistology, microbe, and microscope. The prefix *micro-* can also mean millionth, as in microgram.

mal-

The Latin and French prefix *mal-* means bad, ill, evil, wrong, defective, or imperfect. It also signifies simple negation. Students should have little difficulty inferring the meaning of the prefix *mal-* in these words:

maladjusted	maldirection	malnutrition
malalignment	maleducation	malodor
malaroma	malfed	maloperation
malarrangement	malfortunate	malproportioned
malconstruction	malinstruction	malshaped

mid-

Unlike most of the prefixes studied thus far, the Old English prefix *mid-* is sometimes followed by a hyphen when it means the middle point or part of, as in these words: mid-act, midafternoon, mid-April, midautumn, mid-career, midcentury, mid-continent, mid-December, midevening, mid-flight, mid-ice, mid-January, mid-life, midmonth, midmorning, mid-orbit, midrange, mid-Renaissance, midseason, midspace, midstory, midstream, mid-strife, mid-zone, midday, and midpoint.

The prefix *mid-* also means in the middle of in these words used as adjectives:

mid-African	mid-European	midmonthly
mid-Arctic	midfacial	mid-Siberian
mid-Asian	mid-Italian	

mis-

The Old English *mis-* means bad, amiss, badly, wrongly, or unfavorably. Students should have little difficulty inferring the meaning of the prefix in the following words:

misadd	misascribe	miscopy
misaddress	misassert	misedit
misadjust	misassociate	miseducate
misaffirm	miscenter	misendeavor
misaim	mischallenge	misenter
misalienate	miscommit	misentitle
misallotment	miscomplain	misentry
misanalyze	miscompute	misguess
misanswer	misconfer	misidentify
misappear	miscook	misincline

misinfer	mislie	misreform
misinflame	mismeasure	misrehearsal
misinform	misnumber	misrender
misinstruct	misoccupy	misrepeat
misintend	misopinion	mis-send
misjoin	mispossessed	misstart
mislabel	misprove	mistaught

Students should determine the meaning of the prefix *mis-* in these words:

misadventure	miscalculate	mishap
misadvise	miscarriage	misnomer
misalliance	misconceive	misplace
misapprehend	misconduct	misprint
misappropriate	misconstrue	misrepresent
misarrange	miscount	misspell
misbehave	misdate	misspent
misbelieve	misdemeanor	misunderstanding

mono-

The Greek *monos* means single or one. It is found in the following words: monoacid, monochord, monochromatic, monocle, monocycle, monody, monogamy, monogram, monograph, monolith, monologue, monomania, monomial, mononuclear, monoplane, monopoly, monorail, monosyllabic, monotheism, monotone, monotonous, and monotype.

multi-

The Latin prefix *multi-* means much or many. Students should have little difficulty inferring the meanings of these words:

multiangular	multicourse	multipolar
multibladed	multidimensional	multireflex
multicellular	multifaceted	multisection
multichord	multihued	multispiral
multicoil	multimetallic	multisyllable
multicolor	multimillion	multivoiced

The prefix *multi-* means having more than two in these words: multicylinder, multielectrode, multiengine, multiexhaust, multimotor, and multispeed.

neo-

The prefix *neo-* comes from the Greek *neos* meaning new. It can mean new, recent, or a modern or modified form. Examples: neoclassicism, Neo-Darwinism, neolithic, neologism, neomycin, and neophyte.

non-

The prefix *non-* comes to us both from Latin and French. It simply means not or it negates the action of the free morpheme that follows it. The *Standard College Dictionary* lists 1074 words beginning with *non-* that are "self-explaining." After students have inferred the meanings of the following words, they should be able to compile a long list of *non-* words without difficulty.

noncombatant	nonfiction
noncommissioned	nonobjective
nonconformist	nonpareil
nondescript	nonprofit
nonentity	nonrestrictive

out-

Out- serves as a prefix to form many transitive verbs. It denotes going beyond or surpassing the named action. Some examples include:

outbargain	outdrive	outhunt
outbat	outeat	outjump
outbless	outfight	outkick
outblossom	outfish	outlaugh
outboast	outflatter	outlearn
outcheat	outfloat	outpace
outdance	outglare	outperform
outdo	outgum	outpull
outdress	outhammer	outread
outdrink	outhit	outreason

outshriek	outspell	outwar
outslide	outspy	outwarble
outsmile	outtower	outwrestle
outsparkle	outwander	outyell

over-

Over- as a prefix is used to form nouns, verbs, adverbs, and adjectives. It usually has the meanings of passing a limit, to excess, or too much. A hyphen normally is not used in writing well-established formations such as overlap, overpower, and overweight. A short list of words containing the prefix *over-* follows:

overactive	overdose	overpower
overall	overeat	overreach
overanxious	overflow	override
overbearing	overhead	oversee
overboard	overheat	oversell
overburden	overlap	overspend
overcast	overload	overtax
overcharge	overlook	overturn
overcoat	overnight	overwhelm
overcritical	overpass	overwork
overcrowd	overpopulate	overzealous
overdo		

pan-

The Greek prefix *pan-* means all, every, or whole. It conveys the meaning of comprising or affecting everyone. Students should be familiar with words like Pan-African, Pan-Arab, Pan-Asian, Pan-Islamic, Pan-Russian, Pan-American, Pan-Slavic, panacea, panchromatic, pancreas, pandemonium, panoply, panorama, and pantheism.

para-

The Greek prefix *para-* means beside, nearby, along with, beyond, aside from, or amiss. In medical terminology, it can mean a functionally disordered or diseased condition, an accessory or secondary capacity, or similar to but not identified with the true condition or form. Students may be able to infer the meanings of these words: parable, paradigm, paradise, paradox, paragon, paragraph, parallel, paralysis, paramecium, paraphernalia, paraphrase, and parasite.

post-

The Latin prefix *post-* means after in time or order and is used frequently today in scientific terms. *Post-* appears in words like these: postwar, postglacial, postgraduate, and postpone.

pre-

The prefix *pre-* ultimately comes from the Latin prefix *prae-*, which means before in time or order, prior to, or preceding. Students should have little difficulty with these words:

preacquaintance	preconceived	preheat
preadaptation	precondemn	preinstruct
preamble	preconsent	preliminary
prearrange	predawn	premeditate
preassume	predestine	preordain
precaution	prediscovery	preplan
precede	preeminent	prerequisite
precept	preempt	prescribe
precinct	preenacted	preseason
precipitate	preengage	preshadow
precise	preexamine	presume
preclassical	prefer	pretend
preclude	prefix	prevent

pro-

The Latin prefix *pro-* means forward, to or toward the front, to lead forth, forward in time or direction, in front of, in behalf of, in place of, or in favor of. The prefix *pro-* appears in words like problem, proceed, proclaim, proconsul, procrastinate, procreate, procure, produce, profane, profound, program, profess, progress, prohibit, project, prologue, promise, promote, pronoun, pronounce, propel, proponent, propose, proscribe, prosecute, protect, protest, and provide.

pseudo-

The prefix *pseudo-* comes from the Greek word *pseudes*, meaning false. It conveys the meaning of false, pretended, counterfeit, not genuine, closely resembling, illusory, apparent, abnormal, or erratic. It appears in such words as pseudoascetic, pseudochristian, pseudoclassic, pseudoeducation, pseudoenthusiast, pseudoevangelist, pseudogentleman, pseudo-Gothic, pseudonym, and pseudopatriot.

quasi-

The prefix *quasi-* means resembling or not genuine when it appears with nouns, for example:

quasi-artist	quasi-illness	quasi-market
quasi-bargain	quasi-integrity	quasi-poem
quasi-conservative	quasi-liberal	quasi-protection
quasi-friend	quasi-luxury	quasi-worship

When combined with adjectives, the prefix *quasi-* means nearly or almost, as in these words:

quasi-absolute	quasi-internal
quasi-classic	quasi-jocose
quasi-comic	quasi-religious
quasi-eligible	quasi-scientific
quasi-exempt	quasi-spiritual
quasi-hereditary	quasi-theatrical
quasi-humorous	quasi-willing

In legal terminology the prefix *quasi-* means superficially resembling but intrinsically different, for example: quasi-corporation, quasi-deposit, quasi-legislative, and quasi-partner.

re-

The Latin prefix *re-* means back, again, anew, or over and over. It is a highly productive prefix used with verbs. Students should have little difficulty with these words:

reaccept	realign	reassume
reacquire	reappear	reattack
readjourn	reapply	reavow
readorn	reassert	rebloom

rechallenge
reconfirm
recopy
rededicate
redefine
redescribe
redo
reecho
reelect
reenact
refurnish
regroup
reimpose
reinhabit
reinsert
reintroduce
rekindle
reoccur
repack
repolish
reread
reroute
reseed
reshape
resharpen
restrengthen
restring
retype
reuse
rework

retro-

The Latin prefix *retro-* means back, backward, or behind. It appears in words like retroact, retrocede, retrofire, retrograde, retrogressive, retrorocket, and retrospect.

semi-

The Latin prefix *semi-* means not fully, partially, partly, exactly half, or occurring twice in the period specified in the morpheme that follows the prefix. A highly productive prefix, it appears in words like these:

semiaffectionate
semiagricultural
semiannual
semiarid
semiattached
semibarbaric
semiblind
semi-Christian
semicolon
semiconscious
semicooperative
semidependent
semidomestic
semifinal
semifit
semihistorical
semi-independent
semi-intoxicated
semi-invalid
semiliberal
semimobile
semimonthly
semimystical
semiorganized
semipermanent
semipolitical
semirebellious
semireligious
semiroyal
semisatiric
semisoft
semisocial
semistarved
semisweet
semitruth
semivoluntary

sub-

The Latin prefix *sub-* means under, beneath, below, almost, nearly, slightly, imperfectly, lower in rank or grade, secondary, subordinate, or forming a subdivision. Students should be able to infer the meaning of *sub-* in these words:

subacid
subacute
subagent
subalkaline
subalpine
subaltern
subalternate
subarctic
subassembly
subatomic
subbasement
subcaliber
subcentral
subclass
subclimax
subcommittee
subconscious
subcontinent
subcontract
subculture
subdeacon
subdebutante
subdistrict
subgroup
subhead
subhuman
subindex
subject
subjoin
subjugate
subjunctive
subkingdom
sublease
subliminal
submachine gun
submarine
submit
subnormal
suborbital
subordinate
subpoena
subscription
subservient
subset
subside
subsist
substance
substandard
substantive
substitute
subtitle
subtle
subtract
subtropical
suburban
subversive
subway

If the free morpheme begins with *c*, the prefix *sub-* may become *suc-*, as in succeed, success, succinct, succor, and succumb.

If the free morpheme begins with *f*, the prefix *sub-* may become *suf-*, as in suffer, suffice, suffix, suffocate, and suffuse.

In the word suggest, the prefix *sub-* becomes *sug-*.

If the free morpheme begins with *m*, the prefix *sub-* may become *sum-*, as in summon.

If the free morpheme begins with *p*, the prefix *sub-* may become *sup-*, as in supple, supply, support, suppose, supposition, and suppress.

If the free morpheme begins with *r*, the prefix *sub-* may become *sur-*, as in surreptitious, and surrogate.

If the free morpheme begins with *c*, *p*, or *t*, the prefix *sub-* may become *sus-*, as in susceptible, suspect, suspend, suspicion, and sustain.

super-

The Latin prefix *super-* means above, over, beyond, more than, excessively, extra, additional, or greater than others of its class.

In the words below, the prefix *super-* denotes excess or high quality:

superacute
superambitious
superarduous
superarrogant
supercolossal
supercomplex
supercritical
supercynical
superdiabolical
supereffective
superelegance
supereloquent
superexcellence
superexcited
superfriendly
superhero
superimportant
superindependent
superindignant
superman
supermasculine
superobese
superpositive
superrighteous
superromantic
supersarcastic
superscientific
supersensitive
superspecial
superworldly

Students should be able to infer the meaning of the prefix *super-* in these words:

superabundant
superannuated
supercargo
supercharger
superficial
superfluous
superhighway
superhuman
superimpose
superlative
supermarket
supernatural
supersonic
superstition
superstructure
supertax

syn-

The prefix *syn-* comes from the Greek *syn,* meaning with, together with. In the following words it means with, together, associated with, or accompanying:

synagogue
synchronize
syndrome
synecdoche
synod
synonym
synopsis
syntax
synthesis
synthetic

If the free morpheme begins with *b, p,* or *m,* the prefix *syn-* becomes *sym-*, as in symbol, symmetrical, sympathy, symphony, symposium, and symptom. *Syn-* becomes *syl-* if the free morpheme begins with *l,* as in syllable and syllogism.

trans-

The Latin prefix *trans-* means across, beyond, through, or on the other side of, as in transarctic, transcontinental, transition, and transpolar. With adjectives and nouns denoting specific places, the prefix *trans-* may denote on the other side of or across. In some cases, because of long usage, the words are written as single words, such as transalpine and transatlantic. In most cases, however, the words are hyphenated, as in the following: trans-African, trans-American, trans-Arabian, trans-Canadian, trans-Iberian, trans-Mediterranean, and trans-Scandinavian.

The prefix *trans-* means surpassing or beyond, as in transconscious, transhuman, transmental, transnational, and transrational.

In anatomy, the prefix *trans-* means across as in transcortical and transduodenal.

Students should determine the meaning of the prefix *trans-* in these words:

transaction	transgress
transcend	translucent
transcribe	transmit
transcription	transparent
transfer	transpire
transfigure	transplant
transfix	transport
transform	transpose
transfuse	transverse

tri-

The Latin prefix *tri-* means three, threefold, thrice, or occurring at an interval of three. Examples include triangle, tricolor, triennial, trilingual, trilogy, tripartite, and triumvirate.

ultra-

The Latin prefix *ultra-* means on the other side of or beyond, as in ultra-Arctic, ultralunar, and ultraviolet. It may mean going beyond the limits of or surpassing, as in ultra-atomic, ultra-human, ultranatural, ultrasonic.

It means beyond what is usual or natural, or extremely, as in:

ultra-ambitious	ultraliberal	ultrareligious
ultraconfident	ultraloyal	ultraromantic
ultraconservative	ultramodern	ultrascientific
ultrademocratic	ultraprecision	ultraspiritual
ultrafashionable	ultraradical	ultravirtuous

uni-

The prefix *uni-* comes from the Latin *unus,* meaning one. It simply means having one or consisting of only one, for example: unicellular, unicorn, unicycle, uniform, unify, unilateral, unite, and universe.

vice-

As a prefix, *vice-* is used primarily with words denoting the holder of an office and implies some level of authority. It comes from the Latin *vice,* which means in that place, or instead of. Examples include vice-admiral, vice-chairman, vice-consul, vice-governor, vice-president, and vice-principal.

SUFFIXES

Unlike prefixes, which indicate semantic change only, suffixes change both the semantic value of a word and its grammatical function. (Diminutives, suffixes used to form nicknames or to denote that someone is young or small in stature, do not change the grammatical function of a word. For example, the suffix *-able* may change the meaning of the verb, noun, or phrase to which it is affixed, and it also indicates that the word will function as an adjective in a sentence.

As was done with prefixes, a teacher will probably give students one or two suffixes each week. It would be better to put several words on the board in which a particular suffix appears, ask the students if they can infer the meanings of the suffix, and ask them to use these words in sentences, so they can decide what grammatical function the suffix carries.

-able

The suffix *-able* forms adjectives meaning to, tending to, likely to, fit to, able to, capable of, or worthy of. Depending upon the free morpheme that precedes it, the suffix can be spelled *-able* or *-ible* (or *-ble* in such words as soluble).

The teacher may wish to put all or a part of this list of words on the board and have students infer the meanings of the suffix and also decide, after using several of the words in sentences, what grammatical function the suffix indicates.

acceptable
accountable
achievable
actionable
adaptable
admirable
advisable
agreeable
answerable
appeasable
approachable
attainable
available
believable
changeable
charitable
comfortable
commendable
comparable
conquerable
controllable
convertible
corruptible
countable
credible
damnable
deceivable
demonstrable
dependable
desirable
determinable
dispensable
drinkable
eligible
fashionable
favorable
forcible
honorable
innumerable
invertible
irritable
laughable
livable
marketable
marriageable
measurable
memorable
negotiable
objectionable
palatable
passable
perishable
personable
profitable
readable
reasonable
reliable
reputable
respectable
reversible
serviceable
suitable
tolerable
unavoidable
unbearable
unbreakable
uneducable
unspeakable
untenable

-acy

The suffix *-acy* comes from Old French through Latin through Greek. It forms nouns of quality, state, or condition from adjectives.

aristocracy	effeminacy	literacy
confederacy	efficacy	lunacy
conspiracy	fallacy	obstinacy
delicacy	illiteracy	piracy
democracy	intimacy	primacy
diplomacy	intricacy	privacy

-age

The suffix *-age* came into English through French from Latin. It can indicate a collection of something, a condition, office, or service. This suffix forms nouns.

acreage	dosage	package	spoilage
baggage	drainage	parsonage	steerage
bandage	footage	percentage	storage
bondage	leakage	postage	tutelage
breakage	leverage	poundage	voltage
carriage	luggage	shortage	voyage
coinage	mileage	shrinkage	yardage

-al

The suffix *-al* forms both nouns and adjectives. It means of or pertaining to, characterized by, connected with, or the act of doing that which is expressed by the verb stem. In chemical terms, it denotes a compound having the properties of or derived from an aldehyde.

Students should notice that some of the words in the list below function as adjectives while others function as nouns.

accidental	approval	chemical
acquittal	architectural	circumstantial
actual	arrival	comical
analytical	basal	confidential
ancestral	betrayal	congressional
appraisal	causal	conjectural

conspiratorial
constitutional
continental
contractual
critical
cultural
denial
dictatorial
differential
dismissal
disposal
doctoral
economical
editorial
electoral
equatorial
essential
eventual
existential
factual
federal
fictional
geographical
geometrical
gradual
grammatical
habitual
horizontal
identical
incidental
instrumental
intellectual
logical
magical
manual
musical
pedagogical
periodical
perusal
physical
pictorial
poetical
political
presidential
procedural
professorial
proposal
providential
prudential
reappraisal
recital
removal
renewal
rental
reprisal
residential
revival
rhetorical
senatorial
sensual
spiritual
strategical
substantial
suicidal
surgical
survival
tactical
temporal
theatrical
theological
theoretical
transferral
trial
typical
upheaval

-an and *-ian*

These suffixes are used to form adjectives and nouns denoting of or from a country, person, group, or doctrine.

African
Alaskan
Aristotelian
Asian
Darwinian
Elizabethan
Ethiopian
European
Italian
Jamaican
Johnsonian
Korean
Persian
Puerto Rican
Russian
San Franciscan
Spencerian
Utopian

Students should see that some of these words function both as adjectives and as nouns.

-ance and *-ence*

The suffixes *-ance* and *-ence* come to English through French from Latin. They are used to form nouns of action, quality, state, or condition from adjectives and verbs. According to the *Standard College Dictionary,* the modern spelling of words in this group is unpredictable. "The confusion arose originally in borrowing from the Old French (resistance, assistance) where *-ance* had come to represent Latin *-entia,* as well as *-antia.* Since 1500, however, some have been altered back to *-ence* on the Latin model as in the case of dependence, earlier dependance. Later Latin borrowings in French and in English (through French or directly from Latin) discriminate between *-ance* and *-ence* according to the vowel of the Latin original."

abundance	clearance	negligence
acquaintance	cognizance	nuisance
acquiescence	conference	performance
advance	confidence	procurance
alliance	correspondence	relevance
appliance	dependence	remonstrance
audience	evidence	resistance
brilliance	forbearance	silence
circumstance	independence	variance

-ancy and *-ency*

The suffixes *-ancy* and *-ency* form nouns expressing quality, state, or condition. These suffixes are modern variants of the suffixes *-ance* and *-ence; -ancy* and *-ency* are sometimes used to re-fashion older nouns of quality ending in *-ance* or *-ence,* for example, constancy.

agency	emergency	occupancy
consistency	flippancy	tendency
decency	fluency	trenchancy
deficiency	indecency	truancy
dependency	leniency	vacancy
efficiency	militancy	vagrancy

-ant and *-ent*

The suffixes *-ant* and *-ent* are used to form nouns and adjectives. They imply the act or process of doing something, or someone or something that does what is indicated by the free morpheme.

absorbent	contestant	lubricant
accountant	deodorant	occupant
adherent	dependent	opponent
applicant	inhabitant	participant
aspirant	irritant	propellant
consultant	litigant	stimulant

-arian

The suffix *-arian* comes from the Latin *-arius,* and is used to form adjectives and nouns denoting occupation, age, sect, or religious beliefs. Examples: antiquarian, authoritarian, egalitarian, grammarian, librarian, Parliamentarian, proletarian, sectarian, totalitarian, Unitarian, vegetarian.

-ary

The Latin suffix *-ary* is used to form adjectives and nouns. In the case of adjectives, it means pertaining to what is expressed in the free morpheme. In nouns, it means a person employed as or engaged in what is expressed in the free morpheme. It also means a thing or a place concerned with or dedicated to what is indicated in the free morpheme.

antiquary	evolutionary	revolutionary
complementary	honorary	sanctuary
dictionary	inflationary	secondary
documentary	library	secretary
elementary	probationary	supplementary

-ate

The suffix *-ate* forms adjectives from nouns and carries the meaning possessing or characterized by, as in compassionate. It forms verbs from stems of Latin verbs of the first conjugation and has been extended to make verbs with other stems, for example, fascinate and assassinate. It forms nouns that denote office, function, or agent, as in magistrate, also nouns that denote the object or result of an action, as in mandate.

abbreviate	dedicate	isolate
affectionate	desolate	mitigate
alleviate	dispassionate	mutate
ameliorate	educate	ornate
commentate	equate	recreate
compensate	foliate	separate
contaminate	frustrate	terminate
create	incorporate	translate
cremate	inoculate	vaccinate

-ation

The suffix *-ation* forms nouns. It denotes action or process of, as in the word creation. It denotes state or quality of, as in affectation. It denotes the result of, as in reformation. It is also frequently used in the forms *-ion* or *-tion*. Originally it was found in English nouns borrowed from Latin, and it is now used by analogy to form nouns of any stem, as in starvation. It comes into English through the French from the Latin.

accusation	demarcation	information
adaptation	deportation	justification
administration	derivation	modification
adoration	detestation	purification
affiliation	disputation	quotation
affirmation	edification	ratification
alteration	education	sanitation
altercation	expectation	saturation
annexation	exploration	sedimentation
authorization	exportation	situation
certification	expurgation	taxation
civilization	exultation	temptation
colonization	familiarization	vacation
constellation	glorification	verification
contemplation	humanization	vexation
damnation	identification	vilification

-dom

The suffix *-dom* is an Old English suffix used to form nouns denoting the state or condition of being, as in freedom or wisdom; the territory of, as in kingdom, a rank or office, as in earldom; and the totality of those having a certain rank or status, or condition, as in Christendom or officialdom.

-ed

The Old English suffix *-ed* forms the past tense of regular verbs and the past participle of regular verbs. It forms adjectives from nouns to mean having, possessing, characterized by, or resembling.

barelegged	hotheaded	openhanded
black-haired	hunchbacked	peaked
chicken-hearted	ill-mannered	proud-hearted
conceited	ill-tongued	public-spirited
cornered	ironhanded	ragged
crooked	jagged	roofed
cruel-hearted	jointed	rugged
featured	kindhearted	short-lived
flavored	landed	shortsighted
frenzied	left-handed	simple-hearted
hardheaded	lettered	single-handed
heavyhearted	light-footed	spectacled
high-minded	long-lived	spirited
high-spirited	lowbrowed	strong-headed
high-toned	low-spirited	swift-footed
honey-tongued	many-sided	thickheaded
hot-blooded	moneyed	three-cornered

-ee

The suffix *-ee* comes from French *-é* and originally from the Latin *-atus*. It forms nouns, and generally means one who does a particular thing or benefits from something or some action. It is used especially in legal terms and means the opposite of words ending in *-er* or *-or*. Examples: committee, divorcee, enlistee, escapee, grantee, nominee, payee, referee, trainee, transferee, and trustee.

-eer

The suffix *-eer* forms nouns and verbs. It indicates one who is concerned with, or works with, or makes something indicated by the free morpheme.

auctioneer	fictioneer
charioteer	mountaineer
electioneer	pioneer
engineer	profiteer

-en

The Old English suffix *-en* forms verbs from adjectives and from nouns, as in deepen, harden, hearten, and strengthen. It also is a suffix of adjectives, such as woolen and golden, and means made of, or resembling. It is used to form the past participle of many verbs, such as broken and beaten. It is also used in the plurals of certain nouns, e.g., oxen and children. It also is used with nouns to indicate small or little, as in chicken and kitten. Examples:

ashen	deepen	leaden	sadden
blacken	fatten	lengthen	shorten
brazen	freshen	lessen	sicken
brighten	frighten	lighten	silken
chasten	gladden	loosen	slacken
cheapen	harden	moisten	sweeten
dampen	hasten	oaken	waxen
deafen	heighten	redden	weaken

-er

The suffix *-er* comes from Old English through Latin. As a suffix of nouns, it means a person or thing that performs the action of the verb in the free morpheme, such as maker, and reaper. It also means a person concerned with or practicing a trade or profession, e.g., geographer, hatter; or one who lives in or comes from a certain area, such as New Yorker or New Englander. It may mean a person, thing, or action related to or characterized by something, e.g., three-decker. *-Er* is also used to form the comparative degree of adjectives and adverbs. In verbs, it means repeatedly, as in stutter. As a suffix of nouns, it can denote the action expressed by the verb in the free morpheme, as in gardener and rejoinder.

adviser	finisher	poker
baker	flicker	preacher
Berliner	flutter	quiver
bobby-soxer	gambler	retriever
boiler	gardener	sandbagger
carpetbagger	glimmer	scraper
clatter	honeymooner	setter
clincher	hunter	silencer
commander	juggler	stammer
dancer	left-hander	starter
driver	lighter	stopper
eraser	meddler	strainer
eye opener	New Englander	teacher
farmer	New Yorker	teen-ager
faster	pacer	thriller
fertilizer	packer	trotter

-ery and *-ry*

The suffixes *-ery* and *-ry* came into the English through Old French from the Latin. Used to form nouns, these suffixes denote a business, place of business, or place where something is done; a place or residence for certain persons; a collection of things; the qualities, principles, or practices of certain principles, persons, or ideals; an art, trade, or profession; and a state or condition of being.

ancestry	cutlery	masonry
archery	embroidery	nunnery
artistry	finery	pageantry
banditry	greenery	palmistry
brewery	hatchery	quackery
carpentry	husbandry	rabbitry
chemistry	inquiry	ribaldry
citizenry	jugglery	robbery
confectionery	knavery	savagery

scenery	snobbery	thievery
shrubbery	soldiery	treachery
slavery	sophistry	wizardry

-ese

The suffix *-ese* came into English through Old French from the Latin. It is used to form nouns and adjectives. It denotes a native or inhabitant of a particular place, the language or dialect of a particular country, originating in a particular place, or in the manner or style of a particular profession or class of people. Examples include Brooklynese, Burmese, Chinese, Javanese, journalese, Milanese, Portuguese, and Vietnamese.

-esque

The suffix *-esque* comes into English through the French from the Italian *-esco*. It forms adjectives meaning having the manner or style of, resembling, or like.

Dantesque	lionesque	picturesque	sculpturesque
grotesque	picaresque	Romanesque	statuesque

The coining of Dantesque has led to the making of similar words, such as Hemingwayesque, Kiplingesque, and Garboesque.

-ess

Coming into English through French and Latin and ultimately from Greek, the suffix *-ess* is used to form the feminine of some nouns. Some examples are countess, goddess, governess, heiress, hostess, lioness, millionairess, sorceress, stewardess, and waitress.

-ette

The suffix *-ette* means little or small, resembling, imitating, or feminine. The last meaning has given rise to the coining of many words today.

farmerette	majorette	sailorette
launderette	novelette	statuette
leatherette	Rockette	suffragette

-fold

The English suffix *-fold* means having a specified number of parts or being a specified number of times greater or as much as the element indicated in the free morpheme. Some such words are hundredfold, manifold, tenfold, threefold, and twofold.

-ful

The Old English suffix *-ful* means full of, characterized by the element in the free morpheme, able to do the element contained in the free morpheme, having the character of the element contained in the free morpheme, or the quantity or number that will fill the element in the free morpheme. This suffix is used to form adjectives and nouns.

awful	healthful	skillful
bagful	hopeful	sorrowful
bashful	houseful	soulful
beautiful	joyful	successful
bottleful	lawful	tactful
boxful	manful	tearful
canful	masterful	thoughtful
capful	merciful	trustful
careful	mindful	truthful
cheerful	mirthful	undutiful
cupful	peaceful	uneventful
delightful	pipeful	unlawful
doubtful	pitiful	unmerciful
dutiful	plateful	unrightful
eventful	powerful	unskillful
faithful	remorseful	unsuccessful
faultful	resentful	useful
fearful	respectful	wilful
fruitful	restful	wonderful
graceful	shameful	worshipful
harmful	sinful	wrathful

-hood

The Old English suffix *-hood* was once a separate word. Now it is used to form nouns, and it indicates a condition or quality of the element in the free morpheme, a state of being, or a class or totality of those having a certain character.

babyhood	knighthood	priesthood
bachelorhood	likelihood	sainthood
brotherhood	livelihood	sisterhood
childhood	maidenhood	spinsterhood
falsehood	motherhood	statehood
fatherhood	neighborhood	widowhood
girlhood	parenthood	womanhood

-ic

The suffix *-ic* came into English through French or Latin and ultimately from Greek. It forms adjectives with these meanings: of, pertaining to or connected with, resembling, produced by or in the manner of, consisting of, and containing. In some cases, words containing the suffix *-ic* can be used as nouns as well as adjectives, e.g., classic, lunatic. The suffix *-ic* also occurs in nouns derived from Latin and Greek nouns which are formed from adjectives, e.g., logic and music.

The suffix *-ics* is used to form nouns. It normally means an art, science, or field of study, as in mathematics; or methods, practices, or activities, as in athletics.

The *Standard College Dictionary* notes that "nouns ending in *-ics* are construed as singular when they strictly denote an art, science, or system (as, mathematics is difficult; politics offers an uncertain future); they are construed as plural if they denote personal attributes (as, his mathematics are poor; his politics are suspect), if they denote inherent qualities (as, the acoustics are bad), or if they denote specific activities (as, athletics are compulsory; hysterics are unseemly; our tactics are superior to the enemy's)."

A few adjectives ending in *-ic* form adverbs by adding *-ly* directly, as publicly, but in most cases the adverb is formed by adding

-ly to the adjective ending in *-ical,* as musically, or by adding *-ally* when the adjective exists only in the *-ic* form, as athletically.

agnostic	diplomatic	historic
alcoholic	domestic	Icelandic
Arabic	dramatic	lyric
aristocratic	eccentric	metallic
arithmetic	egocentric	microscopic
arsenic	elastic	Miltonic
asthmatic	electric	mimic
astronomic	emblematic	Mongolic
atomic	Gallic	plutocratic
axiomatic	genetic	poetic
barbaric	geographic	rheumatic
Byronic	geometric	rustic
Catholic	Germanic	Semitic
Celtic	gigantic	symbolic
democratic	harmonic	Teutonic
diagrammatic	heroic	tropic

From this list students should be able to see that certain words form adjectives by adding more than simply *-ic* to them, e.g., *-tic,* *-atic,* and *-itic.*

-ician

The suffix *-ician* comes from the French *-icien* and is used to form nouns.* It denotes one skilled or engaged in some specific field.

academician	mathematician	politician
beautician	mortician	rhetorician
clinician	musician	statistician
logician	obstetrician	tactician
magician	physician	technician

-ie and *-y*

The suffixes *-ie* and *-y* are used to form nicknames. They denote little or dear. Students should know many words that contain these

*See also the sections on *-an,* *-ian,* and *-ic.*

suffixes. Therefore, only four examples are given here: auntie, Davy, doggie or (doggy), and Willy (or Willie).

-ify

The suffixes *-ify* and *-fy* came into English through Old French and ultimately from Latin. They mean to cause to be, or to become, or to make. Students should readily see that these suffixes are used to form verbs and they should have little difficulty inferring the meanings of these suffixes and the grammatical function of these words:

amplify	magnify	satisfy
beautify	modify	stupefy
certify	pacify	terrify
deify	purify	typify
glorify	qualify	verify
gratify	rectify	vivify

-ine and *-in*

The suffix *-ine* came to English through French from Latin. It can mean like, pertaining to, of the nature of, or resembling. It is also used to form feminine words, names, and titles, and was used to form originally feminine abstract nouns like medicine and doctrine. In this sense, the suffix ultimately came from the Greek *-ina.* Some examples include alkaline, alpine, feline, feminine, gasoline, glycerine, marine, nicotine, saccharine, and strychnine.

-ing

The modern English suffix *-ing* comes from the Old English *-ung.* Since it is one of the most productive suffixes in the English language, and since it has several uses, it will be treated somewhat differently here.

The suffix *-ing* is used to form the present participle of a verb or a participial adjective.

cooking	fishing
eating	hunting

jumping	speaking
running	talking
skipping	walking

Like some participial adjectives, the gerund ends in *-ing*, but it functions as a noun. As a noun suffix, *-ing* means the act or art of doing the action expressed in the free morpheme. Some examples of this use are, "Hunting is exciting," "Fishing is fun," or "Laughing can be relaxing." The *-ing* suffix also indicates the product or result of an action. Examples:

bedding	lining	standing
binding	lodging	stitching
clothing	marketing	stopping
drawing	opening	stuffing
dwelling	painting	swelling
knitting	plastering	turning
lacing	sewing	winding
landing	shortening	wrapping

When nouns denote the specific result of an action of the verbal element in the free morphene, the *-ing* suffix sometimes appears in plural form.

buildings	pencillings
cuttings	savings
diggings	scrapings
drawings	shavings
earnings	skimmings
etchings	stampings
leavings	surroundings
meltings	sweepings
mowings	writings

The *-ing* suffix can denote material for the element in the free morpheme, e.g., carpeting, fencing, flooring, grating, lettering, matting, pegging, piping, planking, sheathing, siding, and tiling.

It can also mean a descendant of, as in Browning.

-ish

As a suffix of adjectives, *-ish* can mean of or belonging to a specific national group, as in Irish, Spanish, and Turkish; like something, as in girlish, mannish, and roguish; having the bad qualities of the element expressed in the free morpheme, as in childish, selfish, and babyish; inclined to do the element performed in the free morpheme or tending toward that element, as in bookish and clownish; somewhat or rather, as in greenish and smallish; and in informal language, approximately, as in fiftyish.

As a suffix of verbs, *-ish* came into English through Old French and ultimately from Latin. It appears chiefly in verbs of French origin, e.g., brandish and establish.

biggish	Danish	piggish
blackish	elfish	Polish
blueish	fiendish	reddish
bookish	Finnish	sixtyish
boorish	freakish	smallish
boyish	girlish	Spanish
brutish	Irish	stylish
clownish	Jewish	Swedish
coldish	mulish	Turkish

The suffix *-ish* is used frequently in informal conversation or writing, and students should be able to see which words in the above list would probably be so limited.

-ism

Coming into the English language from the Latin *-ismus* and ultimately from the Greek *-ismos, -ism* is used to form nouns. Among its meanings are the beliefs, teachings, or system of something, such as Protestantism or socialism; a characteristic or a peculiarity of something (particularly true of a language), as in Americanism; the act, process, or result of the element found in the free morpheme, as in criticism; and the characteristic action or behavior of the element found in the free morpheme, as in fanaticism or gangsterism.

With a knowledge of the possible meanings of this suffix, students should be able to define many of the abstract nouns formed by this suffix.

absenteeism	heroism	Platonism
alcoholism	hoodlumism	provincialism
Calvinism	idealism	realism
Catholicism	idiotism	rheumatism
classicism	imperialism	romanticism
defeatism	impressionism	scoundrelism
egotism	jingoism	symbolism
expressionism	Judaism	truism
Fascism	Marxism	vulgarism
favoritism	paganism	witticism

-ist

From Greek through Latin through French, English has borrowed the suffix *-ist* to form nouns. Its meanings include: one whose profession is expressed by the element in the free morpheme, as in chemist, linguist, and pharmacist; one who believes in the element found in the free morpheme, as in socialist and nationalist (this is an extension from nouns ending in *-ism*); and a person or thing that does or has to do with the element found in the free morpheme, as in monopolist.

alarmist	essayist	physicist
bigamist	extremist	pianist
botanist	Fascist	psychiatrist
caricaturist	humanist	publicist
cartoonist	humorist	realist
columnist	isolationist	typist
dentist	novelist	ventriloquist
economist	organist	violinist

-istic

The suffix *-istic* is an extension of the suffix *-ic*. It forms adjectives, and conveys the meaning of tending toward or having the qualities of the element found in the free morpheme. Words ending in *-istic* are formed from nouns ending in *-ist* or *-ism*. Examples include communistic, idealistic, nationalistic, optimistic, pessimistic, and socialistic.

-ite

As a suffix used to form nouns, *-ite* comes from French through Latin and earlier from Greek. It carries these meanings: a native or inhabitant of the place mentioned in the free morpheme; a descendant or follower of or sympathizer with the element mentioned in the free morpheme; resembling or related to the person or thing mentioned in the free morpheme. In technical terminology, it means a rock or mineral, a fossil or fossilized substance, or a part of the anatomy.

It is also a suffix used with the past participial forms of certain Latin verbs to produce adjectives such as infinite and polite, verbs such as dynamite, and nouns such as appetite.

Bakelite	Ishmaelite	satellite
Brooklynite	Israelite	socialite
dynamite	laborite	Stalinite
Hitlerite	pyrite	urbanite

-ition

From the Latin *-itio* and *-onis*, English has acquired the suffix *-ition*, used to form nouns. It indicates the condition, state, or quality of the element found in the free morpheme. It may be or result from an act or process of the element found in the free morpheme. Some examples are:

abolition	definition	partition
acquisition	demolition	position
ambition	disposition	premonition
ammunition	erudition	proposition
apposition	exposition	recognition
attrition	ignition	repetition
audition	imposition	requisition
coalition	inquisition	superstition
competition	munition	supposition
composition	opposition	transition

-itious

As a suffix used to form adjectives, *-itious* comes from the Latin *-icius* and *-itius.* It means characterized by or having the quality of the element in the free morpheme. Ambitious, cautious, expeditious, factitious, fictitious, nutritious, propitious, repetitious, and seditious are examples.

-ity

Coming into English through French from Latin, the suffix *-ity* forms nouns. It indicates state, condition, or quality.

ability	infallibility	respectability
amiability	invincibility	responsibility
authenticity	levity	royalty
brutality	liability	rusticity
charity	locality	similarity
commendability	loyalty	sincerity
domesticity	nobility	speciality
eccentricity	peculiarity	superficiality
elasticity	publicity	technicality
excitability	readability	ubiquity
femininity	reality	unreliability

-ive

Coming through French from Latin, the suffix *-ive* forms adjectives. It denotes having a tendency or predisposition to the element found in the free morpheme, or having the nature, character, or quality of the element found in the free morpheme. An extension of *-ive* is *-ative.*

accumulative	competitive	decorative
additive	comprehensive	denotative
affirmative	conductive	distinctive
appreciative	connotative	effective
argumentative	conservative	effusive
attractive	consumptive	executive
collective	creative	expansive

expressive	motive	productive
extensive	native	representative
impulsive	negative	retrospective
inductive	permissive	suggestive
instinctive	persuasive	talkative

-ize

As a suffix of verbs, *-ize* means to resemble, become, or cause to become the element in the free morpheme; to make into or subject to the action of the element in the free morpheme; to act in the manner of or practice the element in the free morpheme. This suffix came into English through French from Latin and ultimately from Greek.

agonize	jeopardize	publicize
apologize	legalize	rationalize
bowdlerize	liberalize	satirize
capitalize	magnetize	scrutinize
centralize	materialize	secularize
colonize	memorize	socialize
deodorize	modernize	stabilize
dramatize	monopolize	standardize
epitomize	moralize	sterilize
eulogize	naturalize	summarize
exorcize	neutralize	symbolize
fertilize	patronize	tenderize
generalize	philosophize	terrorize
humanize	plagiarize	tranquilize
idealize	propagandize	visualize

-kin and *-ikin*

From Middle Dutch, English has borrowed the suffix *-kin* to form a diminutive, as in bumpkin, manikin, and napkin. We also find the suffix *-kin,* or its variants, in surnames such as Atkins, Dawkins, Dickens, Jenkins, Perkins, Watkins, and Wilkins.

-le

From the Old English *-lian,* we get the suffix *-le.* This is used to form verbs that express sound or movement. Usually the suffix denotes quick, rapid, or nimble "repetition of short, small movements, often with a shade of jerkiness."

babble	giggle	rumble
bobble	grumble	rustle
bungle	gurgle	scramble
bustle	hustle	shuffle
crackle	jingle	tattle
dribble	ramble	whistle

-less

From the Old English *-leas,* meaning free from, we have the suffix *-less,* which is used to form adjectives. It usually means devoid of or without.

colorless	joyless	noiseless
countless	lawless	penniless
dauntless	lifeless	reckless
doubtless	listless	restless
faithless	luckless	ruthless
fearless	matchless	shameless
harmless	meaningless	speechless
hatless	mindless	spineless
heartless	needless	spotless

-let

From Old French and ultimately from Latin, English has borrowed the suffix *-let,* which is used to form nouns. It means small, little, or a band or ornament for a specific part of the body, such as anklet or bracelet. Other examples include booklet, eyelet, goblet, islet, leaflet, ringlet, and starlet.

-like

The English suffix *-like* is used to form adjectives. It means resembling or having the characteristics of the element found in the free morpheme. Compound words formed with *-like* are usually written as one word, but they are hyphenated when three *l*'s occur together, as in shell-like.

gentlemanlike	manlike	unsportsmanlike
ladylike	snakelike	warlike
lifelike	statesmanlike	workmanlike

-ling

As a suffix of nouns, the English *-ling* means little, young, minor, pretty, or a person or thing related to or characterized by the element found in the free morpheme. Some examples are darling, duckling, earthling, foundling, kindling, porkling, seedling, shaveling, sibling, starveling, and yearling.

-ly

The Old English suffix *-ly* is used to form adverbs and adjectives. In its adverbial use, it means in a specified manner or at specific intervals. Normally, *-ly* forms adverbs from adjectives; in a few instances, *-ly* can be affixed to a noun to form an adverb. If an adjective already ends in *-ly,* the forms of the adjective and the adverb are often identical. As an example of this, the *Standard College Dictionary* offers these two examples: "he spoke kindly; he is a kindly man." If the adjective ends in *-le,* the adverb is formed by dropping the *-le* ending before adding *-ly,* as in legibly and probably.

To avoid confusion, the adverbs ending in *-ly* are given separately:

breathlessly	exactly	lightly	relentlessly
cautiously	expertly	needlessly	religiously
continuously	flippantly	nervously	shortly
correctly	fluently	obviously	softly
courteously	gallantly	outrageously	sweetly
currently	graciously	perfectly	swiftly
differently	humorously	poorly	uselessly
directly	imminently	quietly	vigorously
enormously	indignantly	radiantly	voraciously

The suffix *-ly* forms adjectives from nouns. The suffix denotes like, characteristic of, pertaining to. It can also mean occurring at specific intervals, e.g., monthly and yearly.

costly	hourly	poorly
courtly	kingly	quarterly
cowardly	lonely	scholarly
daily	lovely	shapely
dastardly	maidenly	sickly
easterly	manly	slovenly
fatherly	masterly	southerly
friendly	miserly	stately
ghostly	motherly	timely
godly	nightly	weekly
heavenly	northerly	westerly
homely	orderly	worldly

-ment

From the Latin *-mentum,* English has borrowed the suffix *-ment* to form nouns. It means the product or result of the element found in the free morpheme; the instrument or means of doing what is indicated in the free morpheme; the process or action of the element in the free morpheme; or the quality or condition or state of being of the element in the free morpheme.

achievement	astonishment	engagement
advancement	bereavement	environment
agreement	betterment	equipment
allotment	chastisement	estrangement
amusement	commencement	increment
appeasement	commitment	involvement
appointment	confinement	judgment
arrangement	consignment	management
assessment	encampment	placement
assignment	endorsement	retirement
assortment	endowment	shipment

-most

From the Old English suffix *-mest,* modern English has taken the suffix *-most,* which it adds to adjectives and adverbs to form superlatives. Generally this suffix is used with adjectives of place, for example:

bottommost	hithermost	outermost	undermost
foremost	innermost	southernmost	uppermost
furthermost	northernmost	topmost	utmost

-ness

From the Old English suffixes *-nes* and *-nis,* we get the modern English suffix *-ness.* It is used to form nouns and denotes the state or quality of being.

beastliness	fairness	nothingness
bitterness	faithfulness	readiness
carelessness	fierceness	righteousness
closeness	firmness	shortsightedness
coolness	forgiveness	sickness
coyness	goodness	steadfastness
darkness	greediness	straightforwardness
deafness	idleness	wilderness
drunkenness	kindness	wistfulness
dullness	lifelessness	witness

-ory

As a suffix of nouns, *-ory* comes through Old French from Latin and means the place or instrument for performing the action indicated by the free morpheme. As a suffix to form adjectives, *-ory* means related to, like, or resembling.

accusatory	hortatory	obligatory
amatory	illusory	observatory
dormitory	laboratory	statutory
explicatory	lavatory	transitory

-ous

As a suffix to form adjectives, *-ous* comes through Old French from Latin *-osus*. It means full of, having, given to, or like. Its variants include *-ious, -eous,* and *-erous.*

adventurous	famous	pugnacious
ambitious	felicitous	rebellious
amorous	fractious	repetitious
amorphous	glorious	monotonous
blasphemous	harmonious	oblivious
boisterous	idolatrous	righteous
ceremonious	industrious	riotous
conscious	infectious	sacrilegious
contiguous	lecherous	superstitious
courageous	momentous	thunderous
dangerous	poisonous	treacherous
erroneous	prosperous	virtuous

-ship

From the Old English *-scipe,* modern English has formed the suffix *-ship* to form nouns. It means the state, condition, or quality, or office, rank, or dignity of the element in the free morpheme. Occasionally it means the skill of doing something.

brinkmanship	guardianship	postmastership
championship	hardship	scholarship
companionship	kinship	showmanship
craftsmanship	leadership	statesmanship
dictatorship	lordship	township
editorship	marksmanship	trusteeship
fellowship	membership	vicarship
gamesmanship	penmanship	workmanship

-some

As a suffix used to form adjectives, *-some* comes from Old English *-sum,* and means characterized by or tending to be what is indicated by the element in the free morpheme. As a suffix of nouns,

-some comes from the Greek *-soma,* meaning a body. In this sense it appears in words like chromosome. As a suffix to form nouns, it also means a group consisting of a specified number, e.g., twosome and threesome.

bothersome	quarrelsome	troublesome
foursome	threesome	twosome
handsome	tiresome	wholesome

-ster

Although the suffix *-ster* originally in Old English indicated the feminine counterpart of the free morpheme, today its use is more broad. A suffix to form nouns, *-ster* means one who makes or does or belongs to something, or one who is described by the element in the free morpheme, e.g., youngster and spinster.

barrister	roadster
gangster	seamster
jokester	songster
mobster	teamster
prankster	tipster

-ward and *-wards*

From the Old English *-weard* and *-weardes,* we have the suffixes *-ward* and *-wards,* meaning toward or in the direction of. A recent trend has been to drop the *-s* from the suffix, especially in American English.

afterward	landward	outward
downward	leeward	seaward
homeward	northward	upward
inward	onward	windward

-wise

The suffix *-wise* has become extremely productive today and, because it has been carelessly attached in speech to almost any word, its usage has fallen into ill repute. It is not unusual to hear persons say dollarwise, economywise, financewise, safetywise, and so forth;

students can probably give many examples. They should be aware, however, that preferable alternatives usually exist.

-y

As a suffix to form adjectives, *-y* comes from the Old English *-ig*, and means being, or possessing, or resembling. It is also used with nouns to denote quality or state of being, as in victory. This suffix is often used in abstract nouns formed from adjectives ending in *-ous* and *-ic*. In this sense, the suffix comes through French and Latin from the Greek *-ian* and *-eia*.

As was previously noted under the suffix *-ie*, the suffix *-y* also may mean little or small, as in kitty. It is often used in nicknames or to express endearment, as in Tommy.

bloody	icy	shadowy
cloudy	juicy	shady
dirty	leafy	shaky
dizzy	lousy	shiny
empty	mighty	silky
faulty	milky	soapy
fiery	misty	speedy
foamy	moody	sticky
foxy	naughty	stormy
gloomy	nervy	stringy
greasy	panicky	thirsty
guilty	plucky	watery
hairy	pretty	wealthy
heavy	rainy	windy
hungry	sandy	witty

PRONUNCIATION KEYS FOR PREFIXES AND SUFFIXES*

Prefix	*As in*	*American College Dictionary*	*Webster's Seventh New Collegiate Dictionary*	*Webster's New World Dictionary*	*International Phonetic Alphabet*
a-	amoral	ā	ā	ā	eI
a-	aflutter	ə	ə	ə	ə
ab-	abdicate	ăb	ab	ab	æb
ab-	abbreviate	ə	ə	ə	ə
ab-	ablaut	äb	äp	äp	*a*p
ac-		ə	ə	ə	ə
ad-	adhere	ăd	ad	əd, ad	æd
ad-	adjacent	ə	ə	ə	ə
ad-	adjective	ă	a	a	æ
af-	affect	ə	ə	ə	ə
af-	affix	ă	a	a	æ
ag-	aggressive	ə	ə	ə	ə
ag-	aggravate	ă	a	a	æ
al-	allow	ə	ə	ə	ə
al-	'ally	ă	a	a	æ
an-	announce	ə	ə	ə	ə
an-	annotate	ă	a	a	æ
ante-	antecede	ăntə	antə	antə	æntə
ante-	anteroom	ăntĭ	anti	anti	æntI
anti-	antiaircraft	ăntĭ	antē	anti	æntI, ænti
anti-	antitrust	ăntĭ	anti	anti	æntI
ap-	appall	ə	ə	ə	ə
ap-	appetite	ă	a	a	æ
ar-		ə	ə	ə	ə
arch-	archangel	ärk	ärk	ärk	*a*rk
arch-	archbishop	ärch	ärch	ärch	*a*rtʃ
as-		ə	ə	ə	ə
at-		ə	ə	ə	ə
auto-	autobiography	ôtə	ȯtə	ôtə	ɔtə
auto-	autosuggestion	ôtō	ȯtō	ôtō	ɔto
be-		bĭ	bi	bi	bI
co-	coagent	kō	kō	kō	ko
co-	cognate	kŏ	kä	ko	k*a*
col-	collide	kə	kə	kə	kə
col-	colloquy	kŏ	k*ä*	ko	k*a*
com-	'combat	kŏm	käm	kom	k*a*ı.ɹ
com-	com'bine	kəm	kəm	kəm	kəm
con-	connect	kə	kə	kə	kə
con-	convene	kən	kən	kən	kən
cor-	correct	kə	kə	kə	kə
cor-	correspond	kô	kȯ, kä	kô, ko	kɔ, k*a*

*Prepared by Ashley Hastings.

(CONTINUED)

Prefix	*As in*	*American College Dictionary*	*Webster's Seventh New Collegiate Dictionary*	*Webster's New World Dictionary*	*International Phonetic Alphabet*
counter-		kountər	kau̇ntər	kountẽr	kaʊntər
de-	deflect	dĭ	di	di	dI
de-	decade	dē	dē	dē	di
de-	derelict	dĕ	de	de	dɛ
dis-	disinherit	dĭs	dis	dis	dIs
dis-	discern	dĭ	di	di	dI
em-		ĕm	im	im	ɛm, Im
en-		ĕn	in	in	ɛn, In
ex-	exit	ĕgz, ĕks	egz, eks	egz, eks	ɛgz, ɛks
ex-	exhale	ĕks, ĭgz	eks	eks, igz	ɛks, Igz
ex-	excruciate	ĭks	iks	iks	Iks
extra-		ĕkstrə	ekstrə	ekstrə	ɛkstrə
fore-		fōr	fōr, fȯr	fôr, fōr	for, fɔr
hyper-		hīpər	hīpər	hīpẽr	haIpər
hypo-	hypodermic	hīpə	hīpə	hīpə	haIpə
hypo-	hypothyroid	hīpō	hīpō	hīpō	haIpo
hypo-	hypothesis	hīpŏ	hīpä	hīpo, hipo	haIp*a*
il-		ĭ	i (l)	i	I
im-	immodest	ĭ	i (m)	i	I
im-	imperfect	ĭm	im	im	Im
in-		ĭn	in	in	In
inter-	intercede	ĭntər	intər	intẽr	Intər
inter-	interrogate	ĭntĕr	inter	inter	Intɛr
intra-		ĭntrə	intrə	intrə	Intrə
ir-	irrational	ĭ	i (r)	i	I
ir-	irredeemable	ĭ	i	i	I
macro-	macrocosm	măkrə	makrə	makrə	mækrə
macro-	macroeconomics		makrō		mækro
micro-	microbe	mīkrō	mīkrō	mīkrō	maIkro
micro-	microscope	mīkrə	mīkrə	mīkrə	maIkrə
mal-		măl	mal	mal	mæl
mid-		mĭd	mid	mid	mId
mono-	monocle	mŏnə	mäni	monə	m*a*nə, m*a*nI
mono-	monogamy	mənŏ	mənä	məno	mən*a*
mono-	monomial	mōnō	mänō	mōnō	mono, m*a*no
multi-	multicolored	mŭltĭ	məlti		mʌltI
multi-	multimillionaire	multə	məlti	multi	mʌltə, mʌltI
neo-	neoclassic	nēō	nēō	nēō	nio
neo-	neolithic	nēə	nēə	nēə	niə
neo-	neologism	nĭŏ	nēä	nēo	nI*a*, ni*a*
non-		nŏn	nän	non	n*a*n
out-	outdo	out	au̇t	out	aʊt
over-	overcrowd	ōvər	ōvər	ōvẽr	ovər

Prefix	*As in*	*American College Dictionary*	*Webster's Seventh New Collegiate Dictionary*	*Webster's New World Dictionary*	*International Phonetic Alphabet*
pan-		păn	pan	pan	pæn
para-	parable	părə	parə	parə	pærə
para-	paralysis	pəră	pəra	pəra	pəræ
post-		pōst	pōst	pōst	post
pre-	preamble	prē	prē	prē	pri
pre-	precaution	prĭ	pri	pri	prI
pre-	precipice	prĕ	pre	pre	prɛ
pro-	problem	prŏ	prä	pro	pr*a*
pro-	proceed	prə	prō, prə	prō, prə	prə, pro
pro-	proconsul	prō	prō	prō	pro
pseudo-	pseudoclassic	so͞odō	südə, südō	so͞odō, sūdō	sudo, sudə
pseudo-	pseudonym	so͞odə	südə	so͞odə, sūdə	sudə
quasi-		kwäsy		kwäsi	kwasI
		kwāzī	kwāzī	kwāzī	kweIzaI
			kwäzē		kw*a*zi
			kwäsI		kw*a*saI
			kwāzē		kweIzi
		kwāsī		kwāsī	kweIsaI
re-	reprint	rē	rē	rē	ri
re-	report	rĭ	ri	ri	rI
retro-	retroactive	rĕtrō	retrō	retrō	rɛtro
retro-	retrograde	rĕtrə	retrə	retrə	rɛtrə
semi-	semiannual	sĕmĭ	semē, semī	semi	sɛmI, sɛmi, sɛmaI
semi-	semicircle	sĕmĭ	semi	semə	sɛmI, sɛmə
sub-	subagent	sŭb	səb	sub	sʌb
sub-	submit	səb	səb	səb	səb
sub-	subpoena	sə, səb	sə	sə, səb	sə(b)
sub-	subtle	sŭ	sə	su	sʌ
suc-	succeed	sək	sək	sək	sək
suc-	succor	sŭ	sə	su	sʌ
suf-	suffer	sŭ	sə	su	sʌ
suf-	suffice	sə	sə	sə	sə
sug-		səg	sə(g)	sə(g)	səg
sum-		sŭ	sə	su	sʌ
sup-	supple	sŭ	sə, sü	su	sʌ
sup-	supply	sə	sə	sə	sə
super-	superman	so͞opər	süpər	so͞opẽr, sūpẽr	supər, sjupər
super-	superfluous	so͞opûr	süpar	soopũr, syoopũr	sʊpɜr, sjupər
super-	superlative	səpûr	süpər	soopũr, syoopũr	səpɜr
sus-	sustain	səs	səs	səs	səs
sus-	suspect	sŭs	sus	sus	sʌs
syl-		sĭ	si	si	sI
sym-	symbol	sĭm	sim	sim	sIm

(CONTINUED)

Prefix	*As in*	*American College Dictionary*	*Webster's Seventh New Collegiate Dictionary*	*Webster's New World Dictionary*	*International Phonetic Alphabet*
sym-	symmetrical	sĭ	sə	si	sI
syn-		sĭn	sin	sin	sI
trans-		(trăns)	(tran(t)s)	(trans)	træns
		(trănz)	(tranz)	(tranz)	trænz
tri-	tricolor	trī	trī	trī	traI
tri-	trilogy	trĭ	tri	tri	trI
un-		ŭn	ən	un	ʌn
uni-	unicellular	ūnə	yüni	ūni	junə, junI
uni-	unicorn		yünə	ūnə	junə
vice-		vīs	vīs	vīs	vaIs
Suffixes					
-able		əbəl	əbəl	əb'l	əbl̩
-acy		əsĭ	əsē	əsi	əsI
-age		ĭj	ij	ij	Idʒ
-al	accidental	əl	əl	'l	əl, l̩
-al	analytical	əl	əl	'l	əl, l̩
-al	barbital	ăl, ôl	ȯl	al, əl	æl, ɔl, əl
-an		ən	ən	ən	ən
-ance	abundance	əns	ən(t)s	əns	əns
-ance	acquaintance	əns	ən(t)s	'ns	əns, n̩s
-ance	advance	ăns, äns	an(t)s	ans, äns	æns, *a*ns
-ancy		ənsĭ	ənsē	ənsi	ənsI, ənsi
-ant	accountant	ənt	ənt	'nt	ənt, n̩t
-ant	applicant	ənt	ənt	ənt	ənt
-art		ərt	ərt	ẽrt	ərt
-arian		ârĭən	erēən	âriən	ɛrIən, ɛriən
-ary	complementary	ərĭ, trĭ	ərē, trē	ẽri	ərI, əri, tri
-ary	dictionary	ĕrĭ	erē	eri	ɛrI, ɛri
-ate	abbreviate	āt	āt	āt	eIt
-ate	affectionate	ĭt	ət	it	It, ət
-ation		āshən	āshən	āshən	eIʃən
-dom		dəm	dəm	dəm	dəm
-ed	ragged	ĭd	əd	id	Id, əd
-ed	frenzied	d	d	d	d
-ed	domed				d
-ed	looped				t
-ee	committee	ĭ	ē	i	I, i
-ee	divorcee	ā, ē	ā, ē	(ā), ē	eI, i
-eer		ĭr	i(ə)r	êr	Ir, i(ə)r
-el		əl	əl	'l	əl, l̩
-en		ən	ən	'n	ən, n̩
-ence	dependence	ən(t)s	əns	əns	əns

Suffix	*As in*	*American College Dictionary*	*Webster's Seventh New Collegiate Dictionary*	*Webster's New World Dictionary*	*International Phonetic Alphabet*
-ence	evidence	əns	ən(t)s, en(t)s	əns	əns
-ency	agency	ənsĭ	ənsē	ənsi	ənsI, ənsi
-ency	complacency	ənsĭ	ənsē	'nsi	ənsI, n̩si
-ent		ənt	ənt	ənt	ənt
-eous		əs	əs	əs	əs
-er		ər	ər	ẽr	ər
-ery		ərĭ	(ə)rē	ẽri	ərI, (ə)ri
-ese		ēz, ēs	ēz, ēs	ēz	iz, is
-esque		ĕsk	esk	esk	ɛsk
-ess		ĭs	əs	is	Is, əs
-ette		ĕt	et	et	ɛt
-fold		fōld	fōld	fōld	fold
-hood		ho͝od	hu̇d	hood	hʊd
-ian	Spencerian	ĭən	ēən	iən	Iən, iən
-ian	Russian	ən	ən	ən	ən
-ian	Italian	yən	yən	yən	jən
-ible		əbəl	əbəl	əb'l	əbəl, əbl̩
-ic		ĭk	ik	ik	Ik
-ics		ĭks	iks	iks	Iks
-ician		ĭshən	ishən	ishən	Iʃən
-ie		ĭ	ē	i	I, i
-ify		əfī	əfī	əfī	əfaI
-ine	gasoline	ēn	ēn	ēn	in
-ine	medicine	ən, ĭn	ən	'n	ən, In, n̩
-ine	doctrine	ĭn	ən	in	In, ən
-ine	alpine	īn, ĭn	īn	īn, in	aIn, In
-ing		ĭng	iŋ	iŋ	Iŋ
-ish		ĭsh	ish	ish	Iʃ
-ism		ĭzəm	izəm	iz'm	Izəm, Izm̩
-ist		ĭst	əst	ist	Ist, əst
-istic		ĭstĭc	istik	istik	IstIk
-ite	infinite	ĭt	ət	it	It, ət
-ite	dynamite	īt	īt	īt	aIt
-ition		ĭshən	ishən	ishən	Iʃən
-itious		ĭshəs	ishəs	ishəs	Iʃəs
-ity		ətĭ	ətē	əti	ətI, əti
-ive		ĭv	iv	iv	Iv
-ize			īz	īz	*a*Iz
-kin		kĭn	kən	kin	kIn, kən
-le		əl	əl	'l	əl, l̩
-less		lĭs	ləs	lis	lIs, ləs
-let		lĭt	lət	lit	lIt, lət
-like		līk	līk	līk	laIk

(CONTINUED)

Suffix	*As in*	*American College Dictionary*	*Webster's Seventh New Collegiate Dictionary*	*Webster's New World Dictionary*	*International Phonetic Alphabet*
-ling		lĭng	liŋ	liŋ	lIŋ
-ly		lĭ	lē	li	lI, li
-ment		mənt	mənt	mənt	mənt
-most		mōst	mōst	mōst	most
-ness		nĭs	nəs	nis	nIs, nəs
-or		ɔr	ər	ẽr	ər
-ory	accusatory	ōrĭ	ōrē, ȯrē	ôri, ōri	orI, ori, ɔri
-ory	illusory	ərĭ	(ə)rē	ẽri	ərI, (ə)ri
-ous		əs	əs	əs	əs
-ship		shĭp	ship	ship	ʃIp
-some		səm	səm	səm	səm
-ster		stər	stər	stẽr	stər
-ward		wərd	wərd	wẽrd	wərd
-wards		wərdz	wərdz	wẽrdz	wərdz
-wise		wīz	wīz	wīz	waIz
-y		ĭ	ē	i	I, i

GRADE 10

American Dialects

Each man's language differs slightly from that of his neighbors. His use of words, his grammatical constructions, and his pronunciation of some words are not exactly the same as his neighbors. Each man has an idiolect, i.e., each man has a speech pattern that sets him apart from his neighbors. The differences may be so minute that they go unnoticed by most people. But when he visits another part of the country, his speech will probably mark him as a stranger. He may learn for the first time in his life that he speaks a dialect.

It's no disgrace to speak a dialect. Everyone does. But some people—teachers and laymen alike—have disparaged dialects for years, not realizing that they themselves speak a dialect. Such people believe that language should be standardized, that all men should say words the same way, that all should use the same words to refer to the same things. In effect, such people would take a rich, colorful language and make it colorless because they do not understand what language is, what dialects are, and how language changes.

A dialect is the language of a speech community. It is not a separate language; it simply differs in some pronunciations, word choices, and grammatical constructions from the same elements of language in another part of the country. A person in Georgia speaks English, but he has a Southern dialect. His pronunciation of words, some of the words he uses, and some of his grammatical constructions differ from those of a native Hoosier. And the Hoosier's speech, although it, too, is English, differs from that of a Bostonian. And the Bostonian's differs from that of the New Yorker, and so on.

To begin this unit and to help students learn for themselves what a dialect is, a teacher might ask questions like these:

> John, does your mother ever wash a *spider?* (skillet, frying pan)
> Mary, have you ever eaten *bird's nest*? (apple cobbler)
> Bill, does your house have a *dog trot*? (porch)
> Jane, how long has it been since the last *toad-strangler*? (short, heavy rain)
> Bob, do you know any student who has *hooked Jack* recently? (played hooky, been truant)
> Alice, have you ever been *kilt*? (tired)

As students try to answer, or probably laugh at, questions like those, one or more might ask: "What kind of language is that? It certainly isn't good English." But it is. In certain areas those words are commonly accepted; in others they sound strange.

Let's concentrate on changes in vocabulary and grammatical constructions first to show students that not all English-speaking people say things exactly the same way. The teacher may wish to mimeograph the groups of sentences that follow and give them to students, or he may simply read them aloud, asking students which sentence in each group they would say. For some groups of sentences, students may note that they would say two or even three of the sentences naturally. (A teacher may get better results if, no matter how he presents groups of sentences like these, he asks students to write down their responses instead of calling them out, which may inhibit some who speak a dialect other than that spoken in the school area. It should be noted that a few of these dialectal differences were common only in rural areas and may be used in those areas today only by people born in the nineteenth century.)

1. It is *8:45*.
   It is a *quarter of nine.*
   It is a *quarter before nine.*
   It is a *quarter to nine.*
   It is a *quarter till nine.*

2. The leaves have clogged the *eaves.*
   The leaves have clogged the *eaves spouts.*
   The leaves have clogged the *eavestroughs.*
   The leaves have clogged the *gutters.*
   The leaves have clogged the *rain troughs.*
   The leaves have clogged the *spouting.*
   The leaves have clogged the *spouts.*
   The leaves have clogged the *water gutters.*

3. I hang my clothes in the *closet.*
   I hang my clothes in the *clothes press.*
   I hang my clothes in the *wardrobe.*
   I hang my clothes in the *press.*
   I hang my clothes in the *clothes closet.*

4. The *faucet* in the kitchen leaks.
   The *hydrant* in the kitchen leaks.
   The *spicket* in the kitchen leaks.
   The *spigot* in the kitchen leaks.
   The *tap* in the kitchen leaks.

5. Mary plays a *French harp.*
   Mary plays a *breath harp.*
   Mary plays a *mouth organ.*
   Mary plays a *Jew's harp.*
   Mary plays a *harmonica.*
   Mary plays a *mouth harp.*

6. Mother always puts her best *counterpane* on the bed in the guest room.
   Mother always puts her best *counterpin* on the bed in the guest room.
   Mother always puts her best *bedspread* on the bed in the guest room.
   Mother always puts her best *coverlet* on the bed in the guest room.
   Mother always puts her best *coverlid* on the bed in the guest room.

7. When it rains that road is *slick.*
   When it rains that road is *slippery.*

8. He got lost in the *bayou.*
   He got lost in the *bog.*
   He got lost in the *draw.*
   He got lost in the *seep.*
   He got lost in the *slough.*
   He got lost in the *swale.*
   He got lost in the *marsh.*
   He got lost in the *swamp.*

9. I like the piece of chicken that has the *pull bone.*
   I like the piece of chicken that has the *breakbone.*
   I like the piece of chicken that has the *lucky bone.*
   I like the piece of chicken that has the *pulley bone.*
   I like the piece of chicken that has the *pulling bone.*
   I like the piece of chicken that has the *wishbone.*

10. Bean Blossom is just a *ways* down the road.
    Bean Blossom is a *little piece* down the road.
    Bean Blossom is a *little way* down the road.
    Bean Blossom is a *little ways* down the road.
    Bean Blossom is a *piece* down the road.

11. I like *corn bread.*
    I like *corn dodger(s).*
    I like *johnnycake.*
    I like *pone bread.*
    I like *corn pone.*
    I like *hoe cake(s).*

12. Mother makes good *flitters.*
    Mother makes good *fritters.*
    Mother makes good *battercakes.*
    Mother makes good *flannel cakes.*
    Mother makes good *griddle cakes.*
    Mother makes good *flapjacks.*
    Mother makes good *wheat cakes.*

Mother makes good *slapjacks.*
Mother makes good *hot cakes.*
Mother makes good *pancakes.*

13. I like *jerked beef* on toast.
I like *chipped beef* on toast.
I like *dried beef* on toast.
I like *jerky* on toast.

14. I *dived* into the water.
I *dove* into the water.

15. How *be* you?
How *are* you?

16. Bill was *scairt.*
Bill was *scared.*

17. They cut down the *buttonwood* tree.
They cut down the *sycamore* tree.

18. I had a *fatcake* and coffee for breakfast.
I had on *olicook* and coffee for breakfast.
I had a *doughnut* and coffee for breakfast.

19. Just put it in a *poke.*
Just put it in a *paper sack.*
Just put it in a *bag.*

20. He *clumb* out the window.
He *climbed* out the window.

21. *You-uns* are first.
You-all are first.
You are first.

22. I *want off* the train.
I *want to get off* the train.

23. I *mind* when you were born.
I *remember* when you were born.

24. He *sot* down.
He *sat* down.

25. Let me *tote* that *turn* of wood.
Let me *carry* that *armload* of wood.

26. I *carried* her home after the dance.
I *took* her home after the dance.

27. He brought a *snake doctor* to biology class.
He brought a *dragon fly* to biology class.
He brought a *darning needle* to biology class.
He brought an *ear-sewer* to biology class.
He brought a *mosquito hawk* to biology class.
He brought a *sewing needle* to biology class.
He brought a *snake feeder* to biology class.
He brought a *devil's darning needle* to biology class.

28. I *disremember* what I did with it.
I *forget* what I did with it.

29. I'm not *for sure.*
I'm not *sure.*

30. I like *goobers.*
I like *peanuts.*

31. I like *sugar corn.*
I like *roasting ears.*
I like *sweet corn.*
I like *garden corn.*
I like *green corn.*
I like *mutton corn.*
I like *corn-on-the-cob.*

32. I do not like *string beans.*
I do not like *snaps.*
I do not like *beans.*
I do not like *sallet beans.*
I do not like *snap beans.*
I do not like *green beans.*

33. That baby *features* his mother.
    That baby *favors* his mother.
    That baby *looks like* his mother.
    That baby *resembles* his mother.
    That baby *takes after* his mother.

34. I am *all in.*
    I am *beat out.*
    I am *bushed.*
    I am *done out.*
    I am *done up.*
    I am *fagged out.*
    I am *give out.*
    I am *killed.*
    I am *perished.*
    I am *petered out.*
    I am *played out.*
    I am *tuckered out.*
    I am *used up.*
    I am *worn out.*

35. I *catch a cold* easily.
    I *catch cold* easily.
    I *get a cold* easily.
    I *take a cold* easily.
    I *take cold* easily.

36. The baby *crawls* across the floor.
    The baby *creeps* across the floor.

The teacher should give students ample time to read (or listen to) and enjoy the sentences and discuss them. He then should establish clearly that these are not "right" and "wrong" ways of saying the same thing. They are examples to show that different people in our own country have different ways of saying the same things. So, just as language is divided into many languages (like Spanish, German, English, Latin, and so on), each language, including English, is divided into smaller systems of communication called dialects.

The teacher will point out that two kinds of difference are illustrated in the thirty-six pairs of sentences. First, there are many examples of vocabulary differences. A second kind of difference, in grammar, is illustrated by dived, dove; be, are; scairt, scared; into, in; clumb, climbed; you-uns, you-all, you; off, to get off; of, till, to; all, all gone; sot, sat; and for sure, sure.

These two kinds of difference—differences in vocabulary and differences in grammar—might be discussed briefly at this point. Students will probably find it interesting to speculate about the causes of these differences. They might look at the differences in grammar and discuss them in terms of what they know about the principles of grammar. They might also look at the differences in vocabulary and try to decide what kinds of people may use certain symbols to refer to specific objects. They may also speculate on the areas in the country in which these people live.

Next the teacher should point out that there is a third very important kind of difference that helps to make a dialect, i.e., difference in pronunciation. This can be illustrated by simply saying that some persons pronounce the word i-d-e-a as though there were an *r* at the end of it. That is, they say "idear" instead of "idea." Some persons do not "wash"; they "warsh." Some find food "greasy" (using a soft *s*); some find it "greazy." And while one batter takes a "third strike," another takes his "toid."

By this time students may be curious as to who speaks in these various ways, since they will never have heard some of these variations of vocabulary, grammar, and pronunciation, and will have heard others only infrequently. It should now be pointed out that we call these variations *dialects* and that people who study language scientifically mean a certain thing when they use the term *dialect*. One linguist has defined dialect as "a variety of *speech* which is used in a certain locality or region and which differs in pronunciation, vocabulary, and grammar from other varieties spoken in other localities or regions. Furthermore, local or regional dialects differ from the standard language—the 'book words' that could be used in any region of the country."*

*Jean Malmstrom and Annabel Ashley, *Dialects—USA*, Champaign, Ill.: National Council of Teachers of English, 1963, p. 2.

In the studies of our language, linguists have found that there are three relatively distinct dialects along the Atlantic Seaboard. These have been named Northern, Midland, and Southern. These three dialect belts extend westward but tend to become less well defined as one goes farther west.

Of course the boundaries indicating dialect areas have to be somewhat arbitrary, and they certainly must be irregular. One cannot sort people as one might sort different sizes of nuts and bolts into a neat row of bins. And certainly along any dialect dividing line there appears another group whose speech includes grammar, vocabulary, and pronunciation peculiarities of both sections. Graphically one might illustrate this overlapping as follows:

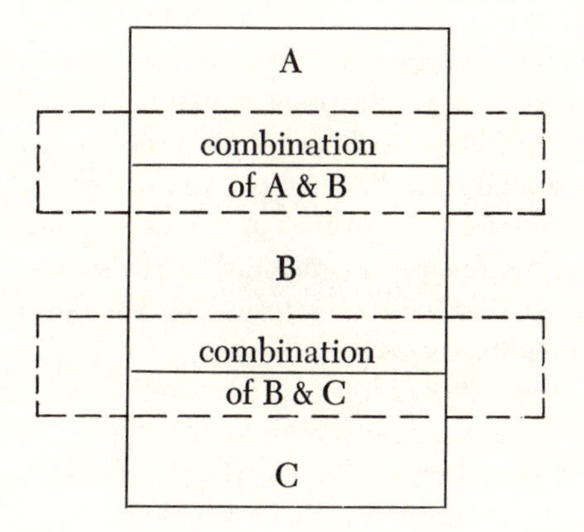

Add to this the fact that people are constantly on the move in and out of all these overlapping areas—traveling, visiting, and changing residence—and it is easy to see that there is no such thing as an unmixed dialect area. Almost any geographic area or community, no matter how small, will be a representation of almost every type of dialect. It is in the proportions of people using the various dialects within any given area that great range is found.

If one pursues the course of dividing language into languages and languages into dialects, taking into account all the overlappings, he will probably conclude eventually that there are, within our own language, as many kinds of speech as there are people. This is almost literally true; the term *idiolect* means the speech pattern of one individual at one particular time of his life. The speech pattern of the individual does constantly change and is not the same at any two times in his life.

One major question remains to be answered: What are the causes of our American English dialects?

Dialect differences have been more clearly defined in the area along the Atlantic Seaboard, in other words, in the area that was first settled. In the earliest stages of the settlement of our country the colonists tended to cluster together in more or less non-overlapping communities. The populace of a community was small and tended much more toward homogeneity than would be true in the larger communities of today. Different nationalities, with their distinctive languages and dialects, were also represented in the early settlement of this country.

As our country grew, migration tended strongly toward the west, tending only slightly toward the south or north. Consequently, as we have mentioned, the dialect belts tend to extend from east to west across our country. Because the western section of the country has not been settled nearly so long and because the process of westward migration led to so much intermixing, the dialect belts are not so clearly defined in the West.

For many language differences from area to area tended to persist because people tended to remain in one place. Transportation was slow, and travel was difficult. Means of easy communication over very great distances have been developed only recently.

Another very important factor contributing to dialect differences is education, or the lack of it. The more formal education an individual has, the less likely he is to use or to persist in using those elements of a dialect that we have classified as differences in grammar. The more reading and traveling an individual does, the more likely he is to learn and to use a wider vocabulary and to be conscious of, and to change, his pronunciation habits.

Caution to the teacher: It is very important that we not give students the impression that educated people do not speak the dialect of their area. Certainly they do. It is not exactly the same dialect as that of the uneducated people of the area, but many elements are the same. As we noted before, most dialect differences in grammar tend to be eliminated from the speech of the educated. As far as vocabulary is concerned, the well-educated people *tend* to use the same dialect vocabulary as others in the area but, because of their broader vocabulary, are more likely to know and use alternate terms that are prominent in other areas. In any given dialect area, the greatest similarity between the dialect of the well-educated and that of those who are not so well educated is in pronunciation (rather than in grammar or even in vocabulary). In an area (Midland) where "Mary" sounds like "merry," everyone is likely to pronounce that name the same way. But in the same Midland area, educated people will probably say "wash the clothes," and most others will say "warsh the clothes." The reason is probably that the well-educated people pay more attention to and are more concerned about their speech and become conscious of speech differences of which other people are hardly aware.

At this point in their study of dialects, students might well be encouraged to speculate concerning the future of American dialects. It is probable that they will conclude that dialects are already becoming less pronounced as a result of (1) more extensive programs of formal education for all youth, (2) the increased mobility of the American people, (3) the change from an agrarian to an urban society, and (4) the impact of radio, television, and other rapid, large-scale means of communication. Students may have noticed that many radio and TV broadcasters, regardless of the area in which they are working, speak what has become known as standard American English. The fact that millions of Americans listen to radio and TV daily may soften the distinctions among existing dialects. It should seem inevitable that these kinds of social force will continue to change and almost eliminate dialects. But when we have shown that language can be subdivided all the way down to idiolects, students will probably conclude also that dialects will never be erased, though they may become much more difficult to distinguish.

A teacher might review a few points:

1. The existence of dialects is a natural and inevitable fact of language.

2. American English is essentially the same throughout the coun-

try. The vocabulary, pronunciation, and grammatical features that account for dialect differences represent a relatively small proportion of the total language elements.

3. No one has the right to say of dialects that one way of speaking is right and another is wrong. It is rather a matter of appropriateness.

4. There *are* some dialectal characteristics—especially those that represent violations of the principles of grammar—which cultured, better-educated people almost invariably will have eliminated from their speech.

5. It is important that each student be aware of kinds of dialect and elements of dialect so that he may not be guilty of thinking others are speaking incorrectly simply because they may speak differently. The student might also carefully evaluate his own speaking habits and identify any features of his speech which could prove embarrassing or detrimental to him as he pursues his own goals.

6. The increased awareness of language which the student should now have can add much to his understanding of literature and of people. Every gain in language awareness helps to reduce by that much the omnipresent danger of misinterpretation and misunderstanding.

Suggested Activities

1. Students should make a list of local terms and classify them according to source: family, friends, reading, and so on. Students should then write a short paper on the influences that have affected their own vocabularies.

2. Students should explain dialects found in literary works the class has studied. Some suggested sources include: Harris, *Uncle Remus: His Songs and Sayings;* Frost, "Death of the Hired Man" or others; Lowell, "The Courtin' "; Garland, "Under the Lion's Paw"; Twain, *Huckleberry Finn;* and Van Druten, *I Remember Mama.*

3. Each student should select a poem, short story, or novel which uses dialect and write an essay on the use of the dialect. In his analysis he should consider the purpose of the use of the dialect, such as the development of setting, mood, or character; the devices used

to indicate differences in pronunciation; and the differences in grammar.

4. In order to illustrate one of the influences of foreign language on the American language, students should check one or more good cookbooks for names of foods which have originated in another language.

5. Students might compare the dialects of any two TV characters, showing how the dialects add to or detract from the development of the character.

GRADE 10

Why Worry About Meaning?

A SUGGESTION FOR A UNIT

From grades seven through nine, students have been concerned with what and how words mean; therefore, a separate unit on semantics might seem superfluous at this point. But there are problems of meaning that students need to reexamine and other problems to which they have not yet been exposed.

In grade ten students in many English classes spend several weeks exploring the mass media. (See *Two Units on Journalism for English Class,* Indianapolis: Indiana State Department of Public Instruction, 1964.) As they become better acquainted with their sources of news and information, students become aware of propaganda, the language of advertising, and the use of loaded words. In the tenth grade they also become acquainted with irony and metaphor as they study poetry. (See Professor Paul Zietlow's unit on poetry in *Teaching Literature in Grades Ten Through Twelve,* a volume in this English Curriculum Study Series.) And further, students continue learning how to manipulate language in their own writing in grade ten. (See *Theme Assignments for Grades Seven Through Twelve,* a volume in this English Curriculum Study Series.)

With all that attention to meaning, why suggest additional studies in semantics? Because students need to examine the writings of the general semanticists if they are to become intelligent senders and receivers of messages. But instead of presenting a formal unit on meaning, we suggest that teachers review, when appropriate, some of the concepts presented in earlier units, e.g., denotation, connotation, and how words change meaning in time and context, and also make individual reading assignments from the following books, giving students two or three periods in which to present oral reports.

Chase, Stuart. *The Tyranny of Words.* New York: Harcourt, Brace and Company, 1938. (Harvest paperback)

Hall, Edward T. *The Silent Language.* Garden City, N. Y.: Doubleday, 1959. (Premier paperback)

Hayakawa, S. I., ed. *The Use and Misuse of Language.* Greenwich, Conn.: Fawcett Publications, 1962.

Salomon, Louis B. *Semantics and Common Sense.* New York: Holt, Rinehart and Winston, 1966.

GRADE 11

A Suggestion for a Unit on the History of the English Language

As students study English literature in grade eleven, they usually become aware of some of the changes in the English language from Beowulf to the present. In several units presented thus far, students have become acquainted with the nature of language, how words are formed, how English has borrowed words from other languages down through the years, and how words change meaning in time and context. In a second unit for grade eleven, students will consider the role of the lexicographer from the earliest English dictionary in 1604 to the publication of *Webster's Third.* Therefore, they have had more than a brief introduction to some of the changes that have occurred in the language during its 1500-year history.

Instead of preparing a separate unit, we have included a brief treatment of the history of the English language by J. N. Hook and E. G. Mathews, in Appendix C, and we have also given teachers examples of changes from Wycliffe to the present by including twelve different translations from the Book of Ruth, in Appendix B. We suggest that teachers, with the help of those two appendices and after reading several of the following books, prepare several lectures on the history of the English language and also assign students the task of reporting on various aspects of the language. Why do we suggest several short lectures at this point? Because we feel that students must have the opportunity to listen to several short lectures before they go on to college and to take notes so that they will learn how. We further suggest that the teacher collect the notes, comment on them, give students advice as to how to take better notes, but not grade them.

Baugh, Albert C. *A History of the English Language*, 2nd ed. New York: Appleton-Century-Crofts, 1957.

Bloomfield, Morton W., and Leonard Newmark. *A Linguistic Introduction to the History of English*. New York: Alfred A. Knopf, 1965.

Francis, W. Nelson. *The English Language—An Introduction*. New York: W. W. Norton, 1965.

Hook, J. N., and E. G. Mathews. *Modern American Grammar and Usage*. New York: Ronald Press, 1956.

Myers, L. M. *The Roots of Modern English*. Boston: Little, Brown, 1966.

Pyles, Thomas. *The Origin and Development of the English Language*. New York: Harcourt, Brace & World, 1964.

Robertson, Stuart, and Frederic G. Cassidy. *The Development of Modern English*, 2nd ed. Englewood Cliffs, N. J.: Prentice-Hall, 1953.

Schlauch, Margaret. *The Gift of Language*. New York: Dover Publications, 1955.

Lexicography from Cawdrey to *Webster's Third**

In an article for *The Saturday Review of Literature* in 1941, Mortimer Adler wrote: "In its various sizes and editions, the dictionary is an unlisted best-seller on every season's list. To be able to get along without one would be a sign of supreme literacy—of complete competence as a reader and writer. The dictionary exists, of course, because there is no one in that condition. But, if the dictionary is the necessity we all acknowledge, why is it so infrequently used by the man who owns one? And, even when we do consult it, why do most of us misuse the dictionary or use it poorly?"† The situation has not changed too much in 26 years. The dictionary, in its various sizes and forms, still remains an unlisted best-seller, and it still is one of the most abused books on any bookshelf.

For years teachers of English have been introducing students to the proper use of dictionaries, and for years teachers have hoped that their efforts will pay dividends. In many cases their teaching has borne fruit; in other cases the fruit has dropped from learned trees in the form of unripened articles about the function of lexicographers and the "passel of double-domes" who produced *Webster's Third International Dictionary.*

The recent controversy over *Webster's Third* indicates that dictionary users still have many misconceptions about the functions of

*This unit was prepared by James R. Jones, chairman of the Department of English, Würzburg American High School, Würzburg, Germany, and Edward B. Jenkinson.

†Mortimer Adler, "How To Read A Dictionary." Reprinted in Jack C. Gray's *Words, Words, and Words about Dictionaries* (San Francisco: Chandler Publishing Company, 1963), p. 55.

lexicographers and the uses they can make of the lexicographers' products—the hundreds of dictionaries available today. This unit concentrates on the role of the lexicographer; it is not a simple repetition of units on dictionaries and words that have already been taught in grades seven and eight. Instead, it is a reexamination of the dictionary from a different point of view—the role of the lexicographer. It serves to correct some misconceptions that have arisen from misinterpretations of the function of a lexicographer from the time of Robert Cawdrey. It also serves to underscore the contributions of Samuel Johnson to lexicography, and thus ties in with the study of English literature in grade eleven.

As an introductory activity the teacher may wish to divide the class into four or five small groups and give each group a different dictionary from which one member of each group will read aloud to the class the entire dictionary entry for at least half of the following words: paradox, paragon, parallel, paraphrase, passion, pause, penalty, period, pioneer, and popular. As the entries from the different dictionaries are read for each word, students should note how entries vary from dictionary to dictionary. The teacher should make certain that all students understand each part of the entries, referring students to the front matter of the dictionaries when questions arise.

THE FIRST ENGLISH DICTIONARY

After students have listened to and discussed the entries from four or five dictionaries for the words suggested above, the teacher may wish to tell them about the first English dictionary of record. In 1604, Robert Cawdrey and his son Thomas, both teachers, compiled a list of some three thousand difficult words and published them in *A Table Alphabeticall.* The entries in the Cawdreys' dictionary were limited to words that had been borrowed from other languages and that gave students trouble. Since the main purpose of the first English dictionary of record was to serve as an aid to students in dealing with foreign words, the Cawdreys were not deeply concerned with such items as alternate spellings, word etymologies, and lengthy definitions. They entered only one spelling for each word. They confined their treatment of etymology to a simple parenthetical g. or gr. if the word were of Greek origin or to the symbol ʃ if the word had been borrowed from the French; in the case of Latin, the Cawdreys did not indicate any origin. They also gave only one definition for most of the words. Thus the Cawdreys offered students a dictionary containing restricted treatment of spelling, etymology, and definition.

The slim volume produced by the Cawdreys went into four editions. It was filled with material that today's students would not quite accept because they are accustomed to something better. It was also an example of poor proofreading and an indiscriminate selection of any spelling of words that were borrowed from other languages and were widely used in the early part of the seventeenth century. A close examination of the Cawdrey dictionary, particularly in the light of the entries in modern dictionaries, would indicate that Robert Cawdrey was most optimistic when he wrote:

> By this Table (right Honourable & Worshipfull) strangers that blame our tongue of difficultie, and uncertaintie may heereby plainly see, & better understand those things, which they have thought hard. Heerby also the true Orthography, that is, the true writing of many hard English words, borrowed from the Greeke, Latine & French, and how to know one from the other, with the interpretation thereof by plaine English words, may be learned and knowne.

After telling students a little bit about the Cawdrey dictionary, the teacher may wish to write several of these entries from the Cawdrey dictionary on the chalkboard or have them mimeographed and given to students.

paradoxe, (g) marueilous, or strange speech:
ʃ paragon, patterne, example
paraleles, (g) lines, or other things as farre off from one another: in one place as in another.
paraphrase, (g) exposition of anything by many words:
passion, suffering, griefe
pause, thinke, stay, or rest
penaltie, losse

period, (g) the end of a perfect sentence
∫ pioneer, digger, or ditcher
popular, seeking the fauour of the people by all meanes possible:

A rapid glance at any modern dictionary will readily reveal to students the changes and expansions that have taken place in the treatment of spelling, etymology, and definition in the three centuries following the Cawdrey publication. Students certainly know that a modern dictionary supplies them with words other than only those taken from foreign languages, and they also know that if a lexicographer were to compile a dictionary only of foreign words, such a dictionary would include many more than the three thousand entries in the Cawdrey dictionary. Students are also aware of the varied spellings a modern dictionary may list for a single word. A closer examination of dictionary entries will quickly reveal the expansions in the treatment of etymology and definition. The average modern dictionary will offer, in most cases, a history of the word and, of course, for many words, a number of definitions.

Suggested Activity

After students have had an opportunity to examine some of the entries in the Cawdrey dictionary, they should compare the entries on the same words that they found in modern dictionaries with those in *A Table Alphabeticall.* Now the teacher may wish to have the students write a paragraph in which they discuss the differences in the entries found in the Cawdrey dictionary and in a modern dictionary. In their paragraphs, students will want to point out what additional information a modern dictionary supplies. They will also want to explain why this information is valuable. They might also want to speculate about the reasons for the differences between the entries in the Cawdrey dictionary and in a modern dictionary. If the teacher makes this speculation a part of the assignment, he should make certain that students know something about the history of the language and the changes that have occurred, and that they are also aware of the differences in scholarship between seventeenth century teachers and scholars and twentieth century teachers and scholars.

THE MODERN DICTIONARY

A modern dictionary contains much more information about words than the Cawdrey dictionary did. According to Mitford Mathews:

> The dictionary has ceased to be merely one book; it is a small library of books brought together into one. These would be suitable titles for the different books that are combined in a good English dictionary:
>
> 1. How to Spell English Words
> 2. How to Capitalize English Words
> 3. How to Divide English Words into Syllables
> 4. How to Pronounce English Words
> 5. A Brief English Grammar
> 6. A Dictionary of English Etymologies
> 7. Levels of English Usage
> 8. The Meanings of English Words
> 9. A Dictionary of Synonyms
> 10. A Dictionary of English Phrases
>
> Ten volumes in one! There is a bargain for everyone who reads and everyone who writes. Become acquainted with its many uses, and you will be many times repaid. As our friend Cawdrey said in 1604, both "delight & judgement" will be yours.*

The listing of suitable titles for the different books combined in a good English dictionary is, of course, concerned only with aspects of the English language and with a standard dictionary of our language. Since we are considering, in this unit, the problems facing lexicographers in general and the science of lexicography itself, we cannot ignore the many other dictionaries that are available to students. As Felicia Lamport reports, the average American "is confronted by yards of dictionaries: multilingual, bilingual, encyclopedic, general, and specialized. In the specialized field alone a single publisher, Dagobert D. Runes . . . claims to have published 250 volumes, including dictionaries of Americanisms, folklore, mys-

*Mitford M. Mathews, "An Introduction to the Dictionary," from *Webster's New World Dictionary,* reprinted in *Words, Words, and Words about Dictionaries,* p. 51.

ticism, psychology, and even tobacco. Narrowing the field to the general English dictionary, there are still some eighty-odd titles, ranging in price from 25 cents to $300, in size from a few ounces to 90 pounds, and in quality from hastily patched-up offsets to fine scholarly works."* All of these dictionaries are concerned basically with words and with knowledge about them. In the true sense of the word, they are all *lexicons,* a term which, although no longer too common in our language, is still used in speaking of, and as a title for, some specialized works and many foreign dictionaries.

Suggested Activity

The teacher may send students to the school or community library to compile a list of the different types of dictionaries that they find there, checking both the card catalog and the shelves for the various kinds of dictionary. Students should select two or three from the list that are totally different and they should inspect those dictionaries carefully. Students may then write a brief paragraph in which they discuss the elements that the two or three dictionaries they selected have in common.

THE LEXICOGRAPHER

Long before Cawdrey, literate men began compiling dictionaries. The first dictionaries were glossaries of Homeric words. Although the Greeks were the first to compile such glossaries, the Greeks themselves did not use the glossaries but prepared them for the Romans who wanted to read Greek. "The Greeks did not have a dictionary, even though 'lexicon' is the Greek word for it. They had no need for foreign language dictionaries because there was no literature in a foreign language they cared to read. They had no need for a Greek word-book because the small educated class already knew what such a book would contain."†

*Felicia Lamport, "Dictionaries: Our Language Right or Wrong," from *Scrap Irony,* by permission of the original publisher, Houghton Mifflin Co.; reprinted in *Words, Words, and Words about Dictionaries,* p. 69.

†Adler, p. 57.

This early attitude of the Greeks has carried over to the present day. A dictionary, after all, is designed to make a literate man more literate. The purpose of a dictionary is to help a man understand words that he is reading or to help him select the appropriate words for his writing. Only literate men can use dictionaries. And since only literate men use them, many decide that they already know the meanings of words or know which words they wish to select; therefore, many men refer to dictionaries occasionally only to check spelling or pronounciation. Or if they need to look up a definition of a word, they sometimes accept the wrong entry because they are not familiar with the arrangements of entries in various dictionaries. Some literate men think that they can move from one dictionary to another, obtaining the same information in the same order. They do not realize that some dictionaries arrange their definitions chronologically. Other dictionaries work from present-day meanings backwards. Therefore, a person unfamiliar with the arrangement of the entries in various dictionaries is likely to come up with an obsolete meaning of a word if he does not read the prefatory material first. Although the dictionary is designed to make a literate man more literate, it can do so only if the man's literacy includes his ability to handle dictionaries well.

The first dictionaries were not too difficult to handle. Since they were primarily glossaries of foreign words, they contained the spelling of a word and, usually, a single definition. As Cawdrey pointed out in his dictionary, the one requirement for using the dictionary was knowledge of the alphabet. Cawdrey was not much concerned with spelling or etymology; he was primarily concerned with giving students the meanings of hard words. Like the dictionaries in the Middle Ages, Cawdrey's dictionary was intended for a limited audience, mainly as an aid to reading the most worthy literature.

The first dictionary makers then were concerned with helping the literate man to read literature written in a foreign language, or to help a literate man understand the meanings of foreign words that had been borrowed by his language. The early lexicographers were not concerned with purifying language or with setting standards of usage. The idea "that the lexicographer is the man who lays down the *lex*" came into being in the late sixteenth century. "The *Academia della crusca* was formed to refine the Italian language and preserve its purity for all time in an official dictionary. The *Académie française* was organized a few years later in France to assure the permanent inviolability of that country's excitable tongue."*

To repeat, the earliest lexicographers were definers of foreign words or terms. Late in the sixteenth century the lexicographer became a prescriptivist. He felt that his duty was to purify and to refine the language, calling attention to words that were used by vagabonds and uneducated men. This movement started, as was indicated above, in Italy and France, and it did not affect England until the eighteenth century "began with a trumpeting of the 'prescriptive' note when Swift, writing to the Lord Treasurer 'in the name of all the learned and polite persons of the nation,' complained of the corruption, absurdities, and gross improprieties of the language. Remedial action was undertaken by Samuel Johnson,"† the giant of English lexicographers and one of the most colorful men of letters.

Dr. Johnson's dictionary first appeared in 1755, and it has been reissued, in whole or in part, periodically ever since. Any student of English literature is no doubt familiar with the story of the struggles Johnson experienced in the writing of this mammoth work, a project which took him eight years. Upon its publication, it became the standard work for nearly a hundred years. The recent McAdam-Milne volume of selections (New York: Random House, 1963) is ample evidence of the interest Dr. Johnson's dictionary still commands after more than two centuries. The purpose of this section on the Johnson dictionary is not to reweave the nostalgic web that has already been woven many times around Johnson's work, but rather to examine some of his views on the function of a lexicographer and to make students aware of the changes that have taken place since Johnson's time.

One of Johnson's original ideas was to purify the language by in-

*Lamport, p. 67.

†Ibid.

cluding words used by only those writers "whose works I regard as *the wells of English undefiled.*" In his famous preface Dr. Johnson wrote:

> I have . . . attempted a Dictionary of the *English* language, which, while it was employed in the cultivation of every species of literature, has itself been hitherto neglected; suffered to spread, under the direction of chance, into wild exuberance; resigned to the tyranny of time and fashion; and exposed to the corruptions of ignorance, and caprices of innovation.
>
> When I took the first survey of my undertaking, I found our speech copious without order, and energetick without rules: wherever I turned my view, there was perplexity to be disentangled, and confusion to be regulated; choice was to be made out of boundless variety, without any established principles of selection; adulterations were to be detected, without a settled test of purity; and modes of expression to be rejected or received, without the suffrages of any writers of classical reputation or acknowledged authority.
>
> Having therefore no assistance but from general grammar, I applied myself to the perusal of our writers; and noting whatever might be of use to ascertain or illustrate any word or phrase, accumulated in time the materials of a dictionary, which, by degrees, I reduced to method, establishing to myself, in the progress of the work, such rules as experience and analogy suggested to me; experience, which practice and observation were continually increasing; and analogy, which, though in some words obscure, was evident in others.
>
> So far have I been from any care to grace my pages with modern decorations, that I have studiously endeavoured to collect examples and authorities from the writers before the restoration, whose works I regard as *the wells of English undefiled,* as the pure sources of genuine diction. Our language, for almost a century, has, by the concurrence of many causes, been gradually departing from its original *Teutonick* character, and deviating towards a *Gallick* structure and phraseology, from which it ought to be our endeavour to recall it, by making our ancient volumes the ground-work of style, admitting among the additions of later times, only such as may supply real deficiencies, such as are readily adopted by the genius of our tongue, and incorporate easily with our native idioms.
>
> But as every language has a time of rudeness antecedent to perfection, as well as of false refinement and declension, I have been cautious lest

my zeal for antiquity might drive me into times too remote, and crowd my book with words now no longer understood. I have fixed *Sidney's* work for the boundary, beyond which I make few excursions. From the authors which rose in the time of *Elizabeth,* a speech might be formed adequate to all the purposes of use and elegance. If the language of theology were extracted from *Hooker* and the translation of the Bible; the terms of natural knowledge from *Bacon;* the phrases of policy, war, and navigation from *Raleigh;* the dialect of poetry and fiction from *Spencer* and *Sidney;* and the diction of common life from *Shakespeare,* few ideas would be lost to mankind, for want of *English* words, in which they might be expressed.

It is not sufficient that a word is found, unless it be so combined as that its meaning is apparently determined by the tract and tenour of the sentence; such passages I have therefore chosen, and when it happened that any author gave a definition of a term, or such an explanation as is equivalent to a definition, I have placed his authority as a supplement to my own, without regard to the chronological order, that is otherwise observed.

Some words, indeed, stand unsupported by any authority, but they are commonly derivative nouns, or adverbs, formed from their primitives by regular and constant analogy, or names of things seldom occurring in books, or words of which I have reason to doubt the existence.

As Dr. Johnson labored on his dictionary, he realized that he could not fix the language as he originally had hoped to do. He wrote in his preface:

Of the event of this work, for which, having laboured it with so much application, I cannot but have some degree of parental fondness, it is natural to form conjectures. Those who have been persuaded to think well of my design, will require that it should fix our language, and put a stop to those alterations which time and chance have hitherto been suffered to make in it without opposition. With this consequence I will confess that I flattered myself for a while; but now begin to fear that I have indulged expectation which neither reason nor experience can justify. When we see men grow old and die at a certain time one after another, from century to century, we laugh at the elixir that promises to prolong life to a thousand years; and with equal justice may the lexicographer be derided, who being able to produce no example of a nation that has preserved their words and phrases from mutability, shall imagine that his dictionary can embalm his language, and secure it from corruption and decay, that it is in his power to change sublunary nature, and clear the world at once from folly, vanity and affectation. . . .

Total and sudden transformation of a language seldom happen; conquests and migrations are now very rare: but there are other causes of change, which, though slow in their operation, and invisible in their progress, are perhaps as much superior to human resistance, as the revolutions of the sky, or intumescence of the tide. Commerce, however necessary, however lucrative, as it depraves the manners, corrupts the language; they that have frequent intercourse with strangers, to whom they endeavour to accommodate themselves, must in time learn a mingled dialect, like the jargon which serves the traffickers on the *Mediterranean* and *Indian* coasts. This will not always be confined to the exchange, the warehouse, or the port, but will be communicated by degrees to other ranks of the people, and be at last incorporated with the current speech.

There are likewise internal causes equally forcible. The language most likely to continue long without alteration, would be that of a nation raised a little, and but a little, above barbarity, secluded from strangers, and totally employed in procuring the conveniences of life; either without books, or, like some of the *Mahometan* countries, with very few: men thus busied and unlearned, having only such words as common use requires, would perhaps long continue to express the same notions by the same signs. But no such constancy can be expected in a people polished by arts, and classed by subordination, where one part of the community is sustained and accommodated by the labour of the other. Those who have much leisure to think, will always be enlarging the stock of ideas; and every increase of knowledge, whether real or fancied, will produce new words, or combinations of words. When the mind is unchained from necessity, it will range after convenience; when it is left at large in the fields of speculation, it will shift opinions; as any custom is disused, the words that expressed it must perish with it; as any opinion grows popular, it will innovate speech in the same proportion as it alters practice.

As by the cultivation of various sciences a language is amplified, it will be more furnished with words deflected from their original sense; the geometrician will talk of a courtier's zenith, or the eccentrick virtue of a wild hero, and the physician of sanguine expectations and phlegmatick delays. Copiousness of speech will give opportunities to capricious choice, by which some words will be preferred, and others degraded; vicissitudes of fashion will enforce the use of new, or extend the signification of known terms. The tropes of poetry will make hourly encroachments, and the metaphorical will become the current sense: pronunciation will be varied by levity or ignorance, and the pen must at length comply with the tongue; illiterate writers will, at one time or other, by publick infatuation, rise into renown, who, not knowing the original import of words, will use them with colloquial licentiousness, confound distinction, and forget propriety. As politeness increases, some expression will be considered as too gross and vulgar for the delicate, others as too formal and ceremonious for the gay and airy; new phrases are therefore adopted, which must, for the same reasons, be in time dismissed. *Swift*, in his petty treatise on the *English* language, allows that new words must sometimes be introduced, but proposes that none should be suffered to become obsolete. But what makes a word obsolete, more than general agreement to forbear it? and how shall it be continued, when it conveys an offensive idea, or recalled again into the mouths of mankind, when it has once become unfamiliar by disuse, and unpleasing by unfamiliarity?

There is another cause of alteration more prevalent than any other, which yet in the present state of the world cannot be obviated. A mixture of two languages will produce a third distinct from both, and they will always be mixed, where the chief part of education, and the most conspicuous accomplishment, is skill in ancient or in foreign tongues. He that has long cultivated another language, will find its words and combinations crowd upon his memory; and haste and negligence, refinement and affection, will obtrude borrowed terms and exotick expressions. . . .

If the changes that we fear be thus irresistible, what remains but to acquiesce with silence, as in the other insurmountable distresses of humanity? It remains that we retard what we cannot repel, that we palliate what we cannot cure. Life may be lengthened by care, though death cannot be ultimately defeated: tongues, like governments, have a natural tendency to degeneration; we have long preserved our constitution, let us make some struggles for our language.

In his treatment of spelling, Johnson's governing purpose was to distinguish "inherent irregularities" from those which he felt were a result of ignorance or negligence. He felt that the latter irregularities "require only to be registered, that they may not be increased, and ascertained, that they may not be confounded." The main duty of the lexicographer here, he believed, was "to correct or proscribe improprieties and absurdities." On the whole, Johnson followed Cawdrey's method in dealing with etymology, although he did provide, in some cases, a breakdown of the foreign term with English definitions for each part. Most of his entries, however, simply listed the name of the language from which the term had been taken. A sample entry follows:

CANT. *n.s.* [probably from *cantus,* Lat. implying the odd tone of voice used by vagrants; but imagined by some to be corrupted from *quaint.*]

1. A corrupt dialect used by beggars and vagabonds.
2. A particular form of speaking, peculiar to some certain class or body of men.

    I write not always in the proper terms of navigation, land service, or in the *cant* of any profession.

    Dryden

3. A whining pretension to goodness, in formal and affected terms.

    Of promise prodigal, while pow'r you want, And preaching in the self-denying *cant.*

    Dryden

4. Barbarous jargon.

    The affectation of some late authors, to introduce and multiply *cant* words, is the most ruinous corruption in any language.

    Swift

5. Auction.

    Numbers of these tenants, or their descendants, are now offering to sell their leases by *cant,* even those which were for lives.

    Swift

Johnson expected the strongest attacks to fall on his approach to definitions (or "explanations") of the words. In explanation and defense he wrote:

To interpret a language by itself is very difficult; many words cannot be explained by synomies, because the idea signified by them has not more than one appellation; nor by paraphrase, because simple ideas cannot be described. When the nature of things is unknown, or the notion unsettled and indefinite, and various in various minds, the words by which such notions are conveyed, or such things denoted, will be ambiguous and perplexed. And such is the fate of hapless lexicography, that not only darkness, but light, impedes and distresses it; things may be not only too little, but too much known, to be happily illustrated. To explain, requires the use of terms less abtruse than that which is to be explained, and such terms cannot always be found; for as nothing can be proved but by supposing something intuitively known, and evident without proof, so nothing can be defined but by the use of words too plain to admit a definition. . . .

Oddly enough, the very section of his work in which Johnson felt most vulnerable is the section that has probably been most responsible for the popularity of the dictionary itself. Johnson's wit showed through every entry. A few examples will show this:

BEAUTY

1. That assemblage of graces, or proportion of parts, which pleases the eye.

Beauty consists of a certain composition of colour and figure, causing delight to the beholder. *Locke*

Your *beauty* was the cause of that effect,
Your beauty, that did haunt me in my sleep—
If I thought that, I tell thee, homicide,
These nails should rend that *beauty* from my cheeks.
Richard III

2. A particular grace, feature, or ornament.
3. Any thing more eminently excellent than the rest of that with which it is united.

This gave me an occasion of looking backward on some *beauties* of my author in his former books. *Dryden Fab. Pref.*

4. A beautiful person.

Remember that Pellean conqueror,
A youth, how all the *beauties* of the east,
He slightly viewed, and slightly overpassed.
Milton

JOB (a low word now much in use, of which I cannot tell the etymology.)

1. Petty, piddling work.
2. A low mean lucrative busy affair.
3. A sudden stab with a sharp instrument.

OATS (Saxon)

A grain, which in England is generally given to horses, but in Scotland supports the people.

PATRON

1. One who countenances, supports, or protects. Commonly a wretch who supports with insolence, and is paid with flattery.

2. A guardian saint.

WHIG (Saxon)

1. Whey
2. The name of a faction.

> The south-west counties of Scotland have seldom corn enough to serve them round the year; and the northern parts producing more than they need, those in the west come in the summer to buy at Leith the stores that come from the north; and from a word, whiggam, used in driving the horses, all that drove were called the whiggamors and shorter the *whiggs*. Now in that year, before the news came down of duke Hamilton's defeat, the ministers animated their people to rise and march to Edinburgh; and they came up marching at the head of their parishes with an unheard-of fury, praying and preaching all the way as they came. The marquis of Argyle and his party came and headed them, they being about six thousand. This was called the whiggamor's inroad; and, ever after that, all that opposed the court came in contempt to be called *whigs;* and from Scotland the word was brought into England, where it is now one of our unhappy terms of disunion. *Burnet*
>
> Whoever has a true value for church and state, should avoid the extremes of *whig* for the sake of the former, and the extremes of tory on the account of the latter. *Swift*

Briefly, then, Cawdrey compiled his dictionary primarily as an aid to help students master certain foreign terminology which they found in their studies. Dr. Johnson set out to purify and fix the English language, discovered that it could not be done and gave us the first dictionary to approach the standards we expect in a dictionary today. We may classify Johnson's dictionary as being *prescriptive* in nature, a term that might well be used in discussing early lexicographers in general. The primary purpose of his dictionary was to set down rules to be followed, to tell people what language they ought to use.

Suggested Activities

1. Several students should read parts of Dr. Johnson's preface. According to Johnson, what were the problems that faced a lexicographer? Why did he set out to compile a dictionary? Why did he rely so heavily on Elizabethan writers for his illustrations? What

were Johnson's accomplishments? Why is he considered so important in English literature?

As students read several of the entries from Johnson's dictionary, they should note that Johnson's personality shows through on every page. They should also note that he frequently speaks in the first person in his entries. Students should contrast the prose style of Johnson with the prose style of modern lexicographers.

2. Johnson set out to purify the language. In making his dictionary, he was prescriptive. Students should define both prescriptive and descriptive. To understand the next step in this unit, students must know the differences between prescription and description.

3. Several students in each class should read Johnson's preface very carefully and report on it. Can they, on the basis of the information about language that they have, detect a few errors in Dr. Johnson's original thinking? For example, do they know that it is not possible to fix absolutely the meaning of words? Do they know that when Elizabethan writers used certain words all of the meanings of those words were not the same then as they are today? If students know this, do they realize that it would be impossible to fix an arbitrary cutoff date for the meanings of words?

4. Some students may be interested in the idea of the formation of an academy to prescribe usage. Several students might read about the French Academy and report on its organization and function. A different group of students may want to read about the idea of a formation of an English Academy and why this failed. Students will want to start with Jonathan Swift.

NOAH WEBSTER

Noah Webster compiled the first genuine American dictionary, which was also basically prescriptive in nature. The emphasis in Webster, however, was placed upon the reform of spelling. Felicia Lamport notes:

> Despite Webster's genius for the clear, concise definition, his dictionary was not notably well received during his life. His price was too steep for the public, his etymologies were too unscientific for the scholars, and his attempts to reform spelling met with such frenetic resistance that he was

forced to drop many of them. He succeeded in knocking the "u" out of such words as *honor* and *glamor,* in substituting *jail* for *gaol,* and in making many Americans so unsure of whether they were going to the theater or the theatre that many of them eventually took to the movies; but he failed to popularize *wimen* or to reduce our *tongue* to a reasonable *tung.* Benjamin Franklin, Theodore Roosevelt, and G. B. Shaw all tried in vain to simplify our spelling. It seems unlikely that our letters will ever achieve happy togetherness with our phonemes: fonetik speling stil haz implikashunz uv unejukatid absurditi.*

In *A History of The English Language,* Albert C. Baugh writes:

Accustomed for generations to dependence upon the mother country, the people settled in America imported most of their books and many of their ideas from Europe. It was a natural and entirely just recognition of the superior civilization of the Old World and the greatness of English literature and learning. But with political independence achieved, many of the colonists began to manifest a distaste for anything that seemed to perpetuate the former dependence. An ardent, sometimes belligerent patriotism sprang up, and among many people it became the order of the day to demand an American civilization as distinctive from that of Europe as were the political and social ideals which were being established in the New World.

No one expressed this attitude more vigorously than Noah Webster (1785–1843). . . . The culmination of his efforts to promote the idea of an American language was the publication of his *American Dictionary* in 1828. Residence for a year in England had somewhat tempered his opinion, but it is still fundamentally the same. In the preface to that work he gave final expression to his conviction: "It is not only important, but, in a degree necessary, that the people of this country, should have an *American Dictionary of the English Language*. For, although the body of the language is the same as in England, and it is desirable to perpetuate that sameness, yet some differences must exist. Language is the expression of ideas; and if the people of our country cannot preserve an identity of ideas, they cannot retain an identity of language. Now an identity of ideas depends materially upon a sameness of things or objects with which the people of the two countries are conversant. But in no two portions of the earth, remote from each other, can such identity be found. Even physical objects must be different. But the principal differ-

*Lamport, p. 68.

ences between the people of this country and of all others, arise from different forms of government, different laws, institutions and customs . . .; the institutions in this country which are new and peculiar, give rise to new trends, unknown to the people of England. . . . No person in this country will be satisfied with the English definitions of the words *congress, senate* and *assembly, court,* etc. for although these are words used in England, yet they are applied in this country to express ideas which they do not express in that country." It is not possible to dismiss this statement as an advertisement calculated to promote the sale of his book in competition with the English dictionaries of Johnson and others. He had held such a view long before the idea of a dictionary had taken shape in his mind. Webster was a patriot who carried his sentiment from questions of political and social organization over into matters of language. By stressing American usage and American pronunciation, by adopting a number of distinctive spellings, and especially by introducing quotations from American authors alongside of those from English literature, he contrived in large measure to justify the title of his work. If, after a hundred years, some are inclined to doubt the existence of anything so distinctive as an American language, his efforts, nevertheless, have left a permanent mark on the language of this country.*

Students should realize that few men have made such a great impact on American English as Noah Webster. He attempted to reform spelling and pronunciation and to show that American English is distinct from British English. His monumental *American Dictionary* was the forerunner of a number of dictionaries that followed, to a certain degree, his ideas. When an American thinks of a dictionary, he normally thinks of Webster.

The change from the prescriptive approach of the early lexicographers came with the publication of the *Oxford English Dictionary* in the twentieth century. Dean Richard Chenevix Trench of Westminster, the leader in compiling this 13-volume dictionary, felt that the dictionary should present an inventory of the language and not be a standard for usage. The lexicographer, in this case, should be "a literary historian, not a critic, and collect not merely the 'good' words but all words." The compilers of this dictionary

*Albert C. Baugh, *A History of the English Language,* 2nd ed. (New York: Appleton-Century-Crofts, 1957), pp. 424-28; reprinted by permission.

proposed to include "every word recorded in the English language since the middle of the thirteenth century, the obsolete as well as the current, giving the full biography of each, illustrating every change in form or meaning by a quotation, proving etymology by the word's history—not by ingenious conjecture, as Webster had done."*

Many students leave high school, and college for that matter, without fully realizing that words are their most important tool. Many students never stop to consider how certain words came into the language or how these words have histories that are sometimes very exciting to read. Many students, both in high school and in college, have never been introduced to the *Oxford New English Dictionary* or to the *Dictionary of American English.* Such an introduction—if it comes as an exciting experience and not merely as a classroom assignment—is usually unforgettable. Such an introduction also usually serves to make students aware of the changing character of words.

Suggested Activities

1. If *The Oxford English Dictionary* or *The Shorter Oxford Dictionary* is available in either the school or public library, the teacher may assign groups of students to look up the words that we recorded from the Cawdrey dictionary. (See pages 172-73.) Each group should copy the entries for one of the words and report its findings to the class.

2. This might be an advantageous time to pause and consider with students the relative merits of the two main approaches to lexicography which have been presented above. Students should be ready to discuss both approaches—prescriptive and descriptive—at this point. The following questions might serve to stimulate discussion.

a. Why do you think that compilers of dictionaries began to feel that treatment and analysis of words other than those derived from foreign languages were necessary?

*Lamport, p. 69.

b. Why did early lexicographers, when they decided to deal with words in the English language in general, adopt a prescriptive approach?
c. Why did Webster try to change the spelling of English words? Why didn't Webster or others who agreed with him succeed in their attempts to reform spelling completely? What would be the value of such a reform today? Are reforms still being attempted?
d. How do you feel about the change from a prescriptive approach to a descriptive approach to lexicography? What are the values of the descriptive approach? What aspects of a language would the descriptive approach contain that would not be found in the prescriptive approach? Do you feel that these aspects are important? Why? Can the descriptive approach present problems? List some of the problems that might result from such an approach.

WEBSTER'S THIRD NEW INTERNATIONAL DICTIONARY

Since its publication in 1961, *Webster's Third New International Dictionary* has been alternately hailed as a linguistic triumph and disparaged as an example of the abdication of the authority of the lexicographer. *Webster's Third* adopted the descriptive approach. And for its failure to label levels of usage as they have been labeled in the past, *The New York Times* in a review in 1961 claimed that "Webster's has, it is apparent, surrendered to the permissive school that has been busily extending its beachhead on English instruction in the schools. . . . It serves to reinforce the notion that good English is whatever is popular."*

Few books published in the last decade have been as controversial as *Webster's Third.* And few books published in this century have been as misunderstood as *Webster's Third.* To understand the position of the dictionary's editors, students should read the

**The New York Times,* October 12, 1961, reprinted in *Words, Words, and Words about Dictionaries,* p. 79.

preface written by the editor, Philip B. Gove. If several copies of *Webster's Third* are not available, the teacher may wish to read Dr. Gove's preface to the class.

Dr. Gove clearly outlines the position that the editors took in preparing *Webster's Third.* By comparing his preface with that of Dr. Johnson, students can recognize the changing function of the lexicographer. Students should also be able to see why the controversy over *Webster's Third* is still being waged since many persons would like to look upon a dictionary as a complete authority to which they can go to decide matters of usage.

To understand the controversy over *Webster's Third,* students should read several of the articles both pro and con. Two excellent paperback sources are Jack C. Gray, ed., *Words, Words, and Words about Dictionaries* (San Francisco: Chandler Publishing Co., 1963), and James Sledd and Wilma R. Ebbitt, *Dictionaries and* That *Dictionary* (Chicago: Scott, Foresman, 1962).

Suggested Activities

1. Groups of students should look up these words in *Webster's Third:* paradox, paragon, parallel, paraphrase, passion, pause, penalty, period, pioneer, popular. Students should compare the entries in *Webster's Third* with the same entries in other dictionaries.

2. Students should write a theme in which they describe the function of a lexicographer. They should outline the duties of a lexicographer, decide for themselves whether a lexicographer should be a prescriptivist or a descriptivist, and defend their position.

3. As a concluding activity, the teacher may wish to assign the class to a long-range project which was tried most successfully in New York schools and described at the 1964 National Council of Teachers of English Convention by Neil Postman, author of *Discovering Your Language.* Mr. Postman described how a class of students learned for themselves the functions of a lexicographer by compiling a dictionary of teen-agers' slang. The students first decided what kind of dictionary they wanted to compile. Selecting slang, they decided whether the slang expressions they would include in their dictionary would be limited to the current year or to

a period covering more than ten years. The students were divided into groups. Each group was assigned a specific task, including: the collection of terms to be included in the dictionary, the preparation of the pronunciation key, the preparation of sample sentences in which the terms are used, the listing of various parts of speech in which a word can be used, and the definition of the words. By compiling such a dictionary, students learn firsthand the problems that confront a lexicographer. They also learn a great deal about their language, and they demonstrate how much they actually know about language since they must perform all the duties of a lexicographer.

For such an activity, the teacher needs to explain, in great detail, what each group must do, and he must also give the groups enough time to compile the dictionary. This, for example, could be the assigned homework for four or five weeks. During this time the students would be working exclusively on the compilation of the dictionary, collecting oral samples of slang and recording them. They would learn to sift through hundreds of words that they hear every day to decide which are slang terms. They would have to decide for themselves how many functions these words can perform in sentences, how these words are to be pronounced, and what kind of pronunciation key they would need to prepare so that anyone picking up a copy of the dictionary could pronounce the words.

GRADE 12

Nothing Moves Without Translation

In their senior year students read great works of world literature in translation. To many of them, those works may seem, at first glance, to differ little from the novels, poems, and plays they read in American and English literature. After all, they might think, the stories and poems are in English, and even though the ideas may seem somewhat foreign, e.g., the religious experiences of *Siddhartha,* the language is not. Many students, then, apparently approach a work by Dostoevsky or Hesse as if it were written originally in English; they may never question that what they are reading is not an original work of art but a second work of art—the product of the translator. Therefore, we suggest that teachers present this unit early in the senior year before students begin reading world literature in translation.

Few students have probably ever considered how dependent they are on the translation of ideas from one language to another. E. S. Bates emphasized such dependence in this opening paragraph of his *Intertraffic: Studies in Translation,** from which this unit gets its title:

> Nothing moves without translation. Human experience is covered by three terms: emotions, techniques, thought. Emotions (fear, etc.) do not change in character: thought and techniques do. No change in thought or in techniques spreads without the help of translation, because, if it is to spread it has to spread from people to people, and therefore from language to language.

*E. S. Bates, *Intertraffic: Studies in Translation* (London: Jonathan Cape, 1943) p. 7.

The purposes of this unit are to acquaint students with both the problems and the importance of translation and to help them recognize that not all translations of the same works of literature are of equal value or, indeed, are truly representative of the original work. This is not to be construed as a negative unit—one that leads students to be highly skeptical of every major work they read in translation; on the contrary, its objectives are to make students aware of the problems of translation, of the superior works of art that able translators have given us despite those problems, and of the wide range of ideas and literature that we can enjoy because of the work of able translators.

J. M. Cohen, one of the translators of *Don Quixote,* emphasized the need for several translations of the same work in his *English Translators and Translations:**

> Every great book demands to be re-translated once in a century, to suit the change in standards and taste of new generations, which will differ radically from those of the past. The Elizabethan translations ignored their author's style and background, intent only on producing a book for their own times; the 18th century made the Classics conform to their own aristocratic standards, ruthlessly pruning away all complexities and digressions that might cause a gentleman's interest to flag; the Victorians conferred on all works alike the brown varnish of antiquarianism; and our own age, in its scientific devotion to simplicity and accuracy, demands plain versions which sacrifice sound to sense, and verbal idiosyncracy to the narrative virtues. It is this preference for plainness that has won our modern translations their wide public in countries where English is only the second language.

Perhaps Cohen's statement that "Every great book demands to be re-translated once in a century" can best be illustrated by having students examine several of the opening passages of the *Odyssey* as they have been translated by eighteenth century, by Victorian, and by modern translators. A careful study of each of these opening lines should make students aware of the problems of translation and should also illustrate how the translator, even

*J. M. Cohen, *English Translators and Translations* (London: Longmans, Green, 1962), pp. 9-10; reprinted by permission.

though he may be trying to remain faithful to the text, is, indeed, at times producing a new work of art. Students should also see how the translator attempts to use the idiom of his time for the convenience of his readers.

Alexander Pope's translation of the *Odyssey** appeared in 1725–26. In a postscript to the translation, Pope commented:

Homer, in his lowest narrations or speeches, is ever easy, flowing, copious, clear, and harmonious. He shows not less *invention*, in assembling the humbler, than the greater, thoughts and images; nor less *judgment*, in proportioning the style and the versification to these, than to the other. Let it be remembered, that the same genius that soared the highest, and from whom the greatest models of the *sublime* are derived, was also he who stooped the lowest, and gave to the simple *narrative* its utmost perfection. Which of these was the harder task to Homer himself, I cannot pretend to determine; but to his translator I can affirm (however unequal all his imitations must be) that of the latter has been much more difficult.

Whoever expects here the same pomp of verse, and the same ornaments of diction, as in the *Iliad*, he will, and he ought to be, disappointed. Were the original otherwise, it had been an offence against nature; and were the translation so, it were an offence against Homer, which is the same thing.

It must be allowed that there is a majesty and harmony in the Greek language which greatly contribute to elevate and support the narration. But I must also observe that this is an advantage grown upon the language since Homer's time; for things are removed from vulgarity by being out of use: and if the words we could find in any present language were equally sonorous or musical in themselves, they would still appear less poetical and uncommon than those of a dead one, from this only circumstance, of being in every man's mouth. I may add to this another disadvantage to a translator, from a different cause: Homer seems to have taken upon him the character of an historian, antiquary, divine, and professor of arts and sciences, as well as a poet. In one or other of these characters he descends into many particulars, which as a poet only perhaps he would have avoided. All these ought to be preserved by a faithful translator, who in some measure takes the place of Homer; and

*Rev. J. S. Watson, ed., *Homer's Odyssey Translated by Alexander Pope* (London: George Bell & Sons, 1900), pp. 395-97.

all that can be expected from him is to make them as poetical as the subject will bear. Many arts, therefore, are requisite to supply these disadvantages, in order to dignify and solemnize these plainer parts, which hardly admit of any poetical ornaments.

Some use has been made to this end of the style of Milton. A just and moderate mixture of old words may have an effect like the working old abbey stones into a building, which I have sometimes seen to give a kind of venerable air, and yet not destroy the neatness, elegance, and equality requisite to a new work: I mean without rendering it too unfamiliar, or remote from the present purity of writing, or from that ease and smoothness which ought always to accompany narration or dialogue. In reading a style judiciously antiquated, one finds a pleasure not unlike that of travelling on an old Roman way: but then the road must be as *good,* as the way is *ancient;* the style must be such in which we may evenly proceed, without being put to short stops by sudden abruptness, or puzzled by frequent turnings and transpositions. No man delights in furrows and stumbling-blocks: and let our love to antiquity be ever so great, a fine ruin is one thing, and a heap of rubbish another. The imitators of Milton, like most other imitators, are not *copies* but *caricatures* of their original; they are a hundred times more obsolete and cramp than he, and equally so in all places: whereas it should have been observed of Milton, that he is not lavish of his exotic words and phrases every where alike, but employs them much more where the subject is marvellous, vast, and strange, as in the scenes of heaven, hell, chaos, &c., than where it is turned to the natural or agreeable, as in the pictures of paradise, the loves of our first parents, the entertainments of angels, and the like. In general, this unusual style better serves to awaken our ideas in the descriptions and in the imaging and picturesque parts, than it agrees with the lower sort of narrations, the character of which is simplicity and purity. Milton has several of the latter, where we find not an antiquated, affected, or uncouth word, for some hundred lines together; as in his fifth book, the latter part of the eighth, the former of the tenth and eleventh books, and in the narration of Michael in the twelfth. I wonder indeed that he, who ventured (contrary to the practice of all other epic poets) to imitate Homer's lownesses in the narrative, should not also have copied his plainness and perspicuity in the dramatic parts: since in his speeches (where clearness above all is necessary) there is frequently such transposition and forced construction, that the very sense is not to be discovered without a second or third reading: and in this certainly he ought to be no example.

To preserve the true character of Homer's style in the present translation, great pains have been taken to be easy and natural. The chief merit I can pretend to, is, not to have been carried into a more plausible and figurative manner of writing, which would better have pleased all readers, but the judicious ones. My errors had been fewer, had each of those gentlemen who joined with me shown as much of the severity of a friend to me, as I did to them, in a strict animadversion and correction. What assistance I received from them, was made known in general to the public in the original proposals for this work, and the particulars are specified at the conclusion of it; to which I must add (to be punctually just) some part of the tenth and fifteenth books. The reader will now be too good a judge, how much the greater part of it, and consequently of its faults, is chargeable upon me alone. But this I can with integrity affirm, that I have bestowed as much time and pains upon the whole, as were consistent with the indispensable duties and cares of life, and with that wretched state of health which God has been pleased to make my portion. At the least, it is a pleasure to me to reflect, that I have introduced into our language this other work of the greatest and most ancient of poets, with some dignity; and I hope, with as little disadvantage as the *Iliad.* And if, after the unmerited success of that translation, any one will wonder why I would enterprise the *Odyssey;* I think it sufficient to say, that Homer himself did the same, or the world would never have seen it.

As students read these opening lines of the Pope translation, they should examine Pope's language, and the effect his verse form (couplets) has on the resulting translation. As students read each of the translations of the *Odyssey* presented here, they should note the differences in diction, in tone, and in style. Here are the opening lines of the Pope translation:

> The man, for wisdom's various arts renown'd,
> Long exercised in woes, O Muse! resound;
> Who, when his arms had wrought the destin'd fall
> Of sacred Troy, and raz'd her heaven-built wall,
> Wandering from clime to clime, observant stray'd,
> Their manners noted, and their states survey'd.
> On stormy seas unnumber'd toils he bore,
> Safe with his friends to gain his natal shore:
> Vain toils! their impious folly dar'd to prey

On herds devoted to the god of day;
The god vindictive doom'd them never more
(Ah, men unbless'd!) to touch that natal shore.
Oh, snatch some portion of these acts from fate,
Celestial Muse! and to our world relate.
Now at their native realms the Greeks arriv'd;
All who the wars of ten long years surviv'd,
And 'scap'd the perils of the gulfy main.
Ulysses, sole of all the victor train.
An exile from his dear paternal coast,
Deplor'd his absent queen and empire lost.
Calypso in her caves constrain'd his stay,
With sweet, reluctant, amorous delay:
In vain—for now the circling years disclose
The day predestin'd to reward his woes.
At length his Ithaca is given by fate,
Where yet new labours his arrival wait;
At length their rage the hostile powers restrain,
All but the ruthless monarch of the main.

In the preface to their translation of the *Odyssey,** which was published in 1879, S. H. Butcher and Andrew Lang wrote:

There can be then, it appears, no final English translation of Homer. In each there must be, in addition to what is Greek and eternal, the element of what is modern, personal, and fleeting. Thus we trust that there may be room for "the pale and far-off shadow of a prose translation," of which the aim is limited and humble. A prose translation cannot give the movement and the fire of a successful translation in verse; it only gathers, as it were, the crumbs which fall from the richer table, only tells the story, without the song. Yet to a prose translation is permitted, perhaps, that close adherence to the archaisms of the epic, which in verse become mere oddities. The double epithets, the recurring epithets of Homer, if rendered into verse, delay and puzzle the reader, as the Greek does not delay nor puzzle him. In prose he may endure them, or even care to study them as the survivals of a stage of taste, which is found in its prime in the sagas. These double and recurring epithets of Homer are a softer form of the quaint Northern periphrases,

*S. H. Butcher and Andrew Lang, translators, *The Odyssey of Homer* (New York: P. F. Collier, 1937) pp. vii-viii.

which make the sea the "swan's bath," gold, the "dragon's hoard," men, the "ring-givers," and so on. We do not know whether it is necessary to defend our choice of a somewhat antiquated prose. Homer has no ideas which cannot be expressed in words that are "old and plain," and to words that are old and plain, and, as a rule, to such terms as, being used by the Translators of the Bible, are still not unfamiliar, we have tried to restrict ourselves. It may be objected, that the employment of language which does not come spontaneously to the lips, is an affectation out of place in a version of the *Odyssey*. To this we may answer that the Greek Epic dialect, like the English of our Bible, was a thing of slow growth and composite nature, that it was never a spoken language, nor, except for certain poetical purposes, a written language. Thus the Biblical English seems as nearly analogous to the Epic Greek, as anything that our tongue has to offer.

Here are the first two paragraphs of the Butcher-Lang translation:

Tell me, Muse, of that man, so ready at need, who wandered far and wide, after he had sacked the sacred citadel of Troy, and many were the men whose towns he saw and whose mind he learnt, yea, and many the woes he suffered in his heart upon the deep, striving to win his own life and the return of his company. Nay, but even so he saved not his company, though he desired it sore. For through the blindness of their own hearts they perished, fools, who devoured the oxen of Helios Hyperion: but the god took from them their day of returning. Of these things, goddess, daughter of Zeus, whencesoever thou hast heard thereof, declare thou even unto us.

Now all the rest, as many as fled from sheer destruction, were at home, and had escaped both war and sea, but Odysseus only, craving for his wife and for his homeward path, the lady nymph Calypso held, that fair goddess, in her hollow caves, longing to have him for her lord. But when now the year had come in the courses of the seasons, wherein the gods had ordained that he should return home to Ithaca, not even there was he quit of labours, not even among his own; but all the gods had pity on him save Poseidon, who raged continually against godlike Odysseus, till he came to his own country. Howbeit Poseidon had now departed for the distant Ethiopians, the Ethiopians that are sundered in twain, the uttermost of men, abiding some where Hyperion sinks and some where he rises. There he looked to receive his hecatomb of bulls and rams, there he made merry sitting at the feast, but the other gods were gathered in the halls of Olympian Zeus. Then among them the father of gods and men began to speak, for he bethought him in his heart of noble Aegisthus, whom the son of Agamemnon, far-famed Orestes, slew.

In the twentieth century, T. E. Shaw, better known as T. E. Lawrence of "Lawrence of Arabia," wrote this "translator's note" in his translation of the *Odyssey* in 1935:*

The twenty-eighth English rendering of the *Odyssey* can hardly be a literary event, especially when it aims to be essentially a straightforward translation. Wherever choice offered between a poor and a rich word richness had it, to raise the colour. I have transposed: the order of metrical Greek being unlike plain English. Not that my English is plain enough. Wardour-Street Greek like the *Odyssey's* defies honest rendering. Also I have been free with moods and tenses; allowed myself to interchange adjective and adverb; and dodged our poverty of preposition, limitations of verb and pronominal vagueness by rearrangement. Still, syntax apart, this is a translation.

Unlike most translators, T. E. Shaw does not begin with the incantation to the muse; instead he begins with what is normally considered the second paragraph of Book One, which follows:

By now the other warriors, those that had escaped headlong ruin by sea or in battle, were safely home. Only Odysseus tarried, shut up by Lady Calypso, a nymph and very Goddess, in her hewn-out caves. She craved him for her bed-mate: while he was longing for his house and his wife. Of a truth the rolling seasons had at last brought up the year marked by the Gods for his return to Ithaca; but not even there among his loved things would he escape further conflict. Yet had all the Gods with lapse of time grown compassionate towards Odysseus—all but Poseidon, whose enmity flamed ever against him till he had reached his home. Poseidon, however, was for the moment far away among the Aethiopians, that last race of men, whose dispersion across the world's end is so broad that some of them can see the Sun-God rise while others see him set. Thither had Poseidon gone in the hope of burnt offerings, bulls and rams, by hundreds: and there he sat feasting merrily while the other Gods came together in the halls of Olympian Zeus. To them

*T. E. Shaw, trans., *The Odyssey of Homer* (New York: Oxford University Press, 1956), p. i.

the father of Gods and men began speech, for his breast teemed with thought of great Aegisthus, whom famous Orestes, the son of Agamemnon, had slain.

In his preface to his translation of the *Odyssey** in 1937, W. H. D. Rouse wrote:

This is the best story ever written, and it has been a favourite for three thousand years: not long since I heard its far-off echo in a caique on the Ægean Sea, when the skipper told me how St. Elias carried an oar on his shoulder until some one called it a winnowing-fan. Until lately it has been in the mind of every educated man; and it is a thousand pities that the new world should grow up without it. Indeed it enchants every man, lettered or unlettered, and every boy who hears it; but unless some one tells it by word of mouth, few are likely to hear it or read it unless they know Greek. They cannot get it from any existing translation, because all such are filled with affectations and attempts at poetic language which Homer himself is quite free from. Homer speaks naturally, and we must do the same. That is what I have tried to do in this book, and I ask that it may be judged simply as a story.

The prefatory note sets the tone for the translation that follows. Here are the first two paragraphs of the Rouse translation:

This is the story of a man, one who was never at a loss. He had travelled far in the world, after the sack of Troy, the virgin fortress; he saw many cities of men, and learnt their mind; he endured many troubles and hardships in the struggle to save his own life and to bring back his men safe to their homes. He did his best, but he could not save his companions. For they perished by their own madness, because they killed and ate the cattle of Hyperion the Sun-god, and the god took care that they should never see home again.

At the time when I begin, all the others who had not been killed in the war were at home, safe from the perils of battle and sea: but he was alone, longing to get home to his wife. He was kept prisoner by a witch, Calypso, a radiant creature, and herself one of the great family of gods, who wanted him to stay in her cave and be her husband. Well then, the seasons went rolling by, and when the year came, in which

*W. H. D. Rouse, trans., *The Odyssey* (New York: The New American Library, 1949), p. vii.

by the thread that fate spins for every man he was to return home to Ithaca, he had not yet got free of his troubles and come back to his own people. The gods were all sorry for him, except Poseidon, god of the sea, who bore a lasting grudge against him all the time until he returned.

Now, students should contrast the first two paragraphs of Rouse's *Odyssey* with the translation by E. V. Rieu,* made in 1946. In his preface, Rieu wrote:

> This version of the *Odyssey* is, in its intention at any rate, a genuine translation, not a paraphrase nor a retold tale. At the same time, and within the rules I have set myself, I have done my best to make Homer easy reading for those who are unfamiliar with the Greek world.

The first two paragraphs of the Rieu translation follow:

> The hero of the tale which I beg the Muse to help me tell is that resourceful man who roamed the wide world after he had sacked the holy citadel of Troy. He saw the cities of many peoples and he learnt their ways. He suffered many hardships on the high seas in his struggles to preserve his life and bring his comrades home. But he failed to save those comrades, in spite of all his efforts. It was their own sin that brought them to their doom, for in their folly they devoured the oxen of Hyperion the Sun, and the god saw to it that they should never return. This is the tale I pray the divine Muse to unfold to us. Begin it, goddess, at whatever point you will.
>
> All the survivors of the war had reached their homes by now and so put the perils of battle and the sea behind them. Odysseus alone was prevented from returning to the home and wife he longed for by that powerful goddess, the Nymph Calypso, who wished him to marry her, and kept him in her vaulted cave. Not even when the rolling seasons brought in the year which the gods had chosen for his homecoming to Ithaca was he clear of his troubles and safe among his friends. Yet all the gods were sorry for him, except Poseidon, who pursued the heroic Odysseus with relentless malice till the day when he reached his own country.

Homer, we are told, was the first and one of the most able of the Greek poets. Although the *Odyssey* is an epic poem, few trans-

*E. V. Rieu, trans., *The Odyssey* (London: Penguin Books, 1946), pp. 9, 25.

lators have attempted a poetic translation; instead, they have preferred to translate the *Odyssey* in prose. A recent translation by Robert Fitzgerald attempts to render into English poetry some of the flavor of the Greek poem. In an introduction to the Fitzgerald translation, Dudley Fitts wrote:

The *Odyssey* is a poem, and it was written in Greek—or sung in Greek, since the writing of it came late in its development. We are not sure what it sounded like to its Greek audience, since we have lost the pronunciation of the ancient language and are quite ignorant of the music that went with it. We can be sure of this much: that any translation of Homer, however brilliant, can only begin to suggest the beauty that the original hearers perceived in it. Even so, much of it can be carried over into our language. The story, of course, can be transmitted intact; and there are several reliable prose versions that give us these necessary bare bones. Bare bones is all that they are, though, and the task of the translator into verse is of a difficulty that would have unnerved Odysseus himself: to make a poem in Anglo-Irish-American (the term is Robert Fitzgerald's) that will move us today as the Greeks were moved in their time. Mr. Fitzgerald's own declaration of purpose is both humble and proud. "If you can grasp the situation and action rendered by the Greek poem," he writes, "every line of it, and by the living performer that it demands, and if you will not betray Homer with prose or poor verse, you may hope to make an equivalent that he himself would not disavow." In my opinion, he has more than succeeded: the Fitzgerald *Odyssey* seems to me to belong to the very small group of ideal translations in the English language, an independent and germinating work of art in its own right.*

Robert Fitzgerald begins his verse translation like this:

Sing in me, Muse, and through me tell the story
of that man skilled in all ways of contending,
the wanderer, harried for years on end,
after he plundered the stronghold
on the proud height of Troy.
He saw the townlands
and learned the minds of many distant men,
and weathered many bitter nights and days

*From Dudley Fitts' introduction to the Fitzgerald translation of *The Odyssey;* © 1965 by Houghton Mifflin Co. and reprinted by permission of the publisher.

in his deep heart at sea, while he fought only
to save his life, to bring his shipmates home.
But not by will nor valor could he save them,
for their own recklessness destroyed them all—
children and fools, they killed and feasted on
the cattle of Lord Hêlios, the Sun,
and he who moves all day through heaven
took from their eyes the dawn of their return.

Of these adventures, Muse, daughter of Zeus,
tell us in our time, lift the great song again.
Begin when all the rest who left behind them
headlong death in battle or at sea
had long ago returned, while he alone still hungered
for home and wife. Her ladyship Kalypso
clung to him in her sea-hollowed caves—
a nymph, immortal and most beautiful,
who craved him for her own.
And when long years and seasons
wheeling brought around that point of time
ordained for him to make his passage homeward,
trials and dangers, even so, attended him
even in Ithaka, near those he loved.
Yet all the gods had pitied Lord Odysseus,
all but Poseidon, raging cold and rough
against the brave king till he came ashore
at last on his own land.*

By comparing these translations, students should see that a translator, no matter how close he attempts to remain to the text, does not always translate a word or an idea in the same way a fellow translator does. Students should also recognize that one word does not necessarily translate exactly the same way into a different language; nor does one translator choose precisely the same word in translating from one language to the next.

Thus far we have let the translators point out the problems of translating the poetry of Homer. Now, instead of having students read the prefatory notes of translators on the difficulties of trans-

*From Homer, *The Odyssey*, translated by Robert Fitzgerald; © 1961 by Robert Fitzgerald and reprinted by permission of Doubleday & Co., Inc.

lating poetry, we offer them these two translations of Alexander Pushkin's "I Loved You Once":

I Loved You Once*

I loved you once; that love perchance may yet
Like hidden embers in my soul remain;
But let that not dismay you, and forget:
I would not want to bring you the least pain.

I loved in silence, loved you hopelessly,
Now with a timid, now a jealous, mind;
I loved so deeply, loved so tenderly—
God grant such love you in some other find!

I Loved You Once†

I loved you once, nor can this heart be quiet:
For it would seem that love still lingers here;
But do not you be further troubled by it;
I would in no wise hurt you, oh, my dear.

I loved you without hope, a mute offender;
What jealous pangs, what shy despairs I knew!
A love as deep as this, as true, as tender,
God grant another may yet offer you.

Students should compare those two translations of the same poem, and then they should contrast those translations with this verbatim translation with no attempt to reproduce poetic form:‡

*Ernest J. Simmons, ed., *Pushkin: A Laurel Reader* (New York: Dell, 1961), pp. 48-49. (Translation by Bernard Guilbert Guerney; © the Vanguard Press, Inc., reprinted by permission.)

†Avrahm Yarmolinsky, ed., *The Poems, Prose and Plays of Alexander Pushkin* (New York: Modern Library, 1936), p. 68. (This translation is by Babette Deutsch.)

‡This verbatim translation of "I Loved You Once" was made by Ashley Hastings, former instructor in the Intensive Language Training Center, Indiana University. In making this translation, with no attempt to create a second work of art in English, Mr. Hastings noted: (1) the Russian text makes it clear that the speaker is a male; (2) the distinction between the *familiar* "you" and the *formal* "you" is always observed in Russian. Pushkin uses the *formal* "you" in this poem, and the effect cannot be completely duplicated in modern English.

I Loved You Once

I you used to love; love still, perhaps,
In soul my has become extinct not quite.
But let it you more not trouble;
I not want to sadden you by anything.
I you used to love mutely, hopelessly;
Sometimes by shyness, sometimes by jealousy tormented;
I you used to love so sincerely, so tenderly,
As grant you God loved to be by another.

Striking differences in translations are not limited only to poetry. After comparing the first two paragraphs of these three translations of *Crime and Punishment*, students should decide which they think has the most merit, defend their position, and then decide which of the translations was written first, which second, and which third, and give their reasons for their answers.*

On a very hot evening at the beginning of July a young man left his little room at the top of a house in Carpenter Lane, went out into the street, and, as though unable to make up his mind, walked slowly in the direction of Kokushkin Bridge.

He was lucky to avoid a meeting with his landlady on the stairs. His little room under the very roof of a tall five-storey building was more like a cupboard than a living-room. His landlady, who also provided him with meals and looked after him, lived in a flat on the floor below. Every time he went out, he had to walk past her kitchen, the door of which was practically always open; and every time he walked past that door, the young man experienced a sickening sensation of terror which made him feel ashamed and pull a wry face. He was up to the neck in debt to his landlady and was afraid of meeting her.

On an exceptionally hot evening early in July a young man came out of the garret in which he lodged in S. Place and walked slowly, as though in hesitation, towards K. Bridge.

*Note to the teacher: The first is the 1951 translation by David Magarshack, *Dostoevsky's Crime and Punishment* (London: Penguin, 1951), p. 19; the second is the early twentieth century translation by Constance Garnett, *Crime and Punishment by Fyodor Dostoevsky* (New York: Dell, 1959), p. 23; and and third is the 1953 translation by Jessie Coulson, George Gabian, ed., *Crime and Punishment: The Coulson Translation, Backgrounds and Sources, Essays in Criticism* (New York: Norton, 1964), p. 1; all reprinted by permission.

He had successfully avoided meeting his landlady on the staircase. His garret was under the roof of a high, five-storied house and was more like a cupboard than a room. The landlady who provided him with garret, dinners, and attendance, lived on the floor below, and every time he went out he was obliged to pass her kitchen, the door of which invariably stood open. And each time he passed, the young man had a sick, frightened feeling, which made him scowl and feel ashamed. He was hopelessly in debt to his landlady, and was afraid of meeting her.

Towards the end of a sultry afternoon early in July a young man came out of his little room in Stolyarny Lane and turned slowly and somewhat irresolutely in the direction of Kamenny Bridge.

He had been lucky enough to escape an encounter with his landlady on the stairs. His little room, more like a cupboard than a place to live in, was tucked away under the roof of the high five-storied building. The landlady, who let him the room and provided him with dinners and service, occupied a flat on the floor below, and every time he went out he was forced to pass the door of her kitchen, which nearly always stood wide open. He went past each time with an uneasy, almost frightened, feeling that made him frown with shame. He was heavily in debt to his landlady and shrank from meeting her.

Now students should compare those translations with this verbatim translation by Ashley Hastings:*

In the beginning of July, in extraordinarily (excessively, uncommonly) hot time, towards evening, one young person went out from own small room (closet), which was renting from lodgers (tenants) in S_____ side-street (by-lane), onto street, and slowly, as if in indecision, set out (directed self) towards K_____n bridge.

He luckily (happily) avoided encounter with own landlady on stairway. Small room (closet) his fitted under very roofing of high five-storey house and resembled more clothes-press (cupboard) than apartment. Landlady his, by which he was renting this small room (closet) with dinner and servants (service, attendance), was lodged (placed, put up) by one storey lower, in separate apartment, and each time,

*This verbatim translation of the first two paragraphs of *Crime and Punishment* was made by Ashley Hastings, former instructor in the Intensive Language Training Center, Indiana University.

upon exit to street, to him certainly (by all means, without fail) necessary was to pass by landlady's kitchen, almost always wide open onto stairway. And each time young person, passing by, felt some kind of sickly and cowardly (timid, anxious, fearful) sensation (feeling, perception), of which was ashamed and from which knit brow. He was owing (due) entirely (all round) to landlady, and feared with her to encounter.

Thus far we have concentrated on the problems of translating specific poems or prose into English. Now we turn to the problems of translation presented by the very nature of a language that is difficult to translate into English since the translator must supply so many words. In the introduction to his *Wisdom of Confucius,** Lin Yutang summarizes the complex problems a translator faces.

A little more must be said about the present method of translation. I consider a translation in this case as indistinguishable from paraphrase, and believe that is the best and most satisfying method.

The situation is as follows: The ancient texts were extremely sparing in the use of words, owing of course to the method of inscribing on bamboo sticks. Most of the important ideas and characterizations that covered a whole class of qualities were expressed by monosyllabic words, and in accordance with the general nature of Chinese grammar, the meaning was indicated by syntax or word order rather than by the usual English connectives. Here are two extreme instances in the Chinese form: "Confucius completely-cut-off four—no idea—no must—no *ku*—no I"; "Language expressive only." It is clear that unless connectives are supplied by the translator, the translation would be practically unreadable. The extent to which connectives and amplifying phrases are allowable has by necessity to be left to the discretion of the translator, and for this the translator has no other guide than his own insight into the wisdom of Confucius, assisted, of course, by the commentators.

The first job is of course to determine the scope and connotation of a term in the general classical usage and secondly its particular meaning and shade of meaning in a given sentence. In the above instance of the word *ku,* this word meant several things: "strong," "stubborn," "persis-

*Lin Yutang, ed. and trans., *The Wisdom of Confucius* (New York: Random House, 1943), pp. 42-47; reprinted by permission of the publisher.

tence," "narrow-mindedness," "vulgarity," "limited in knowledge," and "sometimes also." From these different possible meanings, the translator has to make his choice. That is the terrible responsibility and the latitude given to the translator of ancient Chinese texts, and it is clear that a choice of a different word would alter the sense of the line completely. In this particular instance, I have translated the passage as follows: "Confucius denounced (or tried completely to avoid) four things: arbitrariness of opinion, dogmatism, narrow-mindedness and egotism." It is, of course, open to question whether the phrase "no must" should be translated as "don't insist upon a particular course," "don't be persistent," "don't be insistent," or "don't assume that you *must* be right (or don't be dogmatic)." Any of these translations involves as much paraphrasing as the others. In translating the phrase "no idea," I have paraphrased it as meaning "don't start out with preconceived notions," or "don't be arbitrary." That is a sense or shade of meaning won from a knowledge of the general meaning of the word "idea" in the Chinese language, and from an insight into the whole character of Confucius' conduct. But the mere use of the phrase "preconceived notion" or "arbitrariness of opinion" necessarily expresses what at best was only implied in the Chinese word "idea."

In the more fundamental concepts, like *li, jen, hsin, chung,* etc., I have adopted a method of provisionally translating these words in my mind by a certain English concept and going over the body of the texts containing these words to see which one would cover the field of meaning most adequately in the majority of cases, allowing, of course, several meanings for one word. Thus I have come to the conclusion that *li* usually translated as "ritual" or "ceremony" must be translated as "the principle of social order" in the general social philosophy of Confucius, and as "moral discipline" in certain passages dealing with personal conduct. I have also come to the conclusion that the translation of the word *jen* as "kindness," "charity," or "benevolence" is completely inadequate, but represents Confucius' ideal of the "true man," or the "great man," or the "most complete man." Likewise, *hsin* cannot be translated as "honesty" or "keeping one's promise," which latter quality Confucius rather despised and actually didn't care about in his own conduct. Sometimes *hsin* means a condition of "mutual confidence in the state," and sometimes it means "faithfulness."

In the actual act of translation, the translator is faced with two jobs after he has grasped the meaning of the sentence. First he is faced with the choice of one of a number of synonyms, and failure to get at the exact word would completely fail to render the meaning of the remark clear to the reader. I found it impossible, for instance, always to translate the word *teh* as "virtue" or "character," or the meaning would be hopelessly lost for the reader. Thus, Confucius said, "Thoroughbred, don't praise its strength, praise its *character*." The meaning becomes clear only when we translate it as follows: "In discussing a thoroughbred, you don't admire his strength, but admire his *temper*." Now come the same words for "character" in another passage: "Confucius said, 'One having virtue must have words; one having words not always has virtue.' " The meaning becomes clear only when we translate the word for "character" or "virtue" here by the word "soul" in the English language, as follows: "Confucius said, 'A man who has a beautiful soul always has some beautiful things to say, but a man who says beautiful things does not necessarily have a beautiful soul.' " Then again occurs the same word elsewhere in the phrase *teh yin;* to translate this as "virtuous sounds" may give the impression of scholarly fidelity, but merely hides the lack of understanding on the part of the scholarly translator that it means "*sacred* music." Again Confucius said, "Extravagant than not humble; frugal than *ku* (vulgar or stubborn, etc.). Rather than not humble, be *ku*." The connection between extravagance and lack of humility must be quite vague, and becomes clear only when we realize that people who live extravagantly are liable to be *conceited*. A fully clear and adequate translation must therefore involve a sure choice of words. I believe it should be translated as follows: "Confucius said, 'The people who live extravagantly are apt to be snobbish (or conceited), and the people who live simply are apt to be vulgar. I prefer vulgarity to snobbery (or I prefer the vulgar people to the snobs).' "

In the second place, the translator cannot avoid putting the thought in the more precise concepts of a modern language. The translator does not only have to supply the connectives, but has also to supply a finer definition of ideas, or the English will be extremely bald. Thus in the example given above, "Language expressive only," the modern translator is forced to translate it as follows: "Expressiveness is the only *principle* of language," or "expressiveness is the sole *concern*, or *aim*, or *principle*, of rhetoric." It is clear that there are at least a dozen ways of translating this line in any case. But it is inevitable that the translator would have to slip in a word like "principle" or "aim" or "concern" or "standard." It simply cannot be helped, if the translation is not to become unreadable.

The use of parentheses—In the resulting text of the translation, I have to resort to the use of parentheses after dodging the above difficulties. The parentheses are used for two purposes. First, for giving an alternate translation, usually indicated by "(or . . .)." The situation is often such that no one can be sure that a particular interpretation is the only correct one. Secondly, the parentheses are used exclusively for explanatory matter necessary to a clear understanding of the text without reference to footnotes. Without this device, such explanatory references could be endless. In this case, the parentheses are used with the sole purpose of supplying the minimum explanations to enable the reader to read a passage smoothly and understand its meaning with difficulty. The footnotes are then reserved for my comments and other reference material.

It would be fruitless to have students read more translators' notes at this stage or compare additional translations of the same work so long as they now recognize some of the problems of translation and realize that skilled translators give us not the original work of art but a second work—one of their own creation.

Suggested Activities

1. To fully appreciate the problems a translator must overcome, the teacher may wish to assign students who have had two or more years of any foreign language the task of translating one of the following passages into that language. After students have attempted their translations, they should discuss the difficulties involved, pointing to specific problems of diction, syntax, and meaning.

From "Politics and the English Language," by George Orwell: *

Most people who bother with the matter at all would admit that the English language is in a bad way, but it is generally assumed that we cannot by conscious action do anything about it. Our civilization is decadent and our language—so the argument runs—must inevitably share in the general collapse. It follows that any struggle against the abuse of language is a sentimental archaism, like preferring candles to electric light or hansom cabs to aeroplanes. Underneath this lies the half-conscious belief that language is a natural growth and not an instrument which we shape for our own purposes.

*In *Shooting an Elephant and Other Essays*, Harcourt, Brace and World, 1950.

Now, it is clear that the decline of a language must ultimately have political and economic causes: it is not due simply to the bad influence of this or that individual writer. But an effect can become a cause, reinforcing the original cause and producing the same effect in an intensified form, and so on indefinitely. A man may take to drink because he feels himself to be a failure, and then fail all the more completely because he drinks. It is rather the same thing that is happening to the English language. It becomes ugly and inaccurate because our thoughts are foolish, but the slovenliness of our language makes it easier for us to have foolish thoughts. The point is that the process is reversible. Modern English, especially written English, is full of bad habits which spread by imitation and which can be avoided if one is willing to take the necessary trouble. If one gets rid of these habits one can think more clearly, and to think clearly is a necessary first step towards political regeneration: so that the fight against bad English is not frivolous and is not the exclusive concern of professional writers.

From "The Most Dangerous Game," by Richard Connell: *

"Not at all," said the general. "I never joke about hunting. I needed a new animal. I found one. So I bought this island, built this house, and here I do my hunting. The island is perfect for my purposes—there are jungles with a maze of trails in them, hills, swamps—"

"But the animal, General Zaroff?"

"Oh," said the general, "it supplies me with the most exciting hunting in the world. No other hunting compares with it for an instant. Every day I hunt, and I never grow bored now, for I have a quarry with which I can match my wits."

Rainsford's bewilderment showed in his face.

"I wanted the ideal animal to hunt," explained the general. "So I said: 'What are the attributes of an ideal quarry?' And the answer was, of course: 'It must have courage, cunning, and, above all, it must be able to reason.' "

"But no animal can reason," objected Rainsford.

"My dear fellow," said the general, "there is one that can."

"But you can't mean—" gasped Rainsford.

"And why not?"

"I can't believe you are serious, General Zaroff. This is a grisly joke."

"Why should I not be serious? I am speaking of hunting."

"Hunting? Good God, General Zaroff, what you speak of is murder."

From *Huckleberry Finn,* by Mark Twain:

"Why, Huck, doan' de French people talk de same way we does?"

"No, Jim; you couldn't understand a word they said—not a single word."

"Well, now, I be ding-busted! How do dat come?"

"*I* don't know; but it's so. I got some of their jabber out of a book. S'pose a man was to come to you and say Polly-voo-franzy—what would you think?"

"I wouldn't think nuffn; I'd take en bust him over de head—dat is, if he warn't white. I wouldn't 'low no nigger to call me dat."

"Shucks, it ain't calling you anything. It's only saying, do you know how to talk French?"

"Well, den, why couldn't he say it?"

"Why, he *is* a-saying it. That's a Frenchmen's *way* of saying it."

"Well, it's a blame ridicklous way, en I doan' want to hear no mo' 'bout it. Dey ain't no sense in it."

"Looky here, Jim; does a cat talk like we do?"

"No, a cat don't."

"Well, does a cow?"

"No, a cow don't, nuther."

"Does a cat talk like a cow, or a cow talk like a cat?"

"No, dey don't."

"It's natural and right for 'em to talk different from each other, ain't it?"

"Course."

"And ain't it natural and right for a cat and a cow to talk different from *us*?"

"Why, mos' sholy it is."

"Well, then, why ain't it natural and right for a *Frenchman* to talk different from us? You answer me that."

"Is a cat a man, Huck?"

"No."

"Well, den, dey ain't no sense in a cat talkin' like a man. Is a cow a man?—er is a cow a cat?"

"No, she ain't either of them."

"Well, den, she ain't got no business to talk like either one er the yuther of 'em. Is a Frenchman a man?"

"Yes."

"*Well*, den! Dad blame it, why doan' he *talk* like a man? You answer me *dat*!"

Note: The teacher should limit the time students spend translating one of the above or any other prose passages. This assignment could easily take hours if a student attempted an excellent translation of any of the above passages; therefore, the teacher will want to limit translating time to 45 minutes.

2. As they studied this unit, students were told several times that a good translation of an excellent literary work is a second work of art. Students should select several translations of a novel or short story, read the translations carefully (in the case of a novel the reading of several chapters should suffice), and then write a theme in which they compare the translations and decide which is the better work of art. Each student should support his decision by comparing the "best" translation with the inferior ones.

A Selected Bibliography

Books of Essays

Each of these books will give the teacher invaluable help in preparing to teach the units presented in this volume.

Allen, Harold B., ed. *Readings in Applied Linguistics,* 2nd ed. New York: Appleton-Century-Crofts, 1964.

Anderson, Wallace L., and Norman C. Stageberg, eds. *Introductory Readings on Language.* New York: Holt, Rinehart and Winston, 1962.

Bailey, Dudley. *Introductory Language Essays.* New York: W. W. Norton, 1965.

Dean, Leonard F., and Kenneth G. Wilson, eds. *Essays on Language and Usage,* 2nd ed. New York: Oxford University Press, 1963.

Hogan, Robert F., ed. *The English Language in the School Program.* Champaign, Ill.: National Council of Teachers of English, 1966.

Kerr, Elizabeth M., and Ralph M. Aderman. *Aspects of American English.* New York: Harcourt, Brace & World, 1963.

Laird, Charlton, and Robert M. Gorrell. *English as Language: Backgrounds, Development, Usage.* New York: Harcourt, Brace & World, 1961.

Lee, Donald W. *English Language Reader.* New York: Dodd, Mead, 1964.

Sanderson, James L., and Walter K. Gordon. *Exposition and the English Language.* New York: Appleton-Century-Crofts, 1963.

American English and Dialects

Malstrom, Jean, and Annabel Ashley. *Dialects—USA.* Champaign, Ill.: National Council of Teachers of English, 1963.

Marckwardt, Albert H. *American English.* New York: Oxford University Press, 1958.

Mencken, H. L. *The American Language.* Abridged by Raven I. McDavid. New York: Alfred A. Knopf, 1963.

On Dictionaries

Gray, Jack C., ed. *Words, Words, and Words about Dictionaries.* San Francisco: Chandler Publishing, 1963.

Sledd, James, and Wilma R. Ebbitt, eds. *Dictionaries and* That *Dictionary.* Chicago: Scott, Foresman, 1962.

History of the Language

Baugh, Albert C. *A History of the English Language,* 2nd ed. New York: Appleton-Century-Crofts, 1957.

Bloomfield, Morton W., and Leonard Newmark. *A Linguistic Introduction to the History of English.* New York: Alfred A. Knopf, 1965.

Francis, W. Nelson. *The English Language—An Introduction.* New York: W. W. Norton, 1965.

Myers, L. M. *The Roots of Modern English.* Boston: Little, Brown, 1966.

Pyles, Thomas. *The Origin and Development of the English Language.* New York: Harcourt, Brace & World, 1964.

Robertson, Stuart, and Frederic G. Cassidy. *The Development of Modern English,* 2nd ed. Englewood Cliffs, N. J.: Prentice-Hall, 1953.

Schlauch, Margaret. *The Gift of Language.* New York: Dover Publications, 1955.

Semantics

Chase, Stuart. *Power of Words.* New York: Harcourt, Brace, 1954.

———. *The Tyranny of Words.* New York: Harcourt, Brace, 1938. (Reissued as a Harvest paperback.)

Hayakawa, S. I., ed. *The Use and Misuse of Language.* Greenwich, Conn.: Fawcett Publications, 1962.

Salomon, Louis B. *Semantics and Common Sense.* New York: Holt, Rinehart and Winston, 1966.

Word Formation and Word Change

Barber, Charles. *Linguistic Change in Present-Day English.* University, Ala.: University of Alabama Press, 1964.

Greenough, James Bradstreet, and George Lyman Kittredge. *Words and Their Ways in English Speech.* New York: Macmillan, 1900. (Reissued as a Beacon paperback.)

Groom, Bernard. *A Short History of English Words.* New York: St. Martin's Press, 1965.

Laird, Helene and Charlton. *The Tree of Language*. Cleveland: World Publishing, 1957.

Pyles, Thomas. *Words & Ways of American English*. New York: Random House, 1952.

Serjeantson, Mary S. *A History of Foreign Words in English*. New York: E. P. Dutton, 1936.

Usage

Bryant, Margaret M. *Current American Usage*. New York: Funk & Wagnalls, 1962.

Evans, Bergen and Cornelia. *A Dictionary of Contemporary American Usage*. New York: Random House, 1957.

Fowler, H. W. *A Dictionary of Modern English Usage*, 2nd ed. Revised by Sir Ernest Gowers. New York: Oxford University Press, 1965.

Appendix A

On Usage

The tradition of a prescriptive usage is still so firmly impressed on the lay mind that even now the popular stereotype of the English teacher contains elements of the grim-visaged guardian of a citadel dedicated to "good English," constantly on the alert to repel the assaults of the forces of "bad English." More sophisticated manifestations of this misconception caused otherwise intelligent critics like Jacques Barzun and Dwight MacDonald to carry on as they did after the publication of *Webster's Third* and its alleged offenses against the doctrine of correctness.

Actually, working English teachers are much more ready than the rest of the population to accept the view, in Professor Robert Pooley's words, "that usage is what happens in language, and that many factors contribute to the formation of standards by which patterns of usage are to be judged." Thus it hardly seems necessary to belabor this point further in a volume addressed to teachers of English.

In grade ten a teacher may wish to introduce students to such volumes as Margaret Bryant's *Current American Usage* and Bergen and Cornelia Evans' *A Dictionary of Contemporary American Usage*. Some students will also be interested and amused on dipping into the classic H. W. Fowler's *Modern English Usage*, in both the original and the revised editions if both are available.

The following essay by Professor Pooley states very well a sensible modern attitude toward usage.

Usage—Standard vs. Substandard*

Robert C. Pooley

PROFESSOR OF ENGLISH

DIRECTOR OF THE ENGLISH CURRICULUM STUDY CENTER

UNIVERSITY OF WISCONSIN

Since we address ourselves today to the study of English usage, it will be well to start with a consideration of what we mean by usage. The term is subject to a good deal of confusion, especially in relation to the term "grammar," and, indeed, its right to be used at all is challenged. In an article appearing in the *Wisconsin English Journal* of April, 1962, Professor Robert Williams says, " 'Usage' is one of the most abused words in the English teacher's vocabulary . . .; it is time that we looked into the linguists' vocabulary for a new word which would be more honest and descriptive." If we take Dr. Williams literally, the word "usage" is less than satisfactorily honest and descriptive. The word he supplies is "dialect." We are, he says, to avoid "usage" and speak of the "dialect of the privileged or educated classes." I do not accept such a limitation of terms.

The Meanings of Usage

I am impelled first to point out to Dr. Williams that within the compass of any dialect there are many optional choices of form, word, and construction. I may speak of the room's dimensions or the dimensions of the room. Both are "standard English" (the term Dr. Williams prefers) but my choice is a matter of usage. Still speaking standard English, I may say, "May I take your car?" or "Can I take your car?" My choice of *can* or *may* is usage within the dialect. Again in standard English I may inquire, "From whom is it?" or more frequently, "Who is it from?" My selection is again a matter of usage. If these acts of choice cannot be described as usage, then what term does apply? Truly they are not "dialect," for any possible definition of "the dialect of the privileged or

*From *The English Language in the School Program,* Robert Hogan, ed. (Champaign, Ill.: The National Council of Teachers of English, 1966); reprinted by permission of the National Council of Teachers of English.

educated classes" would have to include these and many other alternatives.

It is true indeed that "usage" is also employed as the term to describe the choice between "he done it good" and "he did it well." It is also true that the speaker of "he done it good" and similar constructions speaks a dialect different from that of the one who habitually says, "He did it well." Despite the possible confusion between the two levels of applications of the word "usage," the word is too valuable to suppress. I query whether verbicide is any more respectable than homicide.

A review of the writings of modern linguists reveals no avoidance of the word "usage," and its appearance as a major subject in this institute is further evidence of its acceptability. On one point I would agree with Dr. Williams, namely that the term "usage" must not be considered a synonym for "correctness" nor must it be used to mean only acceptable usage. No one could deny that it has been so abused. But the term is broader than that.

Some years ago I defined usage in a publication (Robert C. Pooley, *Teaching English Grammar,* 1957, p. 106) and I am willing to stand upon this definition still. "Usage is to grammar as etiquette is to behavior. Behavior simply notes what people do; etiquette sets a stamp of approval or disapproval upon actions, or sets up standards to guide actions. The specific business of usage, therefore, is to determine what choices and discriminations are made in the use of English, and then to analyze the forces, social and psychological, which determine the choices. In practical terms, usage is the study which notes the variety of choices made in the use of English, observes the standards set up by such choices or created to influence such choices, and attempts to evaluate the validity of such standards."

Attitudes Toward Usage

The teaching implications of this definition should be reasonably clear. First of all, we note that what we mean by usage is the way people use language: "I ain't got no pencil" is as much a phenomenon of usage as "I don't have a pencil." But second, usage is concerned with the choice between these locutions. The person who says "I don't have a pencil" does so for reasons of habit, choice, or sensibility to the social effects of word patterns. The one who says "I ain't got no pencil" does so from exposure to certain patterns of language use and habits derived therefrom, and is lacking in, or indifferent to, sensitivity to the effects of word patterns in various social situations. Correction of the second speaker is certainly not a matter of punishment or shame, nor is it a matter of grammar, in the sense of studying the structures involved. Actually communication is equally clear in either locution. Correction then becomes a matter of awakening sensitivities to social expectation, similar in approach to teaching a little boy to remove his hat in church, and a little girl to say "please" and "thank you." Usage, therefore, can never be concerned with absolutes. No element of language in use can be said to be entirely right or entirely wrong. Each element has to be evaluated in its linguistic context, with regard to a number of variables, and even after this evaluation is made, no clear right and wrong will appear. Rather there will be a sense of degree of appropriateness, with allowance for a tolerable range of deviations. What is the difference between "I shall be pleased to join you," and "Sure, count me in"? There is no right or wrong, good or bad, here; not even a decision of appropriateness until all the contextual and social factors have been weighed. Ultimately it will be seen that in some situations the second is preferable. The person who can use either pattern in its appropriate place is the person skilled in English usage, the goal toward which our instruction is directed.

The prescriptive view of usage, in which certain patterns are labelled *wrong* and other patterns are labelled *right* without regard to context and social setting, is still evidenced in many school books and courses of study and especially in popular views about language. The large number of well-educated people who say "Between you and I" do so with conscious pride in avoiding the error of "you and me" to which they have attached the label "wrong" as a result of overzealous teachers in early school years. Today a new use of *as* as a preposition is developing from the overteaching of the avoidance of *like*. I see on students' papers now such sentences as, "My mother, as other mothers, would not let me out at night," or "Most of my friends, as John, like the movies." This is clearly a replacement of the preposition *like* by the conjunction *as*. Why? Because prescriptive teachers have so firmly set the stamp of *wrong* on *like* that students avoid it even in its historically proper use. It is not *like* that is wrong, but the teachers who label it so.

We need not wonder at the persistence of the prescriptive view of usage. After all, it developed in the eighteenth century, became firmly established in the nineteenth, dictated the attitudes of textbooks of the early twentieth century, and is still present in many current texts. Only in the late twenties of this century was a clear alternative presented and defended by such leaders as Sterling Andrews Leonard and Charles C.

Fries. They and their followers have established what may be called the observational or relative theory of English usage, namely, that usage is what happens in language, and that many factors contribute to the formation of standards by which patterns of usage are to be judged. It was my privilege as a member of this group to write a definition of good English in these terms in 1931, a definition which was adopted by the National Council of Teachers of English and is now frequently cited without reference to its source. Allow me to repeat it now, as it contains the elements which describe the attitude toward usage I would like to make as my contribution to [the present discussion of language]. . . . "Good English is that form of speech which is appropriate to the purpose of the speaker, true to the language as it is, and comfortable to speaker and listener. It is the product of custom, neither cramped by rule nor freed from all restaint; it is never fixed, but changes with the organic life of the language."

In the Classroom

The question raised by a good many teachers at this point is, "How can I teach students to speak and write correctly if usage is relative and nothing is really right or wrong?" This is a practical question and I shall try to give a practical answer. When the baby in the house says "Me want milk" or "Me want a cookie," the conscientious mother, before providing milk or cookie, helps the infant to say, "I want milk," "I want a cookie." The repetition of these expected patterns aids the child to form the habit of using them. He is more likely to establish these patterns if his parents themselves are accurate and he is gently corrected each time he errs. The teaching of usage in elementary schools should be as much along these lines as possible: a teacher who is himself accurate in socially acceptable usage, and who gently corrects his students when they deviate from accepted forms. In junior and senior high schools this method of ear-training in usage is better than any other, for to a degree beyond common belief, the errors in usage in the written work of students are the reflection of unconsciously retained speech patterns.

The establishment of a curriculum of usage teaching is founded on the application of two simple principles: (1) How much social penalty does the usage item bear? and (2) how frequent is its use? At any grade the basic curriculum in usage consists of those items which carry the heaviest social penalty and are most frequent in use. Items which occur rarely and carry slight social penalty can be postponed or omitted. It is therefore possible to make lists at each grade level, from observation of the spoken and written English of the children, of the items of usage most in need of instruction, and of those items which may be left untaught at that grade. Obviously the needs of individual children will differ widely, but the objective is to bring the class as a group to the minimum acceptable level in all spoken and written work.

Without any violation of the principles of frequency and social penalty we can set a standard of minimum acceptability, provided we stand ready to alter it in accordance with changes which are taking place all the time in English usage. I offer the following list as an example:

1. The elimination of all baby-talk and "cute" expressions.
2. The correct uses in speech and writing of *I, me, he, him, she, her, they, them.* (Exception, *it's me.*)
3. The correct uses of *is, are, was, were* with respect to number and tense.
4. Correct past tenses of common irregular verbs such as *saw, gave, took, brought, bought, stuck.*
5. Correct use of past participles of the same verbs and similar verbs after auxiliaries.
6. Elimination of the double negative: *we don't have no apples,* etc.
7. Elimination of analogical forms: *ain't, hisn, hern, ourn, theirselves,* etc.
8. Correct use of possessive pronouns: *my, mine, his, hers, theirs, ours.*
9. Mastery of the distinction between *its,* possessive pronoun; *it's, it is.*
10. Placement of *have* or its phonetic reduction to *v* before *I* and a past participle.
11. Elimination of *them* as a demonstrative pronoun.
12. Elimination of *this here* and *that there.*
13. Mastery of use of *a* and *an* as articles.
14. Correct use of personal pronouns in compound constructions: as subject (Mary and *I*), as object (Mary and *me*), as object of preposition (to Mary and *me*).
15. The use of *we* before an appositional noun when subject; *us,* when object.
16. Correct number agreement with the phrases *there is, there are, there was, there were.*
17. Elimination of *he don't, she don't, it don't.*

18. Elimination of *learn* for *teach, leave* for *let.*
19. Elimination of pleonastic subjects: *my brother he; my mother she; that fellow he.*
20. Proper agreement in number with antecedent pronouns *one* and *anyone, everyone, each, no one.* With *everybody* and *none* some tolerance of number seems acceptable now.
21. The use of *who* and *whom* as reference to persons. (But note, *Who did he give it to?* is tolerated in all but very formal situations. In the latter, *To whom did he give it?* is preferable.)
22. Accurate use of *said* in reporting the words of a speaker in the past.
23. Correction of *lay down* to *lie down.*
24. The distinction between *good* as adjective and *well* as adverb, e.g., He spoke *well.*
25. Elimination of *can't hardly, all the farther* (for *as far as*) and *Where is he (she, it) at?*

This list of twenty-five kinds of corrections to make constitutes a very specific standard of current English usage for today and the next few years. Some elements in it may require modification within ten years, some possibly earlier. Conspicuous by their absence are these items which were on the usage lists by which many of us were taught, which survive today in the less enlightened textbooks:

1. Any distinction between *shall* and *will.*
2. Any reference to the split infinitive.
3. Elimination of *like* as a conjunction.
4. Objection to the phrase "different than."
5. Objection to "He is one of those boys who *is.* . . ."
6. Objection to "the reason . . . is because. . . ."
7. Objection to *myself* as a polite substitute for *I,* as in "I understand you will meet Mrs. Jones and myself at the station."
8. Insistence upon the possessive case standing before a gerund.

These items and many others like them will still remain cautionary matter left to the teacher's discretion. In evaluating the writing of a superior student I would certainly call these distinctions to his attention and point out to him the value of observing them. But this is a very different matter from setting a basic usage standard to be maintained. I think it is fair to say that the items I have listed in the basic table lie outside the tolerable limits of acceptable, current, informal usage; those I have omitted from the basic table are tolerated at least, and in some instances are in very general use.

Disputed Usage: Making Decisions

We come now to the interesting matter of divided and debatable usage. These are the items of language use which are widely current, which are often heard in public speech and frequently appear in print, yet are condemned by many textbooks and are disliked by conservative teachers, editors, and other language-conscious people. First, let it be granted that anyone may say, "I don't like that word and I won't use it." This is certainly a right which any individual may exercise. But if he says, "I don't like that word and therefore *you* are wrong, ignorant, or malicious when you use it," we have another matter. It is concerning these matters that the good judgment of teachers and editors is called into play. I shall illustrate some cases of disputed usage to show how judgments may be formed.

1. *Proven* as participle of prove. Condemned as an illogical formation. Now fully acceptable.
2. Misplaced *only*. Condemned in many grammar books in the construction, "I *only* had five dollars." Has a long literary history and is now fully acceptable.
3. *Data* as singular. "I had a hard time collecting this *data*." Condemned in the singular because it is a Latin plural. Now widely used in high level journals. Has become a singular collective noun.
4. The *reason* I came late *is because* I wanted to. This construction still evokes howls of rage from some professors. It is condemned by practically all handbooks. Yet it has a long and honorable history and is used by reputable writers today. Why condemn it?

There is a fair and practical test to apply to items of this kind. It is a threefold test in answer to these questions: (a) Is the item in reasonably common use today? (b) Does it have a continuous history of use in English for a century or more? (c) Was it used in the past, and is it used today, by writers of acknowledged reputation? If the answers to these questions are affirmative, then the item is unquestionably in good use, no matter what grammarians and critics may say.

Some of you may have the question in mind, "What about preparation for college? I may allow these debatable usages, but my students, and I also, will be condemned for permitting these errors to go unchecked." This is another practical question, and it has a practical answer. Suppose your student writes, "The reason why Hamlet didn't kill the king immediately was because he was not sure of his guilt." You may in all fairness write in the margin, "Avoid this construction." Do not treat it as an error, but caution the student that college professors and other well-informed persons will take exception to it, and to play safe he had better avoid it.

An Outlook

In conclusion, allow me to suggest a frame of mind toward all usage instruction. Our wonderful English language has enormous resources and is especially rich in the varieties of ways in which the same idea may be expressed. Stimulate your students to explore these varieties of expression to come up with as many different forms as will adequately express the same meaning. In the course of these explorations some patterns will be formal and literary, some easy and colloquial, and some perhaps substandard, or socially subject to penalty. Assist your students to note these varieties of level of expression, not as matters of right and wrong, but as combinations of words establishing a *tone* to the communication. Students can readily discriminate between—"Please leave the room," "Go, now," "Beat it, kid," "Scram." Each utterance has its appropriate place, each conveys the same idea, and each establishes a tone. With such practice students can gain a feeling for words and phrases as carrying not only meaning but the quality of social appropriateness, or tone, as well. The establishment of such sensitivities to the shades of language use is the ideal of instruction in usage. In society, the well-mannered person is one who is sensitive to all aspects of a situation and behaves in a way most appropriate to each situation, formal when it is proper, easy where desirable, familiar where acceptable. English usage is exactly parallel: to say the right thing in the appropriate manner in a suitable tone of expression is the ideal for which we are striving.

A final practical question calls for an answer. It is, "Where do I find help in making judgments in matters of usage about which I am not sure?" One answer is, of course, to develop the habit of observing language usage and spotting the particular item as it occurs in speech and writing. This is the best foundation of usage judgments, and it is one which can be successfully passed on to students, to set them the task of finding evidence for usage decisions in the speech and writing that they observe. For somewhat quicker returns, recent dictionaries and handbooks of usage are the answer. I recommend the latest and most reliable guide to English usage, entitled *Current American Usage, How Americans Say It and Write It,* by Margaret M. Bryant, published by Funk and Wagnalls Co., New York, 1962. Margaret Bryant for years has been writing the usage column in the *English Journal* and in this book combines her rich experience with the contributions of many other investigators to form a useful handbook. Somewhat more literary in flavor is *A Dictionary of Contemporary American Usage* by Bergen and Cornelia Evans, published by Random House, New York, 1957. The authors say, "This dictionary . . . is designed for people who speak standard English but are uncertain about some details. It attempts to list the questions that most people ask, or should ask, about what is now good practice and to give the best answers available." On the whole it does these things very well; I refer you to the article on the word *like* as an example. The materials for making sound judgments in matters of usage are reliable and readily available. What is now most needed is the attitude of mind on the part of teachers and the public directed toward seeking information and using it, in the place of repeating worn-out rules which were perhaps once valid, but are superseded by the normal changes of a living language.

Appendix B

A Verse from the Book of Ruth

To illustrate changes in the English language from Middle English to the present, a teacher may wish to show students the following versions of one verse from the Book of Ruth. The first is John Wycliffe's translation in 1382 of the Latin Vulgate of St. Jerome. The second is from the first completed Bible in English which Miles Coverdale published in Zurich in 1535. The third is from the so-called Matthew's Bible, which was published in 1537 and which was probably printed in Antwerp. It is purported to be the work of "Thomas Matthew," which is believed to be the pseudonym of John Rogers, a friend of William Tyndale, who suffered martyrdom for translating the Bible into a "vulgar tongue." The fourth is from the so-called Great Bible, the first English Bible formally authorized for use in churches. Called the Great Bible because of its size, this translation is a revision by Coverdale of Matthew's Bible. The fifth is from the Geneva Bible, published in 1560 by Protestant refugees who fled to the Continent during the reign of the Catholic Queen Mary. The first illustrated Bible, it is popularly known as "the Breeches Bible" from the use of that word in the translation of Genesis 3:7. The sixth is from the Rheims, or Douai Bible, which was translated by the English College at Douai from the Latin Vulgate and published at Rheims in 1609. The seventh is from the King James Version, published in 1611 as the "authorized version," based on the style and method of Tyndale. The eighth is from *The Dartmouth Bible,* which was copyrighted in 1950. The ninth is from *The Oxford Annotated Bible with the Apocrypha,* which was copyrighted in 1952.

Wycliffe (1382)

> . . . she seide to hem, Goth into the hows of youre moder; the Lord do with you mercy, as ye han do with the deed, and with me.

Coverdale (1535)

. . . she sayde vnto both hir sonnes wyues: Go youre waye, & turne backe ether of you to hir mothers house; the Lorde shewe mercy upon you, as ye haue done on them yt are deed & on me.

Matthew's Bible (1537)

Noemi sayde vnto her two daughters in lawe: go & return eche of you unto youre mothers house: the Lorde deale as kyndlye with you/ as ye haue dealt wyth the deed & with me.

The Great Bible (1539)

And Naomi sayde vnto her two daughters in lawe: go and returne eche of you vnto your mothers house: and the Lord deale as kyndlye with you, as ye haue dealt with ye deed, and with me.

The Geneva Bible (1560)

Then Naomi said vnto her two daughters in lawe, Go returne eche of you vnto her owne mothers house: ye Lord shewe fauour vnto you, as ye haue done with the dead, and with me.

The Rheims-Douai (1609)

. . . she said to them: Goe into your mothers house, our Lord doe mercie with you, as you haue done with the dead and with me.

The King James Version (1611)

And Naomi said vnto her two daughters in law, Goe, returne each to her mothers house: the Lord deale kindly with you, as ye haue dealt with the dead, and with me.

The Dartmouth Bible (1950)

And Naomi said unto her two daughters-in-law, Go, return each to her mother's house: the Lord deal kindly with you, as ye have dealt with the dead, and with me.

The Oxford Annotated Bible with the Apocrypha (1952)

But Naomi said to her two daughters-in-law, "Go, return each of you to her mother's house. May the Lord deal kindly with you, as you have dealt with the dead and with me."

Appendix C

On Preparing a Unit on the History of the English Language

As we pointed out in "A Suggestion for a Unit on the History of the English Language," we had not planned to prepare a separate teaching unit on the history of English; instead, we reprint here J. N. Hook and E. G. Mathews' "Changes in the English Language," from their *Modern American Grammar and Usage* (New York: Ronald Press, 1956). We have also included some samples of language change in Appendix B, and we have listed a short bibliography for the teacher in "A Suggestion for a Unit on the History of the English Language."

Changes in the English Language*

J. N. Hook and E. G. Mathews

Examples of Old English

At first glance a selection from Old English appears to be in a foreign tongue. More careful scrutiny reveals that some of the words are almost the same as ours, that others have undergone considerable change, and that still others have vanished. Modern English has lost some of the grammatical constructions that formerly existed.

*From J. N. Hook and E. G. Mathews, *Modern American Grammar and Usage;* copyright © 1956, The Ronald Press Company, New York.

Here is the Lord's Prayer in the Old English (West Saxon) version of approximately a thousand years ago:

Fæder ūre þu þe eart on heofonum sī þīn nama gehālgod. Tō becume þīn rīce. Gewurþe ðīn willa on eorðan swā swā on heofonum. Ūrne gedæghwāmlīcan hlāf syle ūs tō dæg. And forgyf ūs ūre gyltas swā swā we forgyfað ūrum gyltendum. And ne gelǣd þū ūs on costnunge ac ālȳs ūs of yfele. Sōþlīce.

Detailed comment on these few lines would fill many pages; here we shall look at only a few words and constructions. Word order was much less fixed in Old English than it is today: notice the Old English forms of *Father our* and *be thy name hallowed* as examples. Case endings are used with nouns, as in *heofonum* (heaven), *eorðan* (earth), *gyltas* (debts), and *gyltendum* (debtors). Adjectives had to agree in case, number, and gender with their nouns: *ūre, ūrne,* and *ūrum* are today simply *our.* The word *rīce* is now translated as *kingdom,* but it is actually a cognate of *Reich* which survives in German. The symbols þ (thorn) and ð (eth) were both used for *th.* Since Old English times some words have been reduced in the number of syllables: gehālgod (hallowed), gedæghwāmlīcan (daily), forgyfað (forgive). Spelling was much more phonetic than that of today; in general, there were no silent letters. In pronunciation, vowel sounds were more similar to those found in modern continental languages than to those in Modern English; and consonant sounds were not much different from those of Modern English. Punctuation marks other than periods were rare, and even periods were not used very systematically by the scribes.

As a second example consider the following lines from the epic poem *Beowulf.* The manuscript is generally believed to be in the hand of a scribe of the late tenth century. This passage tells of King Hrothgar's sorrow over the killing of his friend and follower by a hideous demon:

Hrothgar spoke — defender of the Scyldings
Hrōðgār maþelode — helm Scyldinga:

Not ask thou about happiness. — Sorrow is renewed
Ne frīn þŭ ǣfter sǣlum — Sorh is genīwod

of the Danes for the people — Dead is Aeschere
Denigea lēodum. — Dead is Æschere

Irmenlaf's
Yrmenlāfes

elder brother
yldra brōþor

my confidant
mīn rūnwita

and my counselor
ond mīn rǣdbora

shoulder-companion
eaxlgestealla

when we in battle
ðonne wē on orlege

head protected
hafelan weredon

when clashed together troops
ðonne hniton fēþan

boar-helmets struck
eoferas cnysedan

Such should hero be
Swylc scolde eorl wesan

nobleman good from old times
ǣþeling ǣrgōd

as Aeschere was
swylc Æschere wǣs.

Even the literal translation of this passage does not seem very clear today. A more free translation might go like this: "Hrothgar, the defender of the Scyldings, spoke: 'Do not ask about happiness, because sorrow has come again to the Danish people. Aeschere is dead. He was Irmenlaf's older brother and my confidant and counselor. He stood at my shoulder when in battle we protected our heads and hewed the boar-helmets as troops clashed. Every hero should be as Aeschere was, a nobleman good to recall from old times.' "

Notice, in comparing these translations, how word order has changed. Observe also how large a proportion of the Old English words have dropped out of the language. Some of them remain, however, in recognizable form: *helm* is a cousin of our *helmets, æfter* is *after, dēad* has changed only its pronunciation, *yldra broþor* is still recognizable, *þonne* has become *then, wē* and *in* are unchanged in spelling, *scolde* is similar to *should, eorl* has altered its meaning and become *earl, ǣrgōd* contains the ancestors of *ere* and *good*, and *wǣs* is obviously *was.*

Inflectional endings are much more important in Old English than in Modern; for example, *Scyldinga* (genitive plural) requires here a three-word translation, *of the Scyldings;* and *lēodum* also requires either a three-word translation, *for* (or *to*) *the people,* or a revised word order. The endings of such words as *rūnwita, fēþan,* and *eoferas* help, along with the context, to show whether the word is to be regarded as a subject or an object. In Modern English we depend more upon word order and upon "function words" such as prepositions than we do upon inflections.

Old English grammar may be made a subject for special study. Here you have seen illustrated only a few of its most obvious characteristics.

Example of Middle English

When we move forward about four hundred years, from the late tenth to the late fourteenth century, we see that the language has changed rather drastically. Here are lines from the Prologue of Chaucer's *Canterbury Tales,* describing the squire, son of the knight:

> With him ther was his sone a yong Squyer
> A lovyere (lover) and a lusty bacheler (aspirant to knighthood)
> With lokkes crulle (curly) as (as if) they were leyd in presse.
> Of twenty yeer of age he was I gesse.
>
> . . . .
>
> Embrouded (embroidered) was he, as it were a mede (meadow)
> Al ful of fresshe floures (flowers) whyte and rede.
> Singinge he was or floyting (playing the flute) al the day.
> He was as fresh as is the month of May.
> Short was his goune with sleves long and wyde.
> Wel coude he sitte on hors and faire (excellently) ryde.
> He coude songes make and wel endyte (compose the words)
> Juste (Joust) and eek (also) daunce and wel purtreye (draw) and
> wryte.
> So hote (hotly) he lovede that by nightertale (in the night-time)
> He sleep namore than dooth a nightingale.

This passage is closer to Modern English in word order than most Old English was. Only in two or three places, such as "He coude songes make," does the order seem very strange to us. Inflectional endings of Middle English were considerably reduced from Old English. In a noun an *-s* or *-es* usually signified either a genitive singular or any case of the plural. (The battle between an *-s* and an *-en* plural was almost decided by Chaucer's time, although in a few words such as *oxen* the *-en* plural never surrendered.) Adjectival forms had in general been reduced to two, one for the "strong" singular, and a second for the strong plural and the "weak" singular and plural. Verbs were somewhat simplified also; in the past tense no distinction was retained between singular and plural or between first, second, and third person, and the past tense and past participle were often identical, as they are in most verbs today.

Of all the things that have happened to English, the reduction of inflectional endings and the increased inflexibility of word order have been most important in giving the language its modern characteristics. Although these changes were not completed in Middle English and will never be completed while the language lives, they were far advanced by the year 1500, a date chosen rather arbitrarily as the beginning of Modern English.

Some of the Developments in Modern English

Since 1500 English word order has become still more fixed, and living inflections have been reduced to seven: an *-s* or *-es* plural for nearly all nouns, an *-s* ending for most third person singular verbs in the present tense, an *-ed* ending for most verbs in the past tense, an *-ing* form for verbs, a special past participle for some verbs, an *-er* ending for the comparative degree of many adjectives and some adverbs, and an *-est* ending for the superlative degree of the same words.

In other ways grammar has changed only slightly. Representative of the many comparatively small changes are the use of *do* in questions (*Does he consent?* rather than Elizabethan *Consents he?*) and the growth in frequency of the progressive tenses (*He was speaking,* for instance, often replacing *He spoke*). Steadily increasing reliance upon prepositional phrases, greater employment of subordinate clauses, the increase in verb-adverb (or verb-preposition) combinations ("*I ran into* an old friend"), and a tendency to use almost any word as more than one part of speech—these are but a few . . Modern English developments. . . .

In the eighteenth century some grammarians, failing to recognize the inevitability of linguistic change, strove to stop or at least retard it. They believed that change in a language is undesirable; since Latin was the most highly regarded language, and since Latin had not changed much in fifteen hundred years or so, change must be bad. (Those who held this theory failed to realize that Latin would probably have changed a great deal if it had not become a dead language, and that in monks' Latin it actually did change considerably.) They believed also that the loss of inflections should be stopped to prevent further "deterioration."

The results of the efforts of these few grammarians may be illustrated by referring to a couple of pronouns and a few verbs. The distinction between *who* and *whom,* which is not essential for clarity, was erratically observed during the eighteenth century. But under pressure from prescriptive grammarians, teachers and editors began to insist upon strict maintenance of *whom* as an object. Several verbs, including *blow, know,* and *throw,* were moving toward a "weak" or "regular" past tense and past participle: *blow, blowed, blowed,* and so on. They were thus following other verbs that had made the shift without hurting the language: as examples, *help* once had *healp* as one past form and *holpen* as the past participle; *climb* had *clamb* and *clumben*; *chew* had *ceaw* and *cowen.* Certainly *blowed* would be no worse than *climbed* or *chewed,* but the prescribers wanted no more "deterioration." As a result of their efforts and those of their intellectual descendants, the use of *blowed, knowed,* and *throwed* may even today keep an able person from being employed for a white collar position.

Similarly, in the eighteenth century, a tendency toward identical forms for past tense and past participle was noticeable. The verb *sing* was tending toward *sing, sung, sung; write* toward *write, wrote, wrote.* The original title of Thomas Gray's most famous poem was "Elegy Wrote in a Country Churchyard." But once more the reactionaries went to work, and the schools ever since have insisted upon different forms for the past tense and past participle of *drink, give, ride, shrink, sing, sink, write,* and other verbs. How many million child-hours have been spent on mastering these forms is beyond calculation. Totally false conceptions of "correctness" have resulted from this wasted effort.

Perhaps the most noticeable change that has occurred since 1500 is not in grammar but in vocabulary. Through borrowings from dead Latin, dead Greek, and most of the important living languages of the world, English has multiplied its store of words manyfold. Since no one can precisely define what a word is, no one can say how many words are now in the language. One clue to the number is that unabridged dictionaries have about 600,000 entries. But since no lexicographer would claim that his dictionary lists every existing word in the language, the total may be much larger.

Why the Language Has Changed

A language changes because things happen to people. If we could imagine the impossible—a society in which nothing happened—there would be no changes in language. But except possibly in a cemetery, things are constantly happening to people: they eat, drink, sleep, talk, make love, meet strangers, struggle against natural perils, and fight against one another. They slowly adapt their language to meet the changing conditions of their lives. Although the changes made in one generation may be small, those made in a dozen generations may enormously affect the language. The big and little phases of history—fashions, fads, inventions, the influence of a leader, a war or two, an invasion or two, travel to a foreign land, the demands of business intercourse—may alter a language so much that a Rip Van Winkle who slept two or three hundred years might have trouble in making himself understood when he awoke. Even in a relatively quiet society, linguistic change proceeds inexorably.

Think, if you will, of the English language as a river. Its headwaters are the closely interrelated Teutonic languages of the Angles, Saxons, and Jutes, who lived mainly in the northern part of what is now Germany. They provided the basic grammatical structure of the language that we call English; they provided most of its linguistic heritage; they provided its basic words, the common everyday words that still are the most important in our simple communications. But to the basic elements brought in by these Teutonic peoples many additions have been made.

When the Teutons began invading and settling in the British Isles in 449 A.D., they found in possession the Celts, who previously had been pushed about by Roman soldiers for several centuries. The Teutons pushed the Celts about some more, finally tending to localize them in what we now call Ireland, Wales, and parts of Scotland. But the Teutonic language was influenced somewhat by the Celtic and indirectly by the Latin which the Celts had fragmentarily learned. So in English we have words of Celtic ancestry such as *brat, cairn,* and *crag,* and the place names *Aberdeen* (*aber* = river mouth), *Avon* (river), *Caerleon, Cardiff, Carlyle* (*caer* or *car* = fortress), *Dundee, Dunbarton, Dunbar* (*dun* = hill), *Inchcape* (*inch* = island), *Kildare, Kilpatrick* (*kill* = church). And as a result of the early and indirect Latin tributary (which existed on the Continent even before the invasions of Britain) we have *wall* and *street* and *port,* words that give promise of enduring even longer than the Roman constructions that they name; and we have place names: Roman *Londinium* (originally Celtic) is now *London, Eboracum* (also once Celtic) has undergone considerable transformation to appear as *York,* and Latin *castra,* a military camp, appears both in England and the United States in *Lancaster, Worcester, Leicester, Gloucester, Chester, Dorchester, Rochester.* Thus Latin and Celtic are early tributaries of English.

By the end of the sixth century Latin was to renew its influence upon English. In 597 Roman missionaries began coming to the British Isles in an attempt to Christianize the inhabitants. They introduced such church words as *altar, creed, mass,* and *nun* and some homely words such as *beet, pine, cheese,* and *cup.* Some of the words that the priests brought over had been borrowed by Latin from Greek: *bishop, deacon, martyr, church, devil, priest, monk, pope, psalm, dish,* and *plum.* So once more a double tributary entered the river of the English language.

In the seventh and most of the eighth centuries the Anglo-Saxon inhabitants of the British Isles lived a relatively peaceful existence—simple by modern standards, but maybe happier than a more complex society can be. But starting in about 790, "Northmen" or Danes began to invade the islands. They were rough and vigorous; in 793, "the heathen men miserably destroyed God's church at Lindisfarne with rapine and slaughter," a contemporary account says. The forays grew into expeditions; the Danes began to colonize; Alfred the Great for a while paid them tribute but then organized military forces and compelled the invaders to sign a peace treaty. One of the terms of the treaty was that the Danes accept Christianity. Since the chief difference between the Danes and the Anglo-Saxons had been in religion, this concession meant that the two groups, already speaking kindred and often mutually intelligible languages, would merge. However, attacks by new groups of Danes, not covered by the treaty, continued, and early in the eleventh century a Danish king, Cnut, ruled in England.

It is often difficult to separate the linguistic contributions of the Danes from the closely related Anglo-Saxon, but apparently we owe to Danish such words as *fellow, husband, law, wrong,* and a number of words with an *sk* sound, as *skill, scale, scare, skirt* (*shirt,* a cognate form, is from Anglo-Saxon), *skin, sky, score,* and *bask.* Numerous English place names are Danish in origin. Danish *thwaite* (piece of ground) appears in many names such as *Stonethwaite, Hallthwaite; thorp* (village) is in names like *Lowthorpe* and *Northrope; by* (town) is in *Derby, Kirkby, Selby, Whitby,* etc.; *toft* (a clearing) is in *Lowestoft.*

The next big tributary came from north via east. Northmen, later called Normans, had begun moving into France at about the time that the Danes invaded England. They were flexible people who adopted French as their language, changing it somewhat in the process. They made of Normandy one of the most vigorous and ambitious states of Europe. In 1066, after the death of England's Edward the Confessor, the Duke of Normandy decided that he would attempt to gain the crown of his late cousin, and at Hastings he earned the more glorious title of William the Conqueror. His people moved into the British Isles, relegated natives to the rank of second-class citizens, and eventually concentrated their grip upon England as they lost their continental footholds.

Now began the period of greatest linguistic turmoil that English has known. England was a country of two languages: the Norman French of the ruling classes and the English of the conquered. The Bishop of Worcester was deposed in 1095 because he was "an idiot who did not know French." French was used in the churches, in the courts, in important business transactions, and in schools. But inevitably the two groups had to meet. A French landowner had to give instructions to his tenants; an English farmer or smith had to try to sell his goods or his skills; intermarriage became frequent. Each group picked up words from the other. However, just as American occupation troops learned only the rudiments of German, Italian, and Japanese after World War II, the Normans did not learn the intricacies of English nor did the English learn the intricacies of Norman French. Each group learned only the fundamentals.

Before the Norman conquest there had been signs that grammatical inflections were being reduced—the dative and accusative cases, for instance, were blending their forms. But the coming of the Normans seems to have expedited such change. At any rate, after the Normans had been in England for about three centuries, English inflections were not nearly so numerous.

The two groups gradually blended. So did their vocabularies, and to a much smaller extent their grammar, although the impact of Norman French upon English was less than one might think. But partly as a result of that impact, and more largely as a result of other, less tangible causes, grammatical gender was replaced by natural gender, word order became less free as inflections were reduced, pronunciations changed, and many words from Norman French, French, and Latin entered the language.

Chaucer's contemporary, John Gower, in the fourteenth century wrote three major works—one in English, one in French, and one in Latin. He chose three languages because he was not sure which language would become standard in England, and he wanted one of his works to be in the language that endured. Had he lived fifty years later, he would have had no difficulty in seeing that English was going to be the winner.

During the Renaissance two more large tributaries entered English. These, of course, were in the form of additional Latin and Greek contributions. Thousands of words came into the English vocabulary during this period, including huge numbers of relatively useless terms that lived briefly and were then buried in soon-to-be-forgotten graves. English spellings were also influenced by the new interest in the Classical languages. Learned men perhaps foolishly proclaimed that the orthography of English words should reveal their Latin backgrounds. They therefore recommended the spellings *debt* and *doubt,* even though the *b's* in these words were not pronounced, and even though the French, from whom the English had borrowed both words, had already dropped the *b's* that existed in Latin. A number of words with *tio,* like *nation,* had also been taken from the French, which often used a phonetically accurate *c* instead of *t;* in English the sound in question was pronounced as *s* or *sh,* but Renaissance scholars insisted that the Latin *t* be retained. Many other of our present illogical spellings may be attributed to the scholars of the Renaissance.

During the Renaissance period and later, the feeling grew that English grammar should be described in the terminology of Latin grammar. Sometimes that procedure was not objectionable, for many elements of the two languages were similar. But when the grammarians insisted upon finding in English everything that existed in Latin, when they made of Latin a procrustean bed into which English must be in some way fitted, and when they ignored the fact that English was basically a Teutonic and not an Italic language, they did irreparable harm to many generations of persons who wanted to acquire a clear understanding of the structure and peculiarities of the language.

Since the Renaissance, many small tributaries have enlarged the stream of English. These cannot be listed in chronological order. Latin has kept appearing, as have French and Greek. Italian has contributed many of the technical terms of music. Dutch has given sailing terms like *ahoy, boom, deck, hoist, skipper, sloop,* and *yacht.* Spanish has given, directly or indirectly, miscellaneous words like *matador, vanilla, armada, alligator,* and *mosquito.* North American Indian has contributed such words as *hominy, Mississippi* (an Algonquin word meaning "big river," not "Father of Waters"), *moccasin, moose, opossum, papoose, pemmican, raccoon, skunk, squaw, toboggan, tomahawk, wampum,* and *wigwam.* Among other contributing languages, with one or two representative words from each, have been Bengali, (*bungalow*); Persian (*azure*); Slavic (*polka, vampire, mammoth*); Hebrew (*amen, hallelujah, behemoth*); Hungarian (*goulash*); Tartar (*khan*); Malay (*gong, cockatoo*); Indian (*rajah, nabob, khaki, yogi*); Australian (*boomerang, kangaroo*); South American Indian (*alpaca, condor, jaguar, quinine*); Polynesian (*taboo, tattoo*); African (*gumbo, mumbo, jumbo, okra*). Even Chinese has given us some words (*tea, typhoon, chop suey,* and *chow mein*);

Chinese Pidgin English has contributed the familiar *chopstick;* Japanese has given us *tycoon, kimono, judo,* and *ju-jitsu.*

The borrowing has of course gone the other way, also, although the details need not concern us here. English and American gastronomic and athletic terms, for instance, have been incorporated in many European languages. An American can use the terms *cocktail* and *beefsteak* with satisfactory results in almost any European restaurant.

Why did English change? Simply because many things happened to many people in many countries. Had the Angles, Saxons, and Jutes moved southeast instead of southwest, the language of the British Isles might never have been Teutonic. Had Harold defeated William the Conqueror at Hastings in 1066, the language of today might have been considerably different, perhaps more complicated in morphology, more simple in syntax. Had the English been stay-at-homes, their language might have lacked some of the versatility, the expressiveness, and the color that we believe it now has.

Appendix D

On Teaching Prefixes, Suffixes, and Roots

A note in the unit on introducing students to phonetic alphabets and to morphemes through prefixes and suffixes warns the teacher: "Students must realize that many prefixes have more than one meaning. Knowledge of a single meaning only will frequently lead a student astray if he attempts to infer the meaning of a new word by drawing solely upon that knowledge." Despite that danger, the unit demonstrates that there is still value in studying prefixes and suffixes.

The analogous extension of fixed literal meanings to root elements is much more complicated and dangerous as the following article by Mr. Lee Deighton demonstrates. For that reason we have not prepared a unit concerned with the part played by root elements in establishing word meanings.

In an era when Latin was an essential part of the secondary school curriculum, a student whose knowledge of Latin served him well could use the system of dividing an English word into prefix, root, and suffix, translating those elements into "literal" meanings and from them inferring a current meaning of the English word. With the decline of the teaching of Latin in the secondary schools, that method of inferring meanings is no longer widely used.

Problems in Word Analysis*

Lee C. Deighton

There is [a] method of dealing with unfamiliar words which has long been established classroom practice. This is the method of word analysis in which the reader breaks up a word into prefix, root, and suffix. Assigning fixed values to each part, the reader translates them into a "literal" meaning and from this literal meaning infers the current meaning. This procedure assigns single-value equivalents to roots and prefixes. Thus *pre-* = "before," *de-* = "of or from," *ad-* = "to or at," *-dic-* = "say," and *-duc-* = "lead." Suffixes are translated into phrases such as "one who," "a place for," "pertaining to."

Difficulties with Prefixes

The briefest consideration will disclose that this arbitrary single-value equivalence is inadequate. Consider, for example, the prefix *de-* which is equated in current texts with "of or from." *Webster's New International Dictionary of the English Language* [*Webster's Third*] gives four meanings for *de-*. It may mean "down" as in *decline* or *depend.* It may indicate separation as in *depart* or *deprive.* It may indicate reversal or undoing as in *decamp, debark, degloss.* It may be used intensively as in *denude,* "to make quite nude." It is impossible to circumscribe all these meanings in the simple equivalence of "of or from." The equivalence is false and misleading.

Similarly, the current practice equates the prefix *trans-* with "across." However, the *New International* dictionary shows that *trans-* may mean "over" in the sense of change of position, as in *transship* and *trajectory.* It may mean "across," as in *transfluent.* It may mean "beyond," as in *transalpine.* It may indicate completeness of change, as in *transform, transfigure.* It may mean "through," as in *transparent.* Here again the single-value equivalence is false and misleading.

If a prefix may have any one of four distinct meanings, how can you determine which of the four it has in a particular unfamiliar word?

*From Lee C. Deighton's *Vocabulary Development in the Classroom* (New York: Bureau of Publications, Teachers College, Columbia University, 1959); reprinted by permission of the publisher.

Either you work with the oversimplified meaning (*de* = "of or from") or you go to the dictionary. In other words, either you deliberately falsify the meaning or you abandon the equation as a way of dealing with unfamiliar words.

ABSORBED PREFIXES

Prefixes create another difficulty in current word analysis. Sometimes the force of the prefix is no longer evident in the English word. There are considerably more than 1000 current English words prefixed by *de-*. In nearly 400 of these the force of the prefix is wholly lost or so attenuated as to be hidden from the average reader. Its force may have been lost in Roman times in the manufacture of a new Latin word. Or its force may have been lost along the way from Latin to current English. There are more than 800 words in current English prefixed by *ad-* and its variant forms. In something over 200 of these, the prefix has lost all or most of its meaning and adds nothing to the meaning of the root. In many of these words, the prefix lost its meaning either in the French or in the Latin. The English word *affranchise* from the French *affranchir* is such a word. *Affreight* from the French *affreter* is another. *Aggroup* from the French *agrouper* is another. These words were taken into English with the force of the prefix wholly absorbed.

In the same way, *desolate* comes from the Latin verb *desolare*, "to forsake." *Desolare* was composed in Latin from *de-* and *solare*, which itself meant "to make lonely." Thus the addition of *de-* to *solare* did not much change the meaning of the root verb. *Dedicate* comes from the Latin verb *dedicare*, "to dedicate." The Latin verb was composed of *de-* plus *dicare*, which itself meant not only "to declare" but also "to dedicate." *Devastate* comes from the Latin verb *devastare*, which was built from *de-* plus *vastare*, and *vastare* itself meant "to lay waste." Clearly in these operations the Romans were not making wholly new meanings but new words only. These new words were useful or ornamental as alternates to words already in current usage.

Sometimes the loss of force of the prefix came after absorption of the word into English. *Precept*, for instance, comes from the Latin *praeceptum* which was composed of *prae-*, "before," and *capere*, "take." In Latin a *praeceptum* was something "taken before." But in current English the impact of *before* is lost. Similarly, *premium* derives from the Latin *praemium* which originally meant "that which one got before or better than others." *Praemium* was composed of *prae-* and *emere*, "to buy." While the impact of the prefix is apparent in Latin, it is almost wholly lost for any meaning of the English word.

It is clear that mechanical word analysis cannot be a satisfactory means of arriving at the meaning of an unfamiliar word if sometimes the prefix has no meaning or force whatever. There is no way except by consulting the dictionary to know whether or not the prefix operates in an unfamiliar word. To give it meaning where it has none is to be misled by the simple sum of prefix, root, and suffix.

SIMULATED PREFIXES

To increase the difficulty with prefixes, there are many current English words in which the introductory letters, even though identical with the letters of familiar prefixes, are not in fact prefixes at all. There is no way of knowing this in advance of consulting the dictionary concerning any particular unfamiliar word. The first three letters in *precarious* and *predatory* are not a prefix. The first two letters in *decorous* and *decoy* are not prefixes. In *foremost* the first four letters are not a prefix. *Dis-* is not a prefix in *dismal, dismay, distaff*. There is no possible escape from this pitfall for the traditional method of word analysis. In this method a prefix must always mean but one thing. And a prefix must always be a prefix. Otherwise, which is the fact, it cannot be applied to unlock the meaning of any unfamiliar word, and the only recourse is to the dictionary.

Difficulties with Roots

The same procedure of single-word equivalence is used currently with roots. Thus, *-duc-* is equated with "lead"; *-dic-* is equated with "speak"; *-fer-* is equated with "bear." For some Latin roots this works very well; for others it does not. It is notorious that Latin verbs have many meanings and greatly variant meanings. To compress this variety into a single equivalent is to oversimplify and distort. The Latin verb *probare* is the root of a great many English words. In the word derivations given in the *New International, probare* is given six different meanings. Thus, as the origin of the English *probate*, the meaning of *probare* is given as "to prove." For the English word, *probe*, the meaning of the root is given as "to try"; for *probable* the meaning of the root is "to approve"; for *approve* itself the meaning of the root is "to esteem as good"; for *reprove* the meaning of the root is "to test." Here is one Latin root with six different definitions. How can it be compressed into a single equivalent of any value in determining the meaning of unfamiliar words? If more than one meaning is recognized in the root, it cannot be used to decipher unfamiliar words because there is no way of knowing in advance of consulting the dictionary which of the multiple meanings applies.

But even granting that this difficulty could be overcome, as it can be for certain roots, there is a question as to how much value these root meanings have in assisting the reader to the full meaning of the English word. Does it advance the pupil's understanding to know that *perceive, receive, deceive* all come from the Latin verb *capere?* What else but this root do *perception, deception, reception* have in common? And if the Latin root is so elastic, how can it be of any value in determining meaning of words which themselves are so far apart in meaning?

There is another very real and practical difficulty in this oversimplified analysis of roots. The spellings of quite different roots in English words are often so close as to be almost indistinguishable. For a pat example, take the following words and their origins:

disseminate	from *seminare,* to sow
emanate	from *manare,* to flow
immanent	from *manere,* to remain
imminent } eminent }	from *minere,* to jut, project

The converse is also true. The spelling of the Latin root is often quite different from the spelling of the English word derived from it. The word derivation noted above, *deceive* composed of *de-* and *capere,* is a case in point. There is nothing about *capere* that would lead the reader either to *-ceive* or to *-cept* in the English derivatives. Hence a knowledge of *capere* as a Latin root is of no help in deducing meaning of many words derived from it.

Many English words come directly from the past participle rather than from the infinitive form of the Latin verb. The past participle forms are different in spelling. Thus *latus* is the past participle of *ferre. Transfer* is composed of *trans-* and *ferre. Translate* is also composed of *trans-* plus the past participle of *ferre.* Both words have the same literal meaning and the same origin, but only the Latin student would know this.

Difficulties with Suffixes

The current practice with suffixes is very much the same as for other word parts. Single equivalents are given for endings that have variant meanings. Thus *-able* is equated with "capable of being." The *New International* indicates that this is an adjective suffix meaning (1) "ability, fitness, worthiness," or (2) "tending to, given to, favoring, causing, liable to." The meanings in this second group are by no means the same. They are distinct and recognizably different elements in a gradient of meanings.

Clearly, the meanings of roots, prefixes, and suffixes vary greatly from one word to another. The greatest number of them do not have fixed, invariant values. The purpose of the traditional method of analysis is largely to equip pupils to deduce the meaning of an unfamiliar word from its parts. But if one of those parts, the prefix, for example, has two or even three possible meanings, the pupil cannot deduce the meaning of the whole word with any certainty whatever.

The Limitations of Literal Meaning

Hence, as a method of deducing meaning of an unfamiliar word, traditional word analysis is ineffective. But there are other objections more important than mere ineffectiveness and so serious as to suggest that the method ought to be abandoned forthwith. The truth is that most words are more than the sum of their parts. Prefix added to root added to suffix does not often give the current meanings of a word. This kind of arithmetic produces a sum traditionally known as the "literal meaning." Occasionally, the literal meaning and the current meanings of a word are identical. For an unfamiliar word there is no way of knowing how close literal and current meanings are without consulting a dictionary. But the aim of much current word analysis is to defer or to escape using the dictionary. Hence even if the right values of the word parts have been drawn together, the result is only something called a "literal meaning," which may or may not fit a particular context. And there is no way to know whether it fits without going to the dictionary.

For many English words there is an extraordinary gap between literal and current meanings. Sometimes the literal meaning is actually misleading. For example, *prehensile* is composed of *prae-*, "before," and *hendere,* "to get." The *New International* dictionary gives as the current meaning "adapted for seizing or grasping especially by wrapping around; as the *prehensile* tail of a monkey." There is nothing in the literal meaning "to get before" which would lead one to the tail of a monkey. Similarly *preposterous* comes from *prae-*, "before," and *posterus,* "after." There is nothing in "before, after" to suggest the current meanings of the word. *Detest* comes from the Latin verb *detestare* which meant among other things "to detest." It was composed of *de-* and *testare* which meant "to be a witness; to testify." It is a long way from "testifying" to the current meaning. The literal meaning of *prevaricate* is "to straddle before"!

Perhaps the most dangerous aspect of traditional word analysis is that it results in *a* meaning for a word. There is only one literal meaning. There are, of course, many English words with only one current meaning. *Prehensile* is one of them. However, most English words have several meanings, and those words in commonest use have the greatest variety of meanings. Sometimes these variant meanings have no relationship to each other. Sometimes they are even opposite or contrary to each other. Thus *disperse* may mean "to scatter in all directions" or in another context "to distribute from a central source." The word *affluent* may mean "flowing to." It may also mean "wealthy." How is it possible to get both meanings from the same combination of prefix and root? *Appreciate* in one context means "to estimate justly." In another context it means "to raise the value of." *Appraise* may mean either "to estimate," which is an impartial act of judgment, or it may mean "to praise," which is neither impartial nor judicial. *Affect* may mean "to be fond of," or it may mean "to counterfeit." It is a safe rule that no word has meaning out of context. Which of several meanings a word may have in a particular context, traditional word analysis cannot reveal.